GROUND STUDIES FOR PILOTS

Fifth Edition
Volume 2

PLOTTING and FLIGHT PLANNING

R. B. Underdown
FRMetS MRAeS
formerly Director of Ground Training and latterly Principal,
College of Air Training, Hamble

b
Blackwell
Science

Fifth edition
© Estate of R. B. Underdown 1993
Blackwell Science Ltd
Editorial Offices:
Osney Mead, Oxford OX2 0EL
25 John Street, London WC1N 2BL
23 Ainslie Place, Edinburgh EH3 6AJ
238 Main Street, Cambridge
  Massachusetts 02142, USA
54 University Street, Carlton
  Victoria 3053, Australia

Other Editorial Offices:
Arnette Blackwell SA
1, rue de Lille, 75007 Paris
France

Blackwell Wissenschafts-Verlag GmbH
Kurfürstendamm 57
10707 Berlin, Germany

Blackwell MZV
Feldgasse 13, A-1238 Wien
Austria

All rights reserved. No part of
this publication may be reproduced,
stored in a retrieval system, or
transmitted, in any form or by any
means, electronic, mechanical,
photocopying, recording or otherwise,
except as permitted by the UK
Copyright, Designs and Patents Act
1988, without the prior permission
of the copyright owner.

First published in Great Britain by
  Crosby Lockwood & Son Ltd 1970
Second edition 1974
Third edition, in three volumes, 1979
Fourth edition published by Collins
  Professional and Technical Books 1986
Fifth edition published by
  Blackwell Science 1993
Reprinted 1995

Set by Best-set Typesetter Ltd, Hong Kong
Printed and bound in Great Britain by
  Hartnolls Ltd, Bodmin Cornwall

DISTRIBUTORS

Marston Book Services Ltd
PO Box 87
Oxford OX2 0DT
(*Orders*: Tel: 01865 791155
         Fax: 01865 791927
         Telex: 837515)

USA
Blackwell Science, Inc.
238 Main Street
Cambridge, MA 02142
(*Orders*: Tel: 800 215-1000
         617 876-7000)
         Fax: 617 492-5263)

Canada
Oxford University Press
70 Wynford Drive
Don Mills
Ontario M3C 1J9
(*Orders*: Tel: 416 441 2941)

Australia
Blackwell Science Pty Ltd
54 University Street
Carlton, Victoria 3053
(*Orders*: Tel: 03 347-5552)

A Catalogue record for this title
is available from the British Library

ISBN 0-632-03602-8

Library of Congress
Cataloging-in-Publication Data

Underdown, R. B.
  Ground studies for pilots.
  Includes various editions of each volume.
  Includes indexes.
  Contents: v. 1. Radio aids — v. 2.
  Plotting and flight planning — v. 3.
  Navigation general and instruments. —
  v. 4. Meteorology.
  1. Navigation (Aeronautics) 2. Aids to
air navigation.   I. Title.
TL586.U48 1993 629.132′51 92-43150
ISBN 0-632-03601-X (v. 1)
ISBN 0-632-03602-8 (v. 2)
ISBN 0-632-03434-3 (v. 3)
ISBN 0-632-03751-2 (v. 4)

CONTENTS

Preface *vi*

Part 1 THE EARTH **1**
   1 Form of the Earth   3

Part 2 NAVIGATION PLOTTING **9**
   2 Basic Navigation Principles   11
   3 Practical Navigation Plotting   29
   4 Plotting on other Charts   43
   5 Grid Navigation   50
   6 Radio Navigation Charts   52
   7 Relative Motion   71

Part 3 FLIGHT PLANNING **83**
   8 Principles of Flight Planning   85
   9 Choice of Route and Area Navigation   102
  10 Weight Calculation   106
  11 Point of No Return   112
  12 Critical Point   121
  13 Flight Planning Re-check   131
  14 Cruise Controls, Fuel Reserves and EROPs   147
  15 Computer and ATC Flight Plans   157

Appendix 1 Glossary of Abbreviations *171*
Appendix 2 Conversion Factors *177*
Appendix 3 Navigation Equipment, Charts, etc. *179*

Answers to Multi-choice Test Questions *182*

Index *183*

PREFACE

As part of the European Community's (EC) intention to harmonise technical standards throughout the common European Market, new syllabuses for pilots' licences have been introduced with effect from 1 January 1993. The European Civil Aviation Conference (ECAC), through wide consultations within and between its member states, has produced the harmonised syllabuses setting the required standards.

To meet these new standards, the text of *Ground Studies for Pilots*, which is published in four volumes:

Volume 1 *Radio Aids*
Volume 2 *Plotting and Flight Planning*
Volume 3 *Navigation General and Instruments*
Volume 4 *Meteorology*

and their companion volume, *Aviation Law for Pilots*, has been completely revised.

This volume deals with aviation practice of the mid-1990s in flight operations and now includes computer flight planning, cruise control, EROPs and ETOPs. It cannot be stressed too strongly that in the subject matter covered by this volume, accuracy combined with speed of execution is essential both operationally and under examination conditions.

I would like to acknowledge particularly the valuable assistance of my former colleague Tony Palmer in writing this volume. The portions of AERAD charts are reproduced by kind permission of British Airways. I am grateful too, for permission from Jeppesen Dataplan to reproduce the computerised flight plan in Chapter 15, for permission from Jeppesen & Co GmbH to reproduce their material in Appendix 3 and for the Civil Aviation Authority's (CAA) permission to reproduce sections of the CAA Instructional Plotting Chart–Europe, for the diagrams in Chapter 2. Copies of the CAA chart may be purchased from the addresses listed in Appendix 3.

Examination practice questions are available by post from the Civil Aviation Authority, Printing and Publication Services, Greville House, 37 Gratton Road, Cheltenham, Glos., GL50 2BN.

Hamble   Roy Underdown

Part 1
THE EARTH

Chapter 1
FORM OF THE EARTH

The earth
The earth is not a true sphere but is flattened slightly at the poles. The more correct description of its shape is an ellipsoid of revolution. Its equatorial diameter of 6884 nm exceeds its polar diameter by about 23 nm. This flattening is known as compression, which is merely the ratio of the difference between the two diameters to the larger diameter. Expressed in mathematical terms:

$$\text{Compression} = \frac{\text{equatorial diameter} - \text{polar diameter}}{\text{equatorial diameter}}$$

and its value approximates $\frac{1}{300}$. However, for our purposes, we will consider the earth as a sphere.

Great circle (GC)
We would all agree that a line which directly joins any two places on the earth represents the shortest distance between them. Now, if we continue one end of this line in the same direction right round the earth until it finally joins up at the other end, we find that the circle we have drawn just divides the earth into two equal halves. Try it on an orange, keeping the knife blade at 90° to the skin. Putting the story in reverse we can state that the smaller arc of a great circle always represents the shortest distance between two places. This is all-important from our point of view.

To define it, a GC is a circle on the surface of the sphere whose centre is the centre of the earth, whose radius is the radius of the earth and which divides the earth into two equal parts. Rather a lengthy one to learn, but know it and keep it in mind when dealing with GC problems. The definition in fact tells us more about the nature of a great circle than just its contents:

- that only one GC could be drawn through any two places – try again on an orange
- but if those two places were diametrically opposite an infinite number of GCs could be drawn. Lines joining the two poles on the earth are examples.

The equator and all the lines of longitude (meridians) are examples of GCs (although, technically, meridians are semi-great Circles).

Small circle

A small circle stands in contrast to a GC. By definition, any circle on the surface of the earth whose centre and radius are not those of the sphere itself is a small circle. All parallels of latitudes (except the equator) are small circles. They do not represent the shortest distance between two places.

Latitude and longitude

A reference system in international use of which you have no doubt heard. First of all, a GC is drawn round the earth through the North and South Poles passing through Greenwich. That half of the GC between the two poles which passes through Greenwich is called the Prime or Greenwich Meridian. The other half is called the Greenwich anti-meridian. The Greenwich meridian is labelled 0° and its anti-meridian, 180°. Thus, with this E–W division established, more GCs in the form of meridians could be drawn, both to the east of Greenwich and to the west.

The next step is to have a datum point for N–S divisions. This is obtained by dividing the earth by a GC mid-way between the two poles, all points on it being equidistant from the poles. Such a GC is called the equator, and labelled 0° latitude. Small circles are now drawn, parallel to the equator, towards both poles – these are parallels of latitude.

Definition of latitude

It is the arc of a meridian intercepted between the equator and the reference point. It is measured in degrees, minutes and seconds, and is termed north or south according to whether the place is to the north or south of the equator.

Definition of longitude

Longitude is the shorter arc of the equator intercepted between the Greenwich Meridian and the reference point. It is measured east or west of the Prime Meridian in degrees, minutes and seconds.

It is the meridians themselves that indicate North–South direction: the parallels run East–West.

The whole network of latitude and longitude (also called parallels and meridians) imagined to cover the earth is called a graticule. Thus, on a complete graticule we would see meridians starting from Greenwich as 0° going right round to the East and West up to 179°59′59″E and 179°59′59″W. 180° is common. Similarly to N–S, we would have parallels right up to 90°N and S, the poles. A degree is divided into 60 minutes, and each minute is divided into 60 seconds (1° = 60′; 1′ = 60″).

And while on the subject of latitudes and longitudes, there are two more definitions you ought to be familiar with. They are: change of longitude (ch long) and change of latitude (ch lat).

Form of the Earth

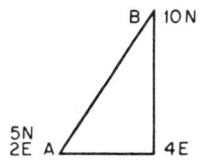

Fig. 1.1 Ch lat and ch long.

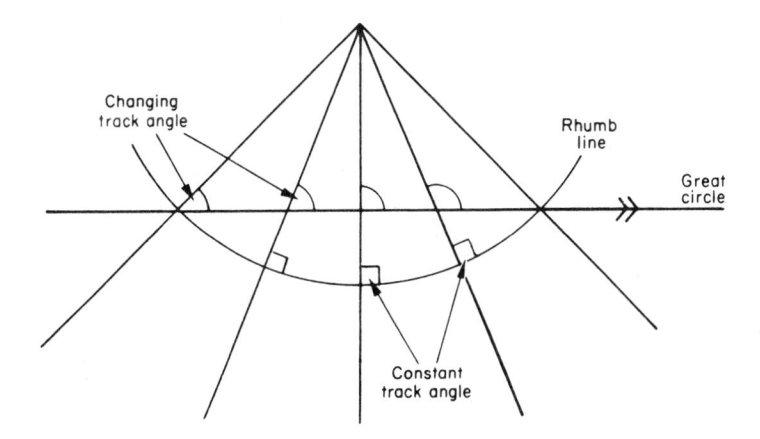

Fig. 1.2 Rhumb line and GC.

Change of longitude
It is the smaller arc of the equator intercepted between the meridians of the reference points. It is named East or West according to the direction of the change.

Change of latitude
It is the arc of the meridian intercepted between the parallels of the two places and is named North or South according to the direction of the change.

In Fig. 1.1, if the flight was made from A to B, the ch long is 2°E; ch lat is 5°N. If the flight was from B to A, the ch long is 2°W and ch lat 5°S.

Rhumb line (RL)

We established above that the shortest distance between any two places is along the GC. This would be the ideal line (call it a track) to fly. However, there is this disadvantage: the GC from one point to another will cross the converging meridians at different angles. Since the meridians form the basis of our track angle measurements, this would mean continuous alterations to the track angles as the flight progresses (Fig. 1.2).

Apart from a 090°/270°RL (i.e. a parallel of latitude or the equator), all others spiral towards the poles. Their curvature and so their disparity from the equivalent GC, which is the nearest approach possible to a straight line

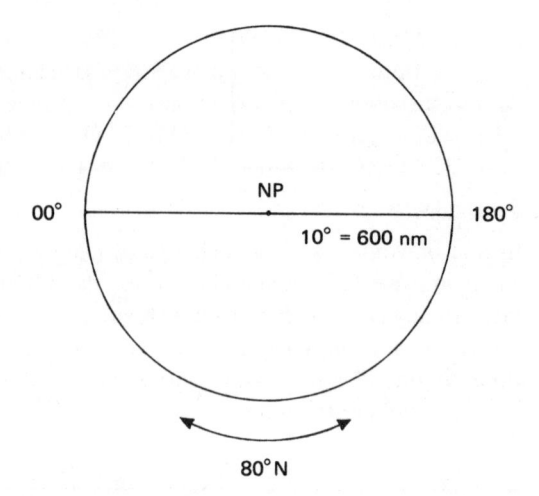

Fig. 1.3 Rhumb line and GC distances.

on the curved surface of the earth, increases with latitude. It follows that, in low latitudes, GC and RL distances will show little difference. After all, the equator is both a GC and an RL. In high latitudes, however, there can be a great and wholly unacceptable difference.

RL and GC distances comparison

Consider a flight from 80°N 00°EW to 80°N 180°EW (Fig. 1.3). The GC route is over the pole and the distance will equal 20° of latitude or 20 × 60 = 1200 nm. Simple plane geometry suggests that the RL distance around the parallel will be 600 π = 1885 nm. In fact, on the spherical earth as opposed to a flat diagram, the exact distance is 180 × 60 × cos 80° = 1875 nm.

RL and GC directions comparison

It is often said that flying a GC, with a need to constantly change true direction unless flying due North or South (meridians are semi-GCs) or East or West along the equator, creates practical steering problems. In practice, only aircraft with automatic (computerised) navigation systems are likely to fly true headings and these will quite easily direct the auto-pilot no matter how many changes are required.

Consider two North Atlantic routes:

Shannon–Gander (GC 1715 nm RL 1748 nm)

	Initial direction		Final direction		Direction change	
	(T)	(M)	(T)	(M)	(T)	(M)
GC	281°	294°	245°	275°	36°	19°
RL	263°	276°	263°	293°	0°	17°

Belfast–Keflavik (GC 747 nm RL 749 nm)

	Initial direction		Final direction		Direction change	
	(T)	(M)	(T)	(M)	(T)	(M)
GC	325°	336°	311°	337°	14°	1°
RL	318°	329°	318°	344°	0°	15°

It will be seen that on some routes less change of magnetic track direction is involved when flying the GC. Remember, also, the GC always has the distance advantage. In any case, on long routes, regular alterations of heading will have to be made to conform with air traffic routes and/or to take account of varying wind conditions. These considerations further blur any clear distinction between the number of direction changes required to fly the two types of route.

Distances on the earth's surface

The basic unit used for aviation track distances is the International Nautical Mile (nm) which is 1852 metres in length. For practical purposes, it can be assumed to be the length of 1' of GC arc on a spherical earth. The true earth is not a perfect sphere. Modern on-board automatic navigation computers make allowances in their calculations for the non-spherical shape of the earth but the differences are not of any significance in any practical calculations that a pilot may have to make for himself.

The equator is a GC and so the 360° of longitude around it represents 360 × 60 = 21 600 nm. As meridians are semi-GCs, 1' of geographical latitude can be assumed to be 1 nm. Do not fall into the trap of treating 1' of longitude as a nm – this is only true at the equator but elsewhere it only equals cos latitude nm (see volume 3). The distance along a meridian from the equator to the pole is 90 × 60 = 5400 nm.

The metric system provides for the decimalisation of the angular system with a right angle being divided into 100 grade (French for degree) and each grade being divided into 100 minuit (French for minute). Using this system, the minuit was established as the basic unit for large distances, i.e. the kilometre (km). It follows that the distance from the equator to the pole will be 100 × 100 minuit of latitude or 10 000 km and so:

and so
or

$$10\,000\,\text{km} = 5400\,\text{nm}$$
$$1\,\text{km} = 0.54\,\text{nm}$$
$$1.852\,\text{km} = 1\,\text{nm}$$
$$(1852\,\text{m})$$

Conversions of distance units

The only other large distance unit encountered, and then only when dealing with the public, is the statute mile (sm). This is an arbitrary legal measure of 5280 ft or approximately 1610 m = 1.61 km.

$$1\,\text{nm} = 1.852\,\text{km} = 1.15\,\text{sm}$$

8 Plotting and Flight Planning

These conversions are available on aviation circular slide rules and can easily be effected using the above values and the electronic calculator. Many maps give scale lines for all three units and these may be used as convenient conversion scales.

Most aviation work is done in nm and it should always be remembered that 1' of geographical latitude for all practical purposes can be used as 1 nm and so, providing a map has a latitude scale that is reasonably well sub-divided, a simple nm scale line is always available.

For shorter distances (runway lengths, visibilities), the metre is gradually becoming the standard unit although feet are still commonly used for altitudes and elevations. The following conversions will be useful:

$$1\,m = 3.28\,ft \text{ or } 39.37\,in$$
$$1\,in = 25.4\,mm$$

Part 2
NAVIGATION PLOTTING

Chapter 2
BASIC NAVIGATION PRINCIPLES

These days it is very unusual to operate an aircraft using just the simple navigational techniques that will be described in this Chapter. However, they represent the basic principles on which all navigation systems operate and should also be regarded as useful 'fall-back' procedures for use when the more sophisticated modern systems fail or become suspect.

The 'art' of navigation
All navigation is the art of being able to give good answers to the following questions:

> Where am I now?
> How did I get here?
> What am I going to do about it?

It is interesting to note that modern technology can give incredibly accurate answers to the first two questions but can only offer suggestions for the third. It is not given to a mere mortal to know what the future holds so any method of forecasting must make assumptions which may or may not prove to be valid. This element of uncertainty is why navigation is often referred to as an art instead of a science. Certain basic procedures will have to be mastered before we can start practising this art.

The velocity triangle
It is easy to appreciate that, to steer a motor-boat directly across a fast flowing river, it will be necessary to head the boat up-stream so that the combined velocities (speeds in defined directions) of the stream and the boat through the water will give a resultant velocity acting at 90° to the flow (Fig. 2.1).

The problem is solved by constructing a velocity triangle. Note that the two component velocities – the boat's 5 kt through the water and the water's flow of 4 kt form two sides of a triangle with the arrows indicating the directions of motion following each other round the triangle and opposing the direction indicated by the arrows on the resultant velocity of the boat's actual motion over the ground (i.e. the river bed). Note that the unit of speed we use is the knot which means one nautical mile per hour. This would seem to be appropriate when talking about boats but we will continue to use it for

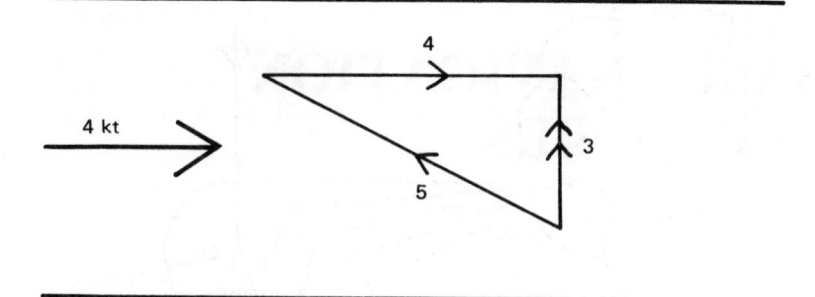

Fig. 2.1 Basic triangle of velocities.

aviation because of the simple relationship of the nautical mile to earth distances (see Chapter 1). The triangle could be solved by a scale drawing or by simple mathematics. In either case the answer would be obtained that the boat should be headed up-stream through an angle of 53° and the resultant speed across the river would be 3 kt. We could say that we are expecting the boat to be drifted 53° to starboard (right) and that its ground speed is 3 kt.

The aircraft velocity triangle
The situation with an aircraft is exactly the same. The air mass in which it is flying will have motion in just the same way as the river. The motion of the air is given by the wind velocity (WV) which is expressed by giving the direction *from which* the wind is blowing (WD) and the speed of the air's motion over the ground (WS) in knots (Fig. 2.2).

A WV of 280°/50 kt would indicate that a free balloon would move in a direction of 100° under its influence at a speed of 50 kt.

The equivalent of the boat's motion through the water is the aircraft's air velocity represented by the True Airspeed (TAS) and the True Heading (Hdg (T)) The aircraft's air velocity would equate to its motion over the ground only in calm or still air conditions.

True airspeed (TAS)
In practice, this will usually be derived from the airspeed indicator (ASI) or the Machmeter – see volume 3 for details. Modern on-board automatic navigation systems will obtain TAS from the air data computer (ADC). Aircraft with ADC may have TAS indicators but all aircraft will have the direct-reading, pressure-actuated ASI, as they play a very important part in pilotage techniques. Critical aircraft speeds are always expressed as Indicated Airspeeds (IAS), i.e. the speeds given by the ASI. Aircraft capable of high speeds will also carry Machmeters which are also direct-reading, pressure-actuated instruments. These will give the aircraft's TAS as a proportion of the speed of sound through the air for the particular temperature conditions.

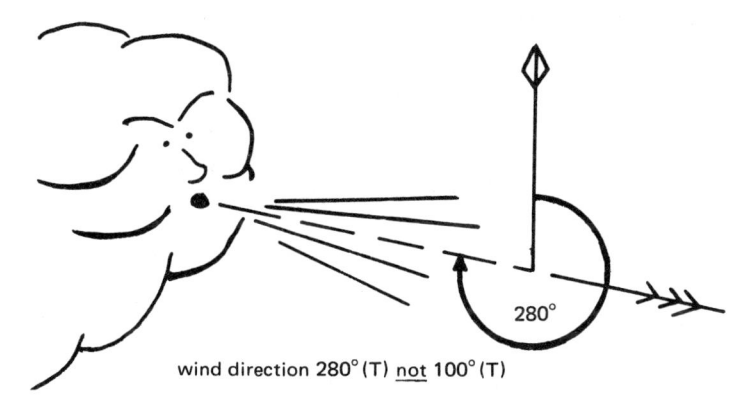

Fig. 2.2 Wind direction.

Standard navigational computers such as the Airtour CRP 5 carry conversion scales which are specially designed to compute the TAS. Refer to the instructional handbook for your computer and note that by setting the corrected outside air temperature (COAT), sometimes referred to as the ambient temperature, against the pressure altitude (PA) (altimeter reading with 1013 mb on the sub-scale) it becomes possible to read off the TAS on the main circular slide rule outer scale against the Rectified Airspeed (RAS) on the inner scale. The RAS or the Calibrated Airspeed (CAS), as the Americans call it, is the IAS corrected for various instrument and installation errors (see volume 3). It will only equal TAS when the air has the calibration density (pressure 1013 mb, temperature +15°C). The computer makes the necessary density correction to produce the TAS.

Check you are doing it correctly with this example:

PA 10 000 ft   COAT −15°C   RAS 150 kt   Solution 171 kt

Be careful if the TAS when calculated exceeds 300 kt. In this case an additional correction is required using an additional sub-scale on the computer. Computers usually refer to this as comp. corr. (compressibility correction). Try this example:

PA 30 000 ft   COAT −45°C   RAS 250 kt

On a first setting a TAS of 400 kt will be obtained but, after adjustment using the comp. corr. scale, a more correct TAS of 394 kt will be obtained.

If you have an electronic navigational computer that has a program for calculating TAS, it will give the correct answer regardless of the TAS. You can test the truth of this statement by solving the last example on an electronic calculator. Incidentally, the CAA do not permit the use of this type of calculator in their examinations.

14 Plotting and Flight Planning

Obtaining TAS from Mach No.

Modern aircraft often cruise at an indicated Mach No. Again the standard navigation computers provide a method of obtaining the TAS. The COAT is set against a Mach Index on a special sub-scale and the TAS can then be read off on the main outer scale against the Mach No. on the inner scale of the circular slide rule. Try this example:

$$\text{Mach No. } 0.82 \quad \text{COAT } -45°\text{C} \quad \text{TAS} = \underline{483\,\text{kt}}$$

An alternative solution, if you are using an electronic calculator, is to make use of this formula which is set out here for the calculator:

$$°\text{C} + 273 = \sqrt{} \times 39 \times \text{Mach No.} = \text{TAS}$$

Remember, if required to make the temperature negative, to use the $+/-$ key after putting in the temperature. Try the previous example by this method.

Now try this calculation by both methods in readiness for when you are flying Concorde:

$$\text{COAT } -57°\text{C} \quad \text{Mach No. } 2.05 \quad \text{TAS } \underline{1175\,\text{kt}}$$

Aircraft heading (Hdg)

The direction in which the aircraft is pointing measured clockwise from a particular direction datum is known as the aircraft heading (Fig. 2.3). In practice the following headings will be encountered:

Hdg(T)	True heading
Hdg(M)	Magnetic heading
Hdg(C)	Compass heading
Hdg(G)	Grid heading (see Chapter 5)

To convert compass direction to magnetic direction, the correction referred to as deviation (see *Ground Studies for Pilots, Volume 3*) should be applied and to convert magnetic direction to true direction, variation should be applied:

$$(\text{C}) \begin{array}{c} +\text{E dev} \\ -\text{W dev} \end{array} = (\text{M}) \begin{array}{c} +\text{E var} \\ -\text{W var} \end{array} = (\text{T})$$

and so conversely:

$$(\text{T}) \begin{array}{c} -\text{E var} \\ +\text{W var} \end{array} = (\text{M}) \begin{array}{c} -\text{E dev} \\ +\text{W dev} \end{array} = (\text{C})$$

See how this works with the examples illustrated in Figs. 2.4 and 2.5.

In modern compass systems, the deviations are usually very slight. Variation can be very large and will be obtained from the isogonals on the chart (see Volume 3 again). It is important to check that the variation is up to date. A

Basic Navigation Principles 15

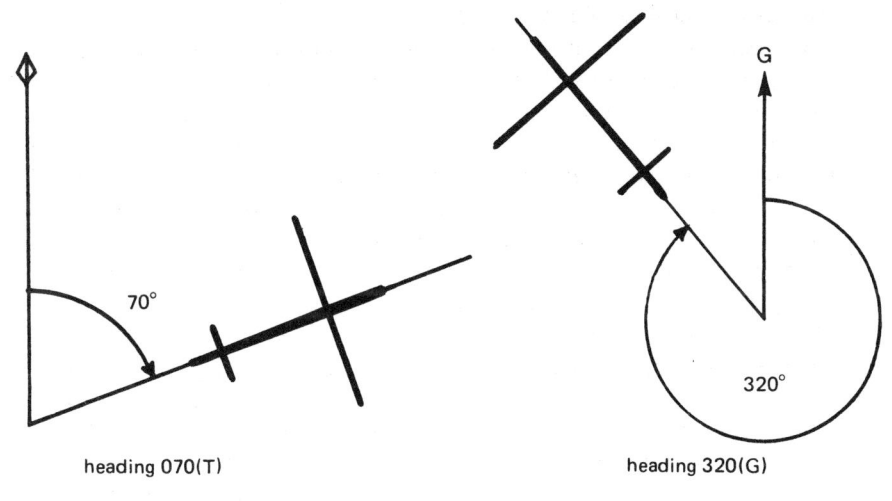

heading 070(T)   heading 320(G)

Fig. 2.3 Expressing aircraft heading.

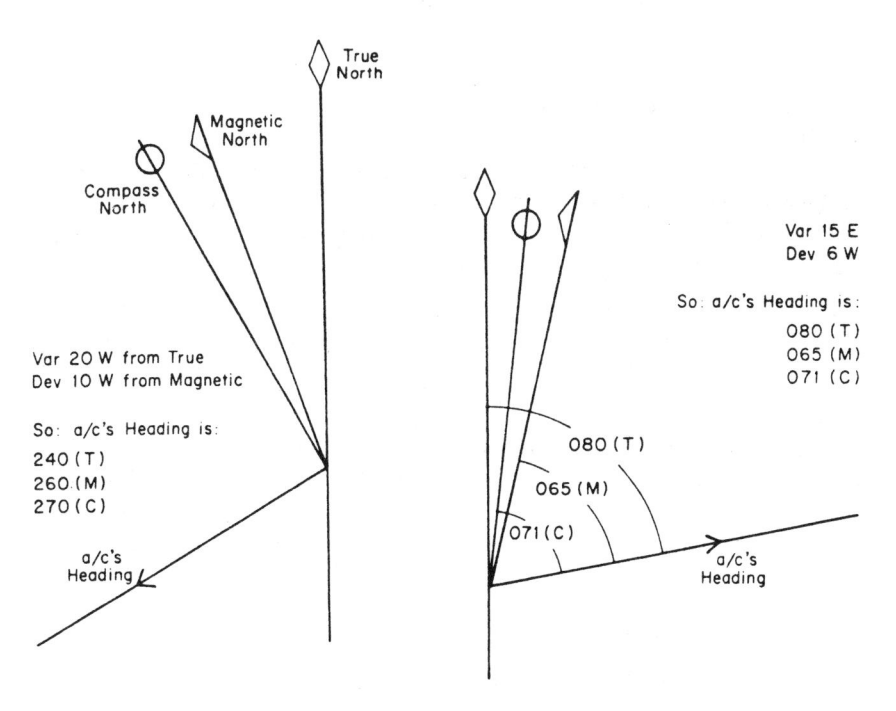

Var 20 W from True
Dev 10 W from Magnetic

So: a/c's Heading is:
240 (T)
260 (M)
270 (C)

Var 15 E
Dev 6 W

So: a/c's Heading is:
080 (T)
065 (M)
071 (C)

Figs. 2.4 and 2.5 Examples of expressing aircraft heading.

note in the margin of the chart or an annotation on the actual isogonals will indicate the year for which the variation is given. If more than two or three years out of date, it may be necessary to up-date the values using the corrections noted on the chart.

Track and groundspeed (Tr and GS)

In UK usage, track refers to the aircraft's actual movement over the ground. It may be the required or desired track, the calculated or DR (dead reckoning) track or the track already achieved usually referred to as the TMG (track made good).

In USA usage, and so often encountered when operating American aircraft and instrument systems, course is used to indicate the required track and track is reserved to describe the actual path over the ground. In radio navigation, a simple VOR set-up will have a course deviation indicator (CDI) which shows if the aircraft is deviating from the required track (course).

The GS is the speed the aircraft is making good or is expected to make good (DR GS) over the ground. Obviously in still air conditions (zero WV), the TAS and the GS will be the same. With a dead tail wind the GS will be the sum of the TAS and WS and with a dead head wind the GS will be the difference of the TAS and the WS.

It is a useful check on calculations to remember these two simple relationships for they place absolute limits on the GS that may be found with given values of TAS and WS and so can be used to reject impossible answers that may be presented.

The aircraft velocity triangle

This is illustrated in Fig. 2.6. It will be noticed that the single arrow on the aircraft air velocity vector is followed round the triangle by the three arrows of the WV vector. The two arrows on the aircraft ground velocity vector are in the opposite direction around the triangle. Try drawing this vector triangle for yourself using a simple and convenient scale such as 1 cm = 10 kt.

   Hdg 090(T)   TAS 180 kt   WV 040/45 kt

                                                     Solution Tr 103(T) GS 156 kt

Drift

Consider the significance of the vector triangle in Fig. 2.6. Try to think yourself into the pilot's seat – you would be pointing the aircraft's nose due

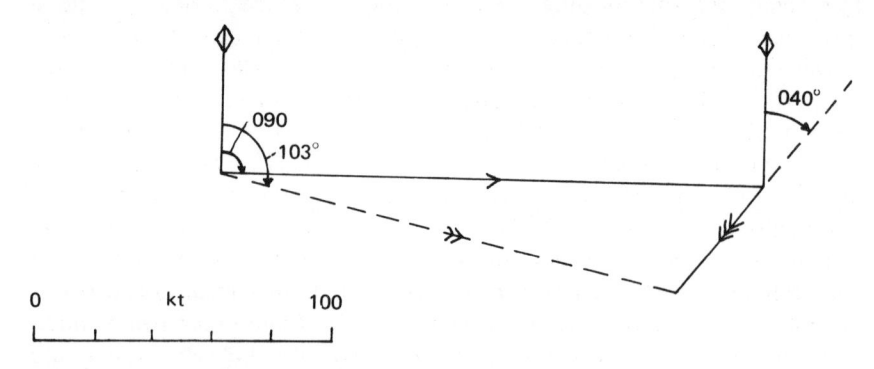

Fig. 2.6 Aircraft velocity triangle.

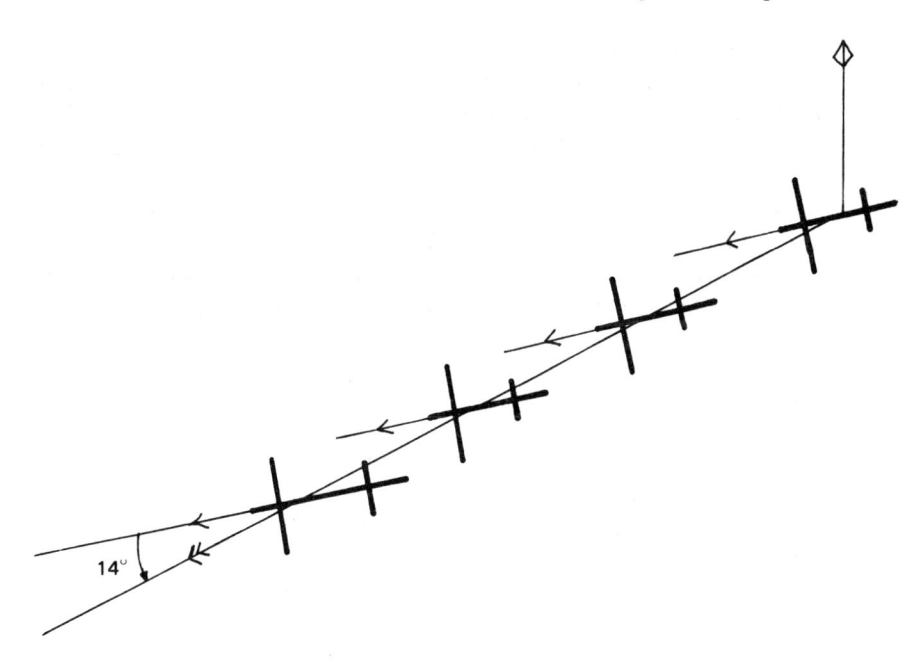

Fig. 2.7 Drift.

East and the wind blowing *from* 040° (round about NE) would be coming at you from ahead and to your left. Naturally it would have the effect of 'drifting' you to the right and slowing you down. In this case the aircraft would be drifted 13° to the right (starboard) and the aircraft would move crabwise along a track of 103°. In Fig. 2.7, the movement of an aircraft with a heading of 256°(T) and a drift of 14°P giving a track of 242°(T) is illustrated.

Navigation computers

In practice, the solution of the vector triangle is accomplished by using a specially designed computer. It may be of the analogue type which effectively provides a simple method of drawing the vector triangle – these are often referred to as Dalton computers after Dr Dalton who invented the system – and typical of these are the CRP series produced by Airtour International. A computer of this type is essential for the CAA exams. There are also electronic digital calculators available where it is only necessary to type in the basic information, e.g. TAS, WD, WS and Tr, and then ask the machine to compute the required heading and GS. At present the use of these is not permitted by the CAA. By their nature they tend to be a little more accurate but they are certainly no more rapid than a Dalton in experienced hands. You must acquire a Dalton-type computer, study the handbook carefully and practise assiduously until it becomes second nature.

18   *Plotting and Flight Planning*

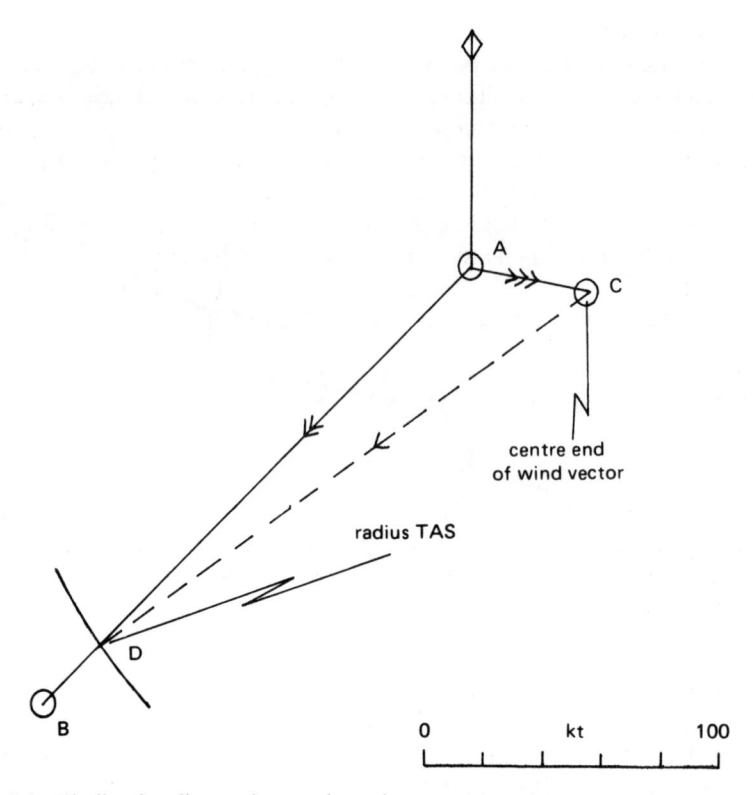

Fig. 2.8   Finding heading and groundspeed.

The heading and GS problem

In practice, finding these is the commonest problem. Before flight, for example, a flight plan will require this problem to be solved for each stage of the flight.

To solve this problem by drawing requires a slightly different sequence of working. In Fig. 2.8, the track required is 225°(T), TAS 200 kt and WV 280°/40 kt.

Before we start on the solution, stop and think yourself into the situation. Sitting in the aircraft, the wind will be coming at you from a direction of 55° to your right (280 − 225) and so will cause left (port) drift and a GS less than the TAS. Make sure that the final answer agrees with this.

The sequence of working is indicated by the letters. Try drawing it for yourself using a scale of 1 cm = 10 kt. The correct answers are: Hdg 234°(T) GS 174 kt drift 9°P. Your answers should be within 2° and 4 kt. Now try the problem on your Dalton computer.

If AB represented on a chart the track required, a pilot would need to leave A and head his aircraft 9° to the right of the required track and rely on the wind to drift him 9° to the left so that the required track of 225°(T) is made good. Notice that as we foresaw the GS less than the TAS.

Wind components

These are often referred to in aviation. Cross-wind components (cwc) are usually identified as such although a more accurate description would be cross-track or cross-runway components. The other type of wind component is usually identified by the addition of 'head' or 'tail' or by the signs '−' or '+'. A word of warning here – in aircraft performance calculations when dealing with take-off and landing problems, the sign convention is reversed. The more common components – head – are given the sign '+' and the tail components are '−'.

Strictly, there are two distinct types of along-track or along-runway components:

'effective' wind components = GS − TAS
'true' wind components   = WV resolved along the Tr or RW direction
                (i.e. WS × cos wind/track angle)

In practice, the expressions effective and true are rarely seen. For flight planning purposes, the tables of wind components produced for a specified TAS are always effective components. In performance manuals tables and diagrams give true components.

(Effective) wind components

A few examples first. Ideally you should have a copy of the CAA's Flight Planning Data Sheet 33 – this is essential for Chapter 8 – and also your Dalton computer. Start by calculating the GS in these cases:

Tr	TAS	WV	Answer (GS)
050	380	140/120	360
050	480	140/120	466

In these cases the (effective) wind components would be:

360 − 380 = −20 kt or 20 kt head wind component (hwc)
466 − 480 = −14 kt or 14 kt hwc

Now compare these results with those given on pages 24 and 25 of Data Sheet 33 entering with a wind/track angle of 90° (140 − 050) and a wind speed of 120 kt. Note, that even in these conditions of maximum drift due to a high wind speed at 90° to track, the effective component only changes by 6 kt with a change of TAS of 100 kt. It will be realised that at a TAS of 430 kt, the correct component would be −17 kt but if interpolation was ignored, the answer from either table in this extreme case would only be in error by 3 kt. In practice therefore, an effective wind table for a specified TAS can be used quite reasonably for any TAS within ±50 kt. Notice that a wind at 90° to track gives a significant effective head wind component and that, if the pilot flew on the reciprocal track, there would be exactly the same effective hwc. This demonstrates that an effective hwc on a track does not necessarily indicate that there will be a corresponding tail wind component (twc) on

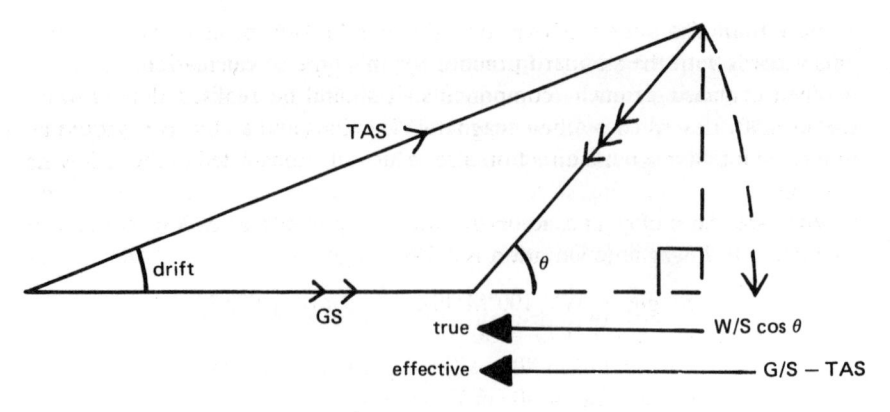

Fig. 2.9 Wind components.

the reciprocal track. Assuming this in the 380 kt TAS case would cause an error of 40 kt (400 − 360) when assessing the GS on the reciprocal track.

(True) wind components

This is the component of the wind resolved along the track or, more commonly, the runway. Unlike (effective) wind components, (true) wind components are not dependent on the TAS. The other significant difference is that the (true) component is zero with a wind at 90° to the track whereas, the (effective) component can be quite a significant head wind as was seen in the previous paragraph. It will be noted in Fig. 2.9, which shows the difference between the two types of component, that the (effective) wind component is less favourable than the (true) wind component. Whenever there is any drift this will always be the case. Naturally, when flying up and down wind, there will be no drift and no difference between the two components, both of which will be equal to the WS. On the other hand, as already noted, the other extreme is with the wind at 90° to track when there will be no (true) component but there will be an (effective) hwc.

(True) components are normally used for landing and take-off performance calculations where the cross-wind (90° to the runway) is also important. Both of these (true) components can be evaluated with the Dalton computer using the square graticule on the slide, or by scale diagrams or tables (both of which may be found in Flight Manuals), or by simple calculation on the electronic calculator:

$$\text{along-runway component WS} \times \theta \cos =$$
$$\text{across-runway component WS} \times \theta \sin =$$

where θ is the difference between the wind direction and the runway.

The above formulae, which are written as they will be entered into the calculator, will give positive results in the case of head winds (θ less than 90°

or more than 270°) but negative for tail winds (θ 090° through 180° to 270°). This accords with the standard practice for this type of calculation.

When evaluating runway components, it should be realised that runways are normally described by their magnetic directions and so the WV should be converted into a magnetic direction also. This is demonstrated in the following example:

What are the along- and across-runway components of a WV 090°T/40 kt on runway 07? Magnetic variation is 10°W.

$$\text{Magnetic WV } 100°M/40\,kt \qquad \text{Runway } 070°M$$
$$\theta = 100 - 070 = 30°$$
$$\text{Head wind} = 40 \cos 30° = \underline{35\,kt} \text{ (nearest kt)}$$
$$\text{Cross wind} = 40 \sin 30° = \underline{20\,kt}$$

Note that if landing in the opposite direction:

$$\text{Headwind} = 40 \cos 150° \, (250 - 100) = \underline{-35\,kt}$$
indicating a 35 kt twc.

Chart work

In aviation in most latitudes, the commonest chart available for general use is the Lambert's Conformal Conic with two standard parallels. In equatorial regions, the standard Mercator chart may be encountered and in polar regions, the Polar Stereographic. *Ground Studies for Pilots Volume 3, Navigation General and Instruments* gives greater detail about these charts. It can be assumed that, provided the use of the chart is confined to the areas for which it is best suited and that it is a conformal (orthomorphic) chart, the following properties may be assumed:

- reasonably constant scale over one chart;
- great circles practically straight lines;
- angles are correctly represented (conformality).

Using the Lambert's Chart

For the purpose of this chapter, we will demonstrate navigation procedures on a Lambert's Chart – reference to using a Mercator or a Stereographic will be found in subsequent chapters. The chart used for demonstration purposes in this Chapter will be the CAA Instructional Plotting Chart–Europe as used in their examinations. This is a 1:1 000 000 Lambert's and so a 20 in (50 cm) 1:1 000 000 scale ruler reading in nm will prove very useful. In addition, a pair of dividers, a pencil compass, a 5 in (13 cm) protractor and a navigational computer will be needed. Using an HB pencil will make it easier to rub out ready for re-use although fairly frequent use of a pencil sharpener may be required to keep a good working point. A draughtsman's clutch pencil will be found very satisfactory.

22 *Plotting and Flight Planning*

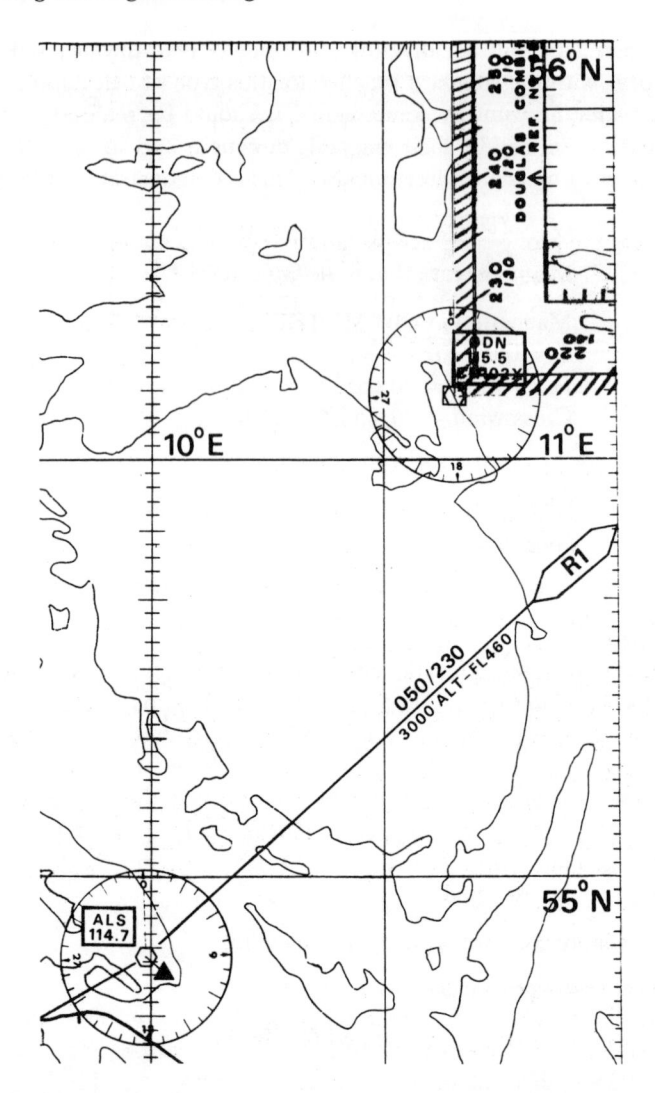

Fig. 2.10 Position on the chart.

Plotting positions on the chart

The chart has a 30′ graticule, so the square protractor will be used to plot and to read off positions accurately. In Fig. 2.10 the corner of the protractor has been placed on the beacon ODN and carefully aligned with the chart graticule enabling the latitude 55°35′N and longitude 10°39′E to be read off. Conversely, the protractor could have been aligned to cut the graduations for 55°35′N and 10°39′E and the corner of the protractor would indicate the required position.

Measuring distances and angles

In many cases on standard routes, directions and distances can simply be read off the chart. For example, in Fig. 2.11, the distance from VOR OSN to

Basic Navigation Principles 23

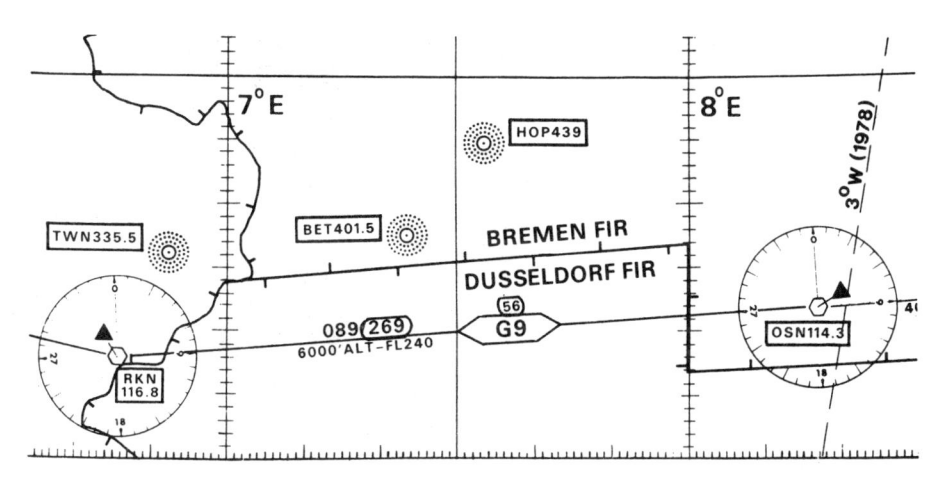

Fig. 2.11 Measuring distances and angles.

VOR RKN is 56 nm. Check this with your dividers using the latitude scale (1′ of latitude = 1 nm) and also using your scale ruler.

The magnetic track can also be read as 269°. Alternatively, measuring the track at the mid-meridian (7°30′E) to be 266°(T) and applying the local variation of 3°W will give the same result. Notice also that the approximate magnetic direction could be read from the compass rose around the OSN VOR which is orientated to Magnetic North (MN).

To improve on this accuracy, try aligning the protractor with MN as indicated by the compass rose and then reading the track direction. Although this technique will not be used for measuring tracks that already have the answer printed on the chart, it will be used for plotting radio bearings.

Plotting radio bearings
As an essential part of fixing an aircraft's position, it could well be required to plot position lines derived from radio bearings or ranges. The information that will normally be available to any aircraft equipped for IFR flight will be:

- VHF or VOR bearings (QDM or QDR)
- ADF bearings (relative or magnetic)
- Radar/DME ranges

(Refer to *Ground Studies for Pilots Volume 1* for more details.)

All of these will give a position line – that is a line along which the aircraft is believed to lie at a given time. It is customary, having drawn this line on the chart, to put a single arrow at each end of it and write the time along it.

Range position lines
These will be derived from DME or by airborne radar measuring the range of an identifiable ground feature such as a small island or headland. Plotting is

24 *Plotting and Flight Planning*

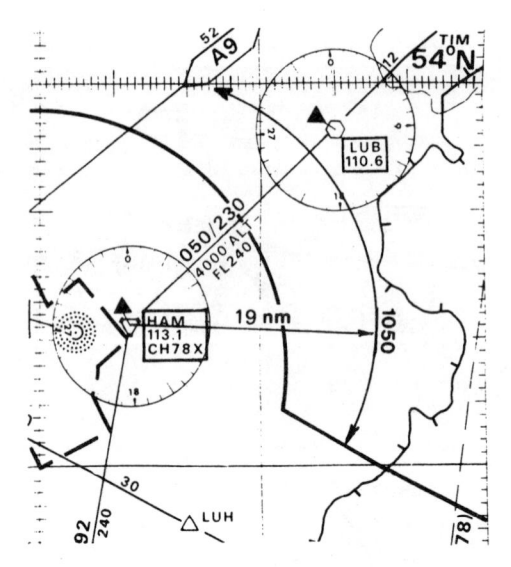

Fig. 2.12 Range position line.

just a matter of drawing the arc of a circle with a radius of the range measured around the DME beacon or ground feature (see Fig. 2.12).

Plotting VHF or VOR bearings
Basically these are GC bearings measured at a ground station – usually the station magnetic variation is applied and then the magnetic bearing (QDR or radial) or its reciprocal (QDM) is transmitted to the aircraft either by electronic means so as to give a display on the cockpit indicator, as in the case of VOR, or by radiotelephony (RTF) to give the bearing to the pilot orally. In each case the procedure for reducing the bearing to obtain the direction to plot on the chart is the same. If it is not in the form of a magnetic bearing from the ground station (QDR or radial) but as its reciprocal (QDM), apply 180°. Then, having aligned the protractor with the magnetic meridian through the ground station, plot the QDR directly. In Fig. 2.13, a QDM of 135° obtained from VOR WSR has been converted, by adding 180°, to get the equivalent QDR of 315°. The protractor is aligned with the magnetic meridian at WSR and the bearing of 315°(M) plotted. The compass rose at the VOR station was not used for measuring the angle because of the difficulty of reading it to the same accuracy as can be achieved with the protractor.

Plotting ADF bearings
These are the bearings of the NDBs measured by the ADF in the aircraft (see Volume 1). It is important to realise that, unlike VOR and VDF, the bearing

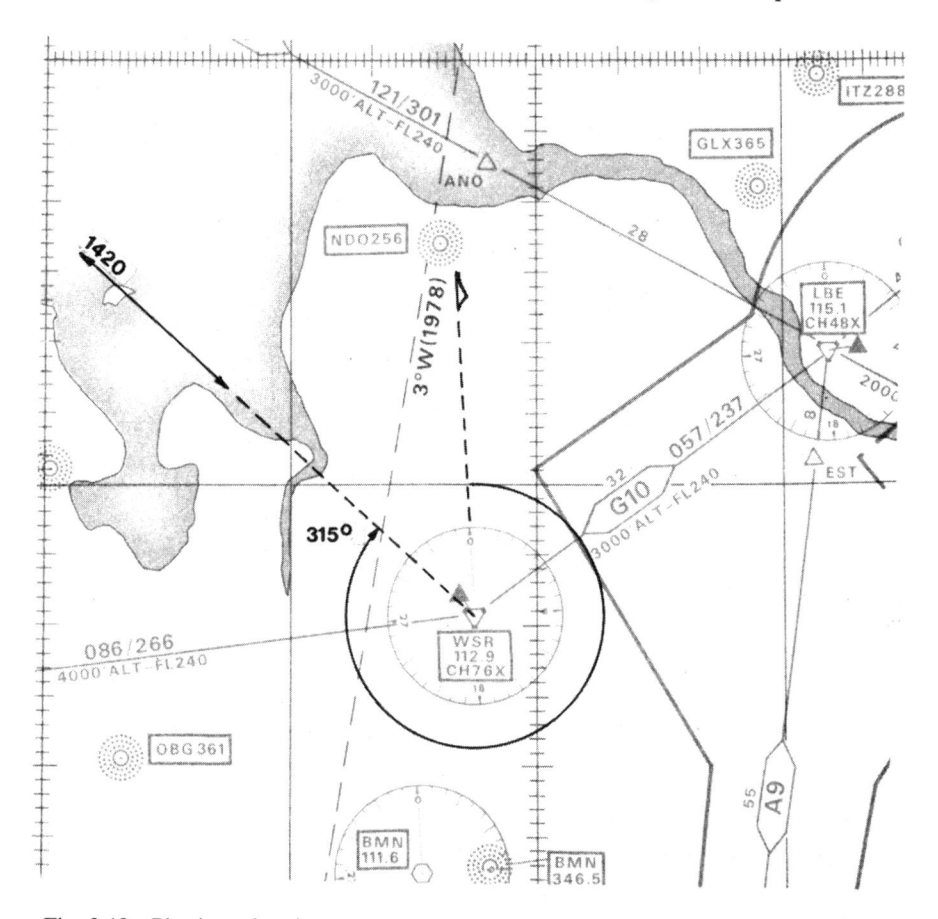

Fig. 2.13 Plotting a bearing.

measurement is actually done in the aircraft, i.e. at the aircraft meridian, but the resulting position line will be drawn from the meridian at the NDB position. GCs do not cut all meridians at the same angle and this will have to be taken into account in our procedure for dealing with these bearings. ADF bearings may be presented in the aircraft either as relative bearings (i.e. measured from the aircraft's nose) or on a radio magnetic indicator (RMI) as magnetic bearings. The reading against the head of the needle on these is often referred as a QDM but this is not strictly correct: QDMs are reciprocals of bearings measured at the ground station meridian whereas these are measured at the aircraft's meridian.

In Fig. 2.14, an aircraft at a calculated (DR) position marked with a square, obtains an ADF bearing of 090°(M) of NDB LO on the RMI. As a double-check, the bearing is noted to be 080° on the relative bearing indicator (RBI) with the aircraft on a heading of 010°(M). Proceed as follows:

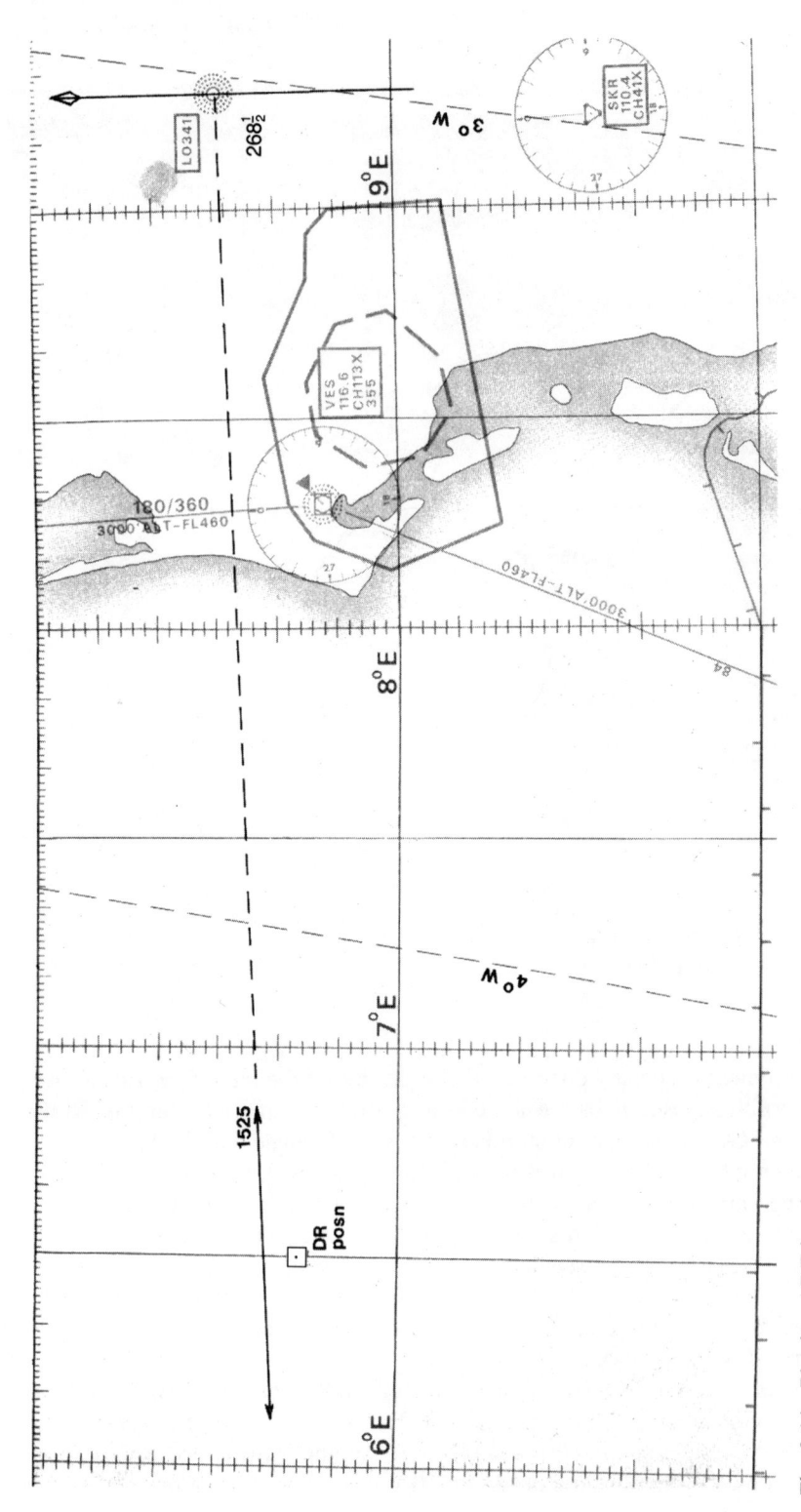

Fig. 2.14 Plotting ADF bearing.

Basic Navigation Principles

	RMI		RBI	
Bearing obtained	090(M)		080(rel)	
Aircraft varn.	−4	Heading	006(T)	010(M) −4
GC bearing	086(T)		086(T)	
		086(T)		

Chart convergency
(ch long $6\frac{1}{2}$E to $9\frac{1}{2}$E) × 0.8
= 3 × 0.8

Reciprocal of bearing to plot

Plot from NDB

$2\frac{1}{2}$ correction applied towards the
$088\frac{1}{2}$ equator, i.e. towards 180°
±180°
$268\frac{1}{2}$(T)

For further details of convergency, see *Ground Studies for Pilots Volume 3*.

On this chart, convergency is approximately 0.8° per degree of ch long. This indicates the change in direction of a GC as it crosses successive meridians turning always towards the equator. The convergency correction is always applied to bring the bearing measured *towards the equator* (i.e. nearer to 180° in Northern latitudes). Having then formed the reciprocal, the bearing is plotted with the protractor aligned with the true meridian through the NDB – note that a small section of the true meridian has been drawn in to facilitate the alignment of the protractor. When the position line has been drawn in, it can be checked with the protractor that its direction in the vicinity of the DR position is indeed 086°.

Practical exercises on the chart

In the next Chapter we deal with obtaining fixes using the position lines obtained at different times. Here, for practice purposes, you are asked to plot the bearings given and then read off the latitude and longitude of the intersection position. These would be referred to as simultaneous fixes. In each case the suggested correct answer is given in brackets. Your answer should normally be within 2′ of latitude and 4′ of longitude.

Questions

(1) 1015   DR position 54°N 03°E
SPY VOR (5232N 0451E) QDM 148
SPY DME   Range 111 nm
(Bearings plotted 328(M)   Fix 5401N 0301E)

(2) 1120   DR position 5430N 0600E
EEL VOR (5310N 0640E) QDM 166
DHE VOR (5411N 0755E) QDM 111
(Bearings plotted 346(M), 291(M)   Fix 5430N 0555E)

28 Plotting and Flight Planning

(3) 1245 DR position 54N 06E
WM NDB (5334N 0748E) bears 116 on RMI
LAK NDB (5231N 0534E) bears 194 on RMI
(Bearings plotted 293(T), 010(T)   Fix 5401N 0602E)

(4) 1415 DR position 5430N 0230E Hdg 050(M)
WM NDB 064(rel)
LAK NDB 093(rel)
(Bearings plotted 292(T), 319(T)   Fix 5448N 0209E)
The cut here is not very good (27°) and so even a slight inaccuracy in a bearing or in its plotting may produce several minutes difference in the answer.

(5) 1520 DR position 5400N 0230E
GV NDB (5206N 0415E) bears 157(M)
EEL VOR   ODM 112
SPY DME   121 nm
(Bearings plotted 332(T), 292(M))
In this case, the three position lines do not meet at a point but form a triangle (cocked hat). In practice, it could well be decided that the VOR/DME information is more reliable than the NDB bearing and so the fix could be taken as the intersection of these two position lines (5355N 0226E). If all position lines are given equal weight, the centre of the cocked hat (strictly the intersection of the bisectors of the angles of the triangle) will be taken as the fix (5357N 0230E).

Chapter 3
PRACTICAL NAVIGATION PLOTTING

Equipment required

All the examples in this Chapter are based on the CAA Instructional Plotting Chart – Europe. It is recommended that each example is plotted as described. Note that examples are given using universal co-ordinated time (UTC), which is gradually replacing GMT in aviation, but is for all practical purposes the same as GMT. In addition to the chart, the following equipment will be needed:

- navigation computer
- electronic calculator (not essential but useful)
- protractor
- dividers
- 1:1 000 000 scale ruler
- pencil compasses
- HB pencil, sharpener and eraser.

Finding initial heading and ETA

1050UTC   Overhead VES VOR (5536N 0818E) SH (set heading)
            EEL VOR (5310N 0640E) TAS 240 kt Forecast WV 230/30 kt
What is the initial Hdg (M) required and the ETA?

Solution
From chart Tr(M) is 205° (printed along the route).
Applying 4°W variation the Magnetic WV will be 234/30 kt and using the computer we can find: Hdg 208° (M), GS 213 kt.

Distance to EEL again using charted data 84 + 73 = 157 nm

Using either the circular slide rule on the back of the computer (see computer handbook) or the electronic calculator:

$$157 \div 213 \times 60 = 44 \text{ min}$$

so ETA = 1050 + 44 = 1134 UTC.

Finding a simple simultaneous fix
1114UTC   VES VOR QDM 027
             VES DME Range 83 nm
What is the aircraft's position at 1114?

Solution

$$\text{VES QDM } 027 + 180 = \text{QDR } 207$$

Plot 207 from VES with the protractor aligned with the magnetic meridian through the VOR beacon. To help in aligning the protractor it may be found helpful to extend the 000/180 points of the compass rose printed at VES.

Now draw in the range position circle of radius 83 nm and centre VES. The intersection of the two position lines (P/L) gives the fix position <u>5420N 0719E</u> (answer should be within 2' latitude and 3' longitude).

Finding Tr and GS WV
Using the information in the preceding paragraph, deduce the average (mean) WV that affected the aircraft since leaving VES, if the pilot steered 205(M).

Solution
Hdg(M) 205   TAS 240 kt   TMG 207 (= QDR) and so the drift is 2° starboard. The GS is 83 nm in 24 min and so by slide rule or calculator:

$$83 \div 24 \times 60 = 207 \, \text{kt}$$

Setting heading 205 and TAS 240 kt on the computer, mark in the point where the drift line for 2° starboard cuts the speed arc for 207 kt (see computer handbook). The WV can then be read off: <u>193M/34 kt</u> (answer should be within 5° and 2 kt).

It will be noted that the magnetic heading was set against the Hdg(T) index on the computer – as a result the WV found is also magnetic. The equivalent true WV would be <u>189/34 kt</u>.

This could be obtained either by using the Hdg(T) of 201° on the computer or by applying the variation to 193°M wind direction already obtained.

Finding a local WV and comparing it with the mean WV
In aircraft fitted with Doppler (see *Ground Studies for Pilots, Volume 1*) or with on-board automatic navigational computers, it is likely that instantaneous values of drift and GS will be available. From these, the value of the local or spot WV can be found using the same procedure as just described. The only difference will be the source of the information.

The question of which is the more accurate and which is the more useful WV cannot be answered without a careful analysis of the circumstances. In its nature the Doppler-derived WV will be a very accurate 'spot' WV, but whether this is a good average WV for the area would have to be a question of subjective judgement. The most useful WV is that which is going to affect the aircraft in the future and who can say what this might be? The WV to use is also, therefore, a question of personal judgement with due regard to the prevailing meteorological situation. It is worth remembering that even the professional Met forecasters can get it wrong so we must not be too disappointed if our estimates do not always work out.

Finding a DR position and revising Hdg and ETA

Using modern radio aids, an aircraft will usually be kept on the required track by a process of continual adjustment of the heading so as to maintain the correct TMG and Tr required readings on the indicators in front of the pilot. The following procedure is not, therefore, likely to be encountered often. It could well be tested in a CAA examination question designed to ensure a candidate could handle the situation in the event of a systems failure.

Carrying on from the previous example – when the position at 1114 was established, you were required to calculate a new heading and ETA from 1117. It is quite common to 'DR ahead' for three or six minutes to give time to complete all the necessary calculations. Choosing three or six minutes (1/20 or 1/10 of an hour) simplifies the calculations.

Solution

Extend the TMG line between VES and the 1114 fix by a distance of 10 nm (3 min at GS 207 kt). This gives the DR position (marked with a square) at 1117 as: 5410N 0712E.

From here the new required Tr to EEL of 198° (T) with a distance to go of 64 nm can be measured. Using the WV found of 189°T/34 kt, the new Hdg required and corresponding GS are: 197(T), 206 kt.

The revised flight time for 64 nm will be 19 min and so the revised ETA will be 1117 + 19 = 1136UTC.

The answers required are: Hdg 201(M), ETA 1136.

It must be emphasised that the solution will only be valid if the calculations are completed within the three minutes after the fix and if the WV used is a fair estimate of what will be experienced until arrival at EEL VOR.

Finding DR position at the top of climb (TOC)

During climb, TAS and WV will be continually changing and so it is not usually possible to establish an accurate top of climb position by calculation. In practice, if climbing away from a VOR/DME, there would be no need for the calculation as the actual position could be established so easily by a simultaneous fix. Similarly, if using an automatic on-board navigation facility, the aircraft position will be continuously available. In the absence of these facilities, calculating the DR position at the top of climb will have to rely on an estimated mean WV – usually the forecast WV for the mean altitude – and on an estimated TAS based on the planned mean RAS and the forecast

32 Plotting and Flight Planning

temperature at the mean altitude. The procedure is best illustrated by an example:

1215UTC Position 5330N 0500E FL 100 COAT +4°C Climbing on Hdg 315(T). Constant RAS 185 kt, mean forecast WV 220/45 kt.
1245   Top of climb FL 240 COAT −24°C
What is the DR position of the top of climb?

Solution
Mean FL = $\frac{1}{2}$(100 + 240) = $\frac{1}{2}$ × 340 = 170
Mean temp = $\frac{1}{2}$(+4 − 24) = $\frac{1}{2}$ × −20 = −10
From circular slide rule (see handbook) Mean TAS = 244 kt.
From computer using Hdg, WV and TAS, DR Tr and GS: 325(T), 252 kt.
On chart draw Tr 325(T) from 1215 position for a distance of 126 nm (30 min at 252 kt) to establish the 1245 DR position: 5513N 0256E.
If your answer does not agree exactly, check that your mean Tr of 325(T) is correctly measured relative to the mean meridian of 4°E.

Finding the DR position at the top of descent (TOD)
Modern aircraft perform better at higher levels and so it is advantageous to delay descending as long as possible − ideally the descent should be timed so that the aircraft arrives at the terminal radio facility at just the required FL for the commencement of the approach procedures. In practice, such perfection is rarely achieved but calculations will often be done in the hope of achieving it. The procedure is very similar to that for the climb and will be illustrated by an example:

1415UTC Fix at SFR (5522N 0500E) on Tr to DHE (5411N 0755E) TAS 200 kt WV 270/50 kt FL 170. Clearance received to descend so as to arrive at DHE at FL 50. Mean RAS for descent 150 kt, mean temp −15°C mean WV 240/35 kt, rate of descent 800 ft/min.

Give the DR position and the latest time to commence descent, ETA at DHE and the Hdg(M) to steer on the descent.

Solution
Tr to DHE = 125°(T)
From computer Hdg(T) and GS for level flight: 133°, 239 kt
Descent mean FL $\frac{1}{2}$(170 + 50) = 110, mean TAS 175 kt
From computer Hdg(T) and GS: 135° 187 kt
Descent time 12 000 feet at 800 ft per min: 15 min
Descent distance 15 min at 187 kt: 47 nm
On chart measure 47 nm back along the Tr from DHE to give the DR position for TOD: 5438N 0648E
Distance from SFR to TOD: 75 nm
At cruising speed 239 kt, time: 19 min

ETA at TOD 1415 + 19: <u>1434</u>
ETA at DHE 1434 + 15: <u>1449</u>
Hdg(M) on descent 135 + 4: <u>139°</u>

Transferring P/Ls to obtain a fix

Situations may arise when, because of the shortage of aircraft equipment or ground facilities, it is not possible to obtain simultaneous fixes as we did in the last Chapter. In these cases, it may be necessary to transfer position lines taken at different times so that they can be used together at a common time to obtain a 'running' fix. The basic technique requires a sensible assessment to be made of the aircraft's ground movement during the period of transfer and then to ensure that all points on the original position line are transferred accordingly. Consider the situation in Fig. 3.1, where three successive position lines have been obtained from one beacon using ADF and an RBI. The aircraft is on a heading of 270°(T) and the best estimate of the TMG is 259°(T) with a GS of 200 kt.

Figure 3.2 illustrates the procedure for obtaining a 'running' fix. Assume the aircraft is actually at position A on the 1705 P/L – this is the point where it cuts the DR Tr line. Twelve minutes later at 1717, the aircraft would be at B. Distance AB = 12 min at 200 kt = 40 nm. Through B the transferred P/L is drawn parallel to the original P/L. The square navigational protractor with

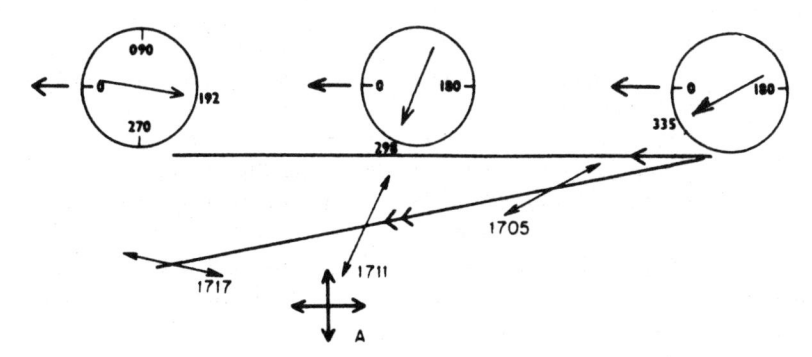

Fig. 3.1 Successive bearings from one station.

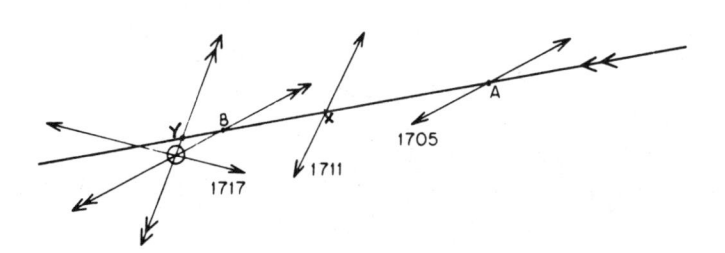

Fig. 3.2 Running fix.

34 Plotting and Flight Planning

its rectangular grid will be found particularly useful for drawing parallel lines. It will be realised that every single point on the original P/L will have been moved to a corresponding point on the transferred P/L assuming that the aircraft movement is correctly represented in direction and distance by the vector AB.

Transferred P/Ls will suffer not only from any original inaccuracy but also additional inaccuracy due to the incorrect assessment of the aircraft's movement during the period of transfer. Of course, these errors could tend to cancel out but they could just as easily add together. In general, the longer the period of transfer, the more suspect the transferred P/L must be. It follows that periods of transfer should be kept to a minimum and the best possible assessment of the Tr and GS prevailing during the transfer should be made. A Doppler Tr and GS, if available, will be particularly useful.

Referring again to Fig. 3.2, which is not drawn to scale, the 1711 P/L is transferred in a similar manner. The point X being moved for 6 min at 200 kt = 20 nm to Y and the transferred P/L drawn through Y parallel to the original 1711 P/L. Note that original P/Ls are marked by single arrows at each end and the time they were obtained is written against them. Transferred P/Ls are marked with double arrows and no times.

The cocked hat

Figure 3.3 shows a situation which often arises in practice – 'a cocked hat'. This has already been referred to in the previous Chapter. While cocked hats indicate that some error is present, it is not necessarily true that the size of the cocked hat indicates the magnitude of the error of the fix. With a consistent error present (e.g. compass deviation error in the case of ADF bearings), a fix obtained from bearings all on the same side of the aircraft as in Fig. 3.1 could give practically no cocked hat but the error would have moved all the P/Ls by approximately the same vector and so the apparently good fix will be in error by this amount.

If the bearings had been taken from beacons spread around the aircraft, ideally at 120° intervals, the constant error would have produced a larger cocked hat but its centre would be quite an accurate fix. The errors would tend to cancel each other out.

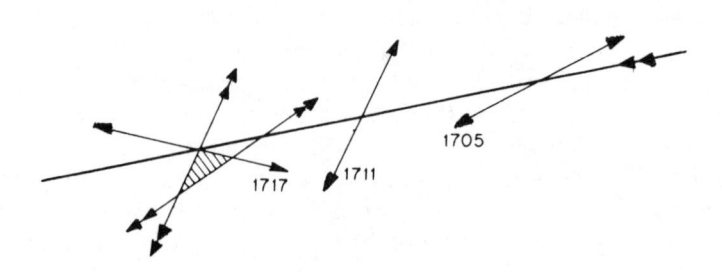

Fig. 3.3 The cocked hat.

Practical Navigation Plotting 35

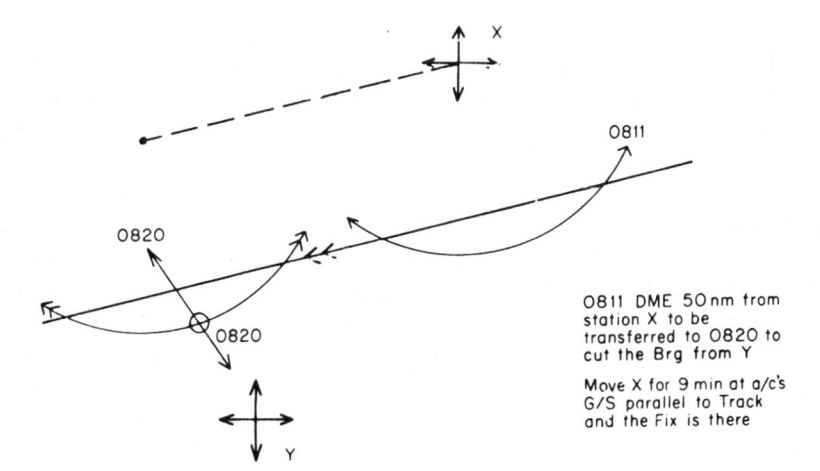

Fig. 3.4 Circular position line transfer.

0811 DME 50 nm from station X to be transferred to 0820 to cut the Brg from Y

Move X for 9 min at a/c's G/S parallel to Track and the Fix is there

Transferring circular P/Ls

The principle here is exactly the same as for linear P/Ls. To ensure all points are transferred for the actual ground movement of the aircraft during the transfer period, we move the centre of the circular P/L (i.e. the DME beacon) as shown in Fig. 3.4 and then draw in the transferred P/L from this new centre. In practice, it would only be necessary to draw in the transferred P/L.

Practical example of a three P/L fix
Referring to Fig. 3.5, suppose the aircraft is in the vicinity of the Dutch coast around latitude 53°N and has been flying various headings and has now settled down on a Hdg of 085°(T) at a TAS of 180 kt with a forecast WV of 000/30 kt. The following readings are then taken:

1215UTC   SPY DME range 25 nm
1218   ENK NDB bears 191(M)
1221   ENK NDB bears 219(M)

Solution
First use the computer to calculate the DR Tr and GS: 095°(T), 180 kt.

In the absence of any other information as to the aircraft's position, just draw in a track line of 095° anywhere in the general area. For transfer purposes we are only interested in the direction and distance of movement – the actual track location is irrelevant unless there was a question of deciding aircraft magnetic variation or the convergency values required with the NDB bearings. Through the SPY position draw in a transfer track of 095°(T) for a length of 6 min at 180 kt = 18 nm and then from this new centre describe the arc of the transferred P/L using a radius of 25 nm. Now calculate the bearings to plot:

36 *Plotting and Flight Planning*

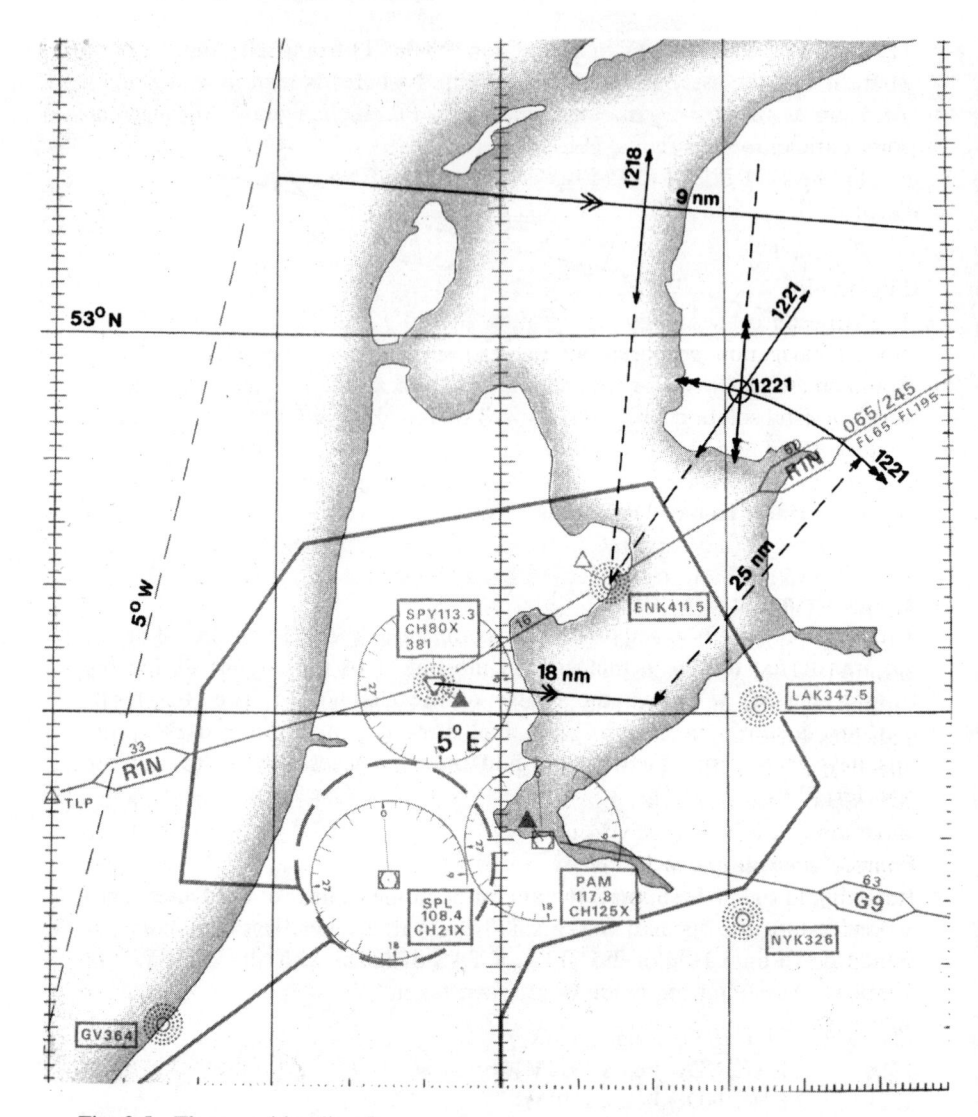

Fig. 3.5 Three position line fix.

Time	1218	1221
Brg(M)	191	219
a/c var	−5	−5
Brg(T)	186	214
convergency	0	0
	186	214
take recip.	180	180
plot (T)	006	034

May have to be revised if area assumed for the aircraft proves to be wrong

The 1218 P/L is now drawn in a direction of 006°(T) from ENK and the point where it cuts the assumed track (drawn in anywhere) is then moved along it for 3 min at 180 kt = 9 nm. The transferred P/L is then drawn through this point parallel to the original P/L.
Finally the 1221 P/L of 034°(T) is drawn in from ENK.
Position of the fix at 1221: <u>5256N 0532E</u>

The airplot

The procedures described up to now should be quite satisfactory for all normal navigation purposes but unusual situations can be visualised which would create problems for the methods just described. The airplot provides a very powerful solution which has the advantage of being comparatively simple to understand and use. An airplot, which is always started from a reliable fix is a graphical method of recording the true headings and air distances flown. In a still air situation, it would be a track plot. In the usual situation, the discrepancy, at any instant, between the airplot position and the actual ground position indicates the effect of the wind since the last fix, presuming all the information used is absolutely accurate.

In Fig. 3.6, if there had been no wind since the 1000 fix, the 1020 air position would also indicate the ground position at 1020. In this case, the aircraft is fixed at a position 244°/12 nm away from the air position. This indicates the effect of a WV blowing away from a direction of 064°(T) at a speed of 12 nm in 20 min = 36 kt. Alternatively, if it was known that the WV for the area was 064/36 kt, drawing in a wind effect (WE) vector of 12 nm in a direction of 244° (i.e. away from 064°) would give a DR position at 1020. Of course, this could also be done by calculating the Tr and GS for both the headings flown and then carrying out a track plot. The final result, if everything is perfect, should be exactly the same. In simple cases, involving only one heading, TAS and WV, the Tr and GS method is probably quicker and simpler but in multi-track cases the airplot will prove much simpler, particularly when a WV has to be found.

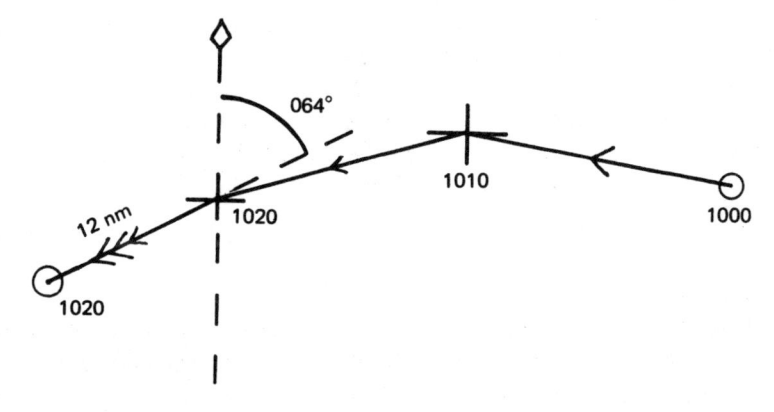

Fig. 3.6 The airplot.

Finding an airplot WV
The following example is illustrated in Fig. 3.7.

1200UTC   Fix 55°N 02°E Hdg 045(T) TAS 240 kt
1210   Alter heading (A/H) 090(T)
1215   Reduce TAS to 210 kt
   25   A/H 120(T)
   33   Fix 5520N 0430E
Find the mean WV from 1200 to 1233.

Figure 3.7 should be self-explanatory. It will be seen that at 1233 the aircraft's position indicates that the average effect of the WV since the airplot started at 1200 has been to blow the aircraft 23 nm in 33 min in a direction of 283°(T), i.e. away from a direction of 103°. The wind effect is therefore 103°/23 nm in 33 min and from this the WV is calculated to be 103°/42 kt (23 ÷ 33 × 60 = 42). Note the single arrow vectors for the airplot and the three arrows for the WE blowing *from* the 1233 air position *to* the 1233 fix position. Note also that the airplot involves a change of TAS and this is dealt with quite simply. Plotting the air position for 1215 when the TAS changed was not essential. The total air distance from 1210 to 1225 could be calculated:

(5 min at 240 kt) + (10 min at 210 kt) = 55 nm

and used to find the 1225 air position from the 1210 position.

Finding a DR position by airplot
Having found an average (mean) WV by airplot, it may be required to 'DR ahead' i.e. to find a DR position for (say) six minutes after the latest fix. From this, having measured the new required track and distance to reach the destination, a new heading and ETA can be obtained. Referring to Fig. 3.7, the procedure to DR ahead for six minutes would be to start a new airplot from the 1233 fix by drawing in an airplot vector 120°(T) for 21 nm (6 min of TAS). From the resulting 1239 air position, a WE vector is drawn parallel to the 1233 WE vector and of length 4.2 nm (6 min at 42 kt). From the resulting DR position (5511N 0453E), the normal procedure of drawing in the Tr and distance required to reach a destination can be carried out. It is worth noting that, if this is done, and then further fixing and wind finding is required before reaching the destination, the airplot should be *continued from the 1239 air position* and *NOT* restarted from the 1239 DR position. If subsequent wind vectors are drawn in they will represent WEs since the fix at 1233 *NOT* from 1239.

Practical exercises
The following exercises are set in the form favoured by the CAA in their navigation papers. Having calculated the required answer and selected the nearest of the four choices offered, it is best to use the CAA answer for further calculations. For example, if you calculated that the TAS should be

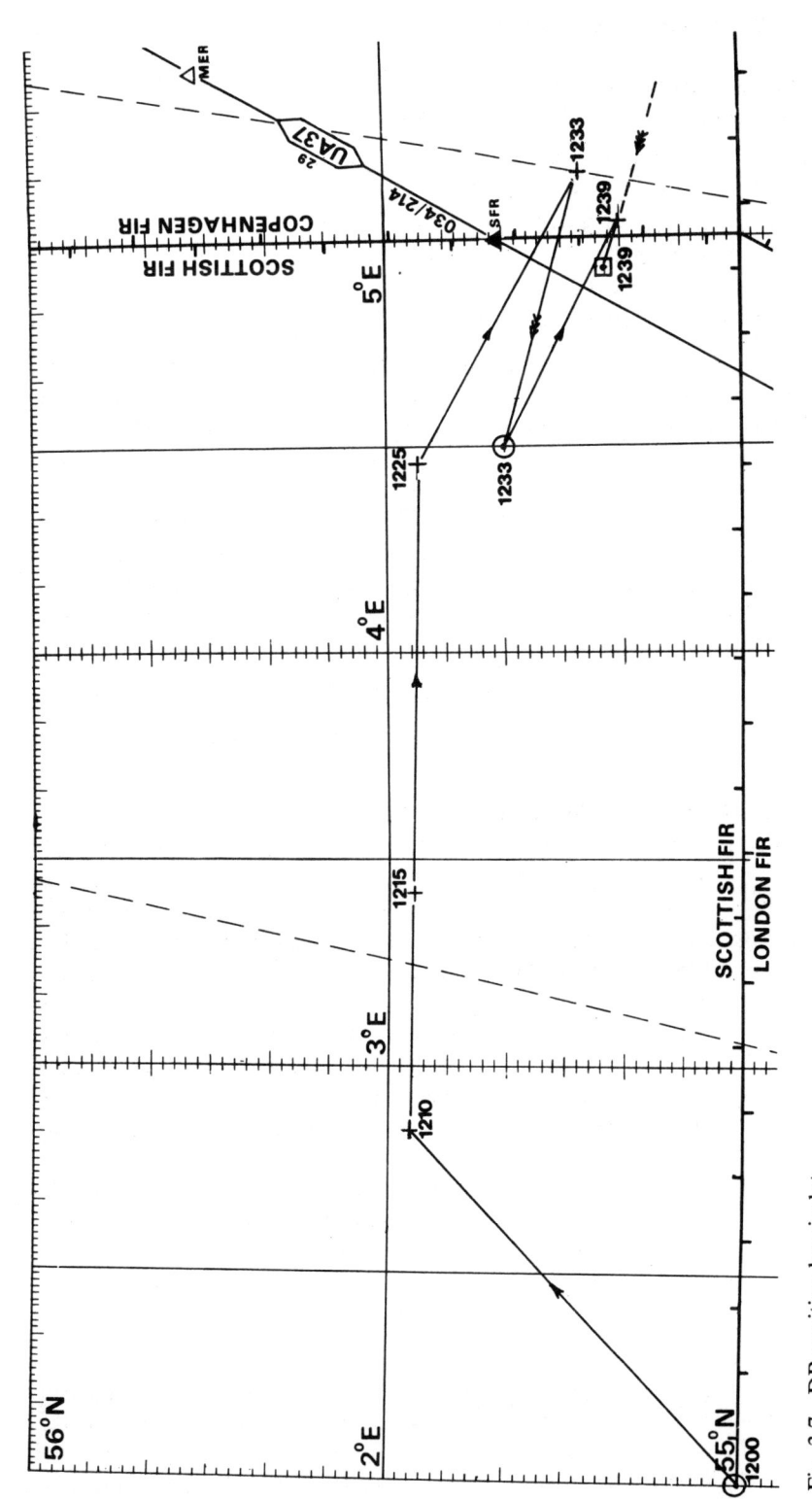

Fig. 3.7 DR position by airplot.

40 Plotting and Flight Planning

182 kt and the nearest answer offered was 180 kt, it is recommended that you then use 180 kt for any subsequent calculations.

The following data relating to a flight should be used together with Instructional Plotting Chart–Europe to answer questions 1 to 9 inclusive.

1027 DR position (5430N 0330E), set heading for SPY VORTAC (5233N 0451E) FL 50, TAS 220 kt, forecast WV 050°/30 kt.
You are cleared to join airway G9 at PAM VOR (5220N 0506E) at FL 90 and to commence the climb when overhead SPY VORTAC.
Assume for the climb: Mean TAS 150 kt.
                        Mean WV 070°/55 kt.
1110 Overhead PAM VOR, FL 90, set heading for RKN VOR (5208N 0645E), WV 130°/60 kt, RAS 200 kt, temperature −10°C.
1133 Overhead RKN VOR, alter heading for OSN VOR (5212N 0817E).
1139 Alter heading 10° to port.
1145 Heading 090°(M) Doppler drift 1°S GS 188 kt.
1152 Overhead OSN VOR.

Questions
(1) The mean heading °(M) required at 1027 is:
    (a) 170   (b) 146   (c) 156   (d) 160

(2) The initial ETA for SPY VORTAC is:
    (a) 1044   (b) 1100½   (c) 1059   (d) 1043

(3) At SPY VOR the heading °(M) for PAM VOR is:
    (a) 169   (b) 128   (c) 118   (d) 159

(4) The rate of climb in ft/min required from SPY VOR is:
    (a) 530   (b) 1060   (c) 400   (d) 800

(5) The cruising TAS from PAM VOR is:
    (a) 235   (b) 232   (c) 223   (d) 226

(6) The mean heading °(M) to steer at 1110 is:
    (a) 116   (b) 098   (c) 112   (d) 104

(7) At 1110 the ETA for RKN VOR is:
    (a) 1130   (b) 1134   (c) 1132   (d) 1147

(8) The mean WV between 1133 and 1152 is:
    (a) 098/48 (b) 088/37 (c) 120/74 (d) 098/70

(9) The local WV at 1145 is:
    (a) 098/48 (b) 088/37 (c) 130/60 (d) 082/37

The following data should be used when answering questions 10 to 16 inclusive:

1707 SPL VOR/DME (5217N 0445E) RMI reads 098°, range 90 nm, FL 110, TAS 258 kt, WV 250°/50 kt, heading 023°(T).

1728 GV NDB (5205N 0415E) RMI reads 178°
1732 NDO NDB (5347N 0849E) RMI reads 100°
1738 Alter heading SFR (5520N 0500E)

(10) The position of the aircraft at 1707 is:
 (a) 5251N 0217E (b) 5229N 0219E (c) 5221N 0343E
 (d) 5221N 0217E

(11) The theoretical range in nm of the SPL VOR/DME assuming its aerials are at sea level will be:
 (a) 131 (b) 95 (c) 38 (d) 48

(12) The DR Tr°(T) and GS in kt at 1707 is:
 (a) 015/288 (b) 023/293 (c) 030/297 (d) 030/293

(13) Assuming a VHF range of 100 nm and a GS of 300 kt, the aircraft will leave the coverage provided by the SPY VOR/DME at:
 (a) 1724 (b) 1728 (c) 1726 (d) 1731

(14) The position of the aircraft at 1732 is:
 (a) 5404N 0408E (b) 5405N 0347E (c) 5423N 0341E
 (d) 5355N 0410E

(15) The mean WV from 1707 to 1732 is:
 (a) 250/50 (b) 146/56 (c) 326/56 (d) 259/56

(16) The DR position at 1738 is:
 (a) 5450N 0402E (b) 5418N 0440E (c) 5429N 0436E
 (d) 5430N 0408E

The following data should be used when answering question 17:

1400 EEL VOR/DME (5310N 0640E) set heading 013°(T), TAS 190 kt on track to VES NDB/DME (5536N 0818E)
1435 Doppler drift 5°S GS 210 kt
1440 HUU NDB (5428N 0905E) bears 121° relative
1440 VES DME (5536N 0818E) range 37 nm
1444 JEV NDB (5331N 0801E) bears 171° relative

(17) The aircraft position is:
 (a) 5458N 0813E (b) 5508N 0814E (c) 5511N 0822E
 (d) 5513N 0815E

The following data should be used when answering questions 18 to 20 inclusive:

1705 Overhead EEL VOR/DME (5310N 0640E) set heading SPY VORTAC (5232N 0450E), TAS 160 kt, FL 80, WV 220°/30 kt.
 You are instructed to cross ENK NDB (5240N 0514E) at 2000 ft. Mean rate of descent 500 ft/min at constant RAS 120 kt, mean temperature +10°C and mean WV 250°/25 kt.

(18) The GS at 1705 is:
(a) 188 (b) 160 (c) 132 (d) 140

(19) The DR position at the top of descent is:
(a) 5251N 0546E (b) 5251N 0516E (c) 5256N 0558E
(d) 5238N 0522E

(20) The ETA at the top of descent is:
(a) $1717\frac{1}{2}$ (b) $1722\frac{1}{2}$ (c) 1719 (d) $1729\frac{1}{2}$

Chapter 4
PLOTTING ON OTHER CHARTS

Up to now all plotting procedures have been done on the Lambert's Conformal Conic. This is quite logical as the chances are that any plotting required will be done on charts which are readily available on the flight deck. These are likely to be Radio Facility Charts and the majority of these are on the Lambert's Projection. It is just possible, however, that other charts may be encountered and this Chapter will highlight any differences encountered in comparison with the Lambert's.

Chart conformality (orthomorphism)
Sensibly, any chart that is used for navigational plotting should be conformal. *Ground Studies for Pilots Volume 3* gives greater detail on this property, but here we should note that, unless a chart is conformal, measuring directions and distances on it will be extremely difficult if accurate results are required. Fortunately, the majority of charts encountered in civil aviation will be conformal (orthomorphic).

Practically every chart used will have its method of projection noted on it. Often the word conformal or orthomorphic will appear in the name. For your information the projections encountered are likely to be as follows:

Conformal	*Not conformal*
Lambert's Conformal Conic	Gnomonic (Polar, Oblique, Equatorial)
(Standard) Mercator (cylindrical conformal)	
Transverse Mercator	Orthographic
Oblique Mercator	Equi-distant
Stereographic (Polar, Oblique, Equatorial)	

Classification of charts for plotting
For plotting purposes, all conformal charts can be placed into two categories:

    Category M (Standard) Mercator
    Category L   All others – usually one of the following:
                      Lambert's Conformal
                      Oblique Mercator
                      Transverse Mercator
                      Polar Stereographic

Using category L (for Lambert's)

The use of Lambert's has already been dealt with in Chapters 2 and 3. Using any of the other charts in this category will not cause any problems if similar procedures are adopted. It will be necessary to remember that the value of chart convergency varies from chart to chart as is explained in Volume 3. In addition, certain problems will occur when flying in polar regions but these can be overcome by using grid navigation techniques as described in the next Chapter. Grid navigation can be used outside polar regions but inside these regions it is essential that it is used.

The suitability of category M charts for navigational plotting

In the past, the standard Mercator chart has been used extensively for plotting. The RAF, for example, produced Mercator plotting charts covering the whole world apart from the Arctic and Antarctic. As is described in Volume 3, the Mercator is an excellent chart for use in equatorial regions (say 15°N to 15°S) but outside these areas, its use is rather impracticable and fraught with all sorts of problems. Measuring distances requires considerable care and straight lines on the chart represent RLs which are not the shortest routes for an aircraft to follow and are not the paths taken by radio signals. It is interesting to note that automatic on-board navigation systems direct aircraft along GC routes, i.e. along curved lines on a Mercator chart. This is why one international airline issued their captains with non-conformal Oblique Gnomonic charts to cover their main routes. Although non-conformal, they had the one great virtue of accurately showing a GC as a straight line, and so a line drawn between two points would precisely represent the route followed by an automatically navigated aircraft.

Using the Mercator in equatorial regions

It is here that the Mercator comes into its own. Everything is right. Consider the properties:

Scale

This is practically constant. In general, the use of scale rulers is quite satisfactory.

Great circles

In equatorial regions these are almost identical with RLs and these are straight lines on the chart.

Graticule

This is rectangular and practically square which makes for great ease when reading off or plotting positions.

Plotting on other Charts

Radio bearings
These are GCs but in these areas almost identical with RLs, i.e. cutting all meridians at the same angle, so no corrections are required when plotting these bearings to allow for convergency.

In short, nothing could be easier. Use it like a Lambert's but forget about convergency corrections for the ADF/NDB position lines.

Using the Mercator in other regions
The best advice here is *Don't*. If nothing else is available, the following points will need to be remembered:

GC routes
Straight lines represent RLs so long routes will need to be broken down into a series of RLs which, taken together, will approximate to the GC required.

Measuring distances
The scale in middle latitudes is already varying quite rapidly, e.g. from 54° to 55° latitude, the scale increases by $2\frac{1}{2}$%! It is very necessary to measure distances very carefully at the correct appropriate latitude. Scale rulers must not be used.

Plotting radio bearings
The best procedure is to convert the GC bearing measured, whether at the station (VDF/VOR) or at the aircraft (ADF), into the equivalent RL bearing and this, or its reciprocal, can then be plotted without further problems.

Plotting radio bearings on Mercator charts in middle latitudes
Two procedures need to be recognised according to whether the bearing is being basically measured at the aircraft (ADF) or at the ground station (VDF/VOR). The following tabulations show the working sequence:

Type of bearing	VOR/VDF	ADF	
	QDM	RMI	RBI
	±180	Brg(M)	Brg(rel)
	QDR	a/c var	Hdg(T)
	Stn var	GC (T)	
	QTE	CA	
	CA	RL (T)	
To plot	RL (T)	±180	
		To plot	RL (T)

46 Plotting and Flight Planning

Notice the two important differences between the methods:

(1) Station variation is used for VOR/VDF but aircraft variation for ADF.

(2) Conversion angle (CA) is applied to the bearing measured at the a/c for ADF and to bearing measured at the station (QTE) for VDF/VOR.

In both cases the CA is applied to bring the bearing nearer to the equator, i.e. nearer to 180° in north latitudes and nearer to 000° in south latitudes.

Obtaining CA

This is dealt with in more detail in Volume 3. Here, we are concerned with the practical methods of obtaining and using it.

CA is the difference between corresponding RL and GC bearings and can be obtained by:

(1) Calculation: $CA = \frac{1}{2}$ch long × sine mean lat

(2) ABAC scale (chart margin), see Fig. 4.1

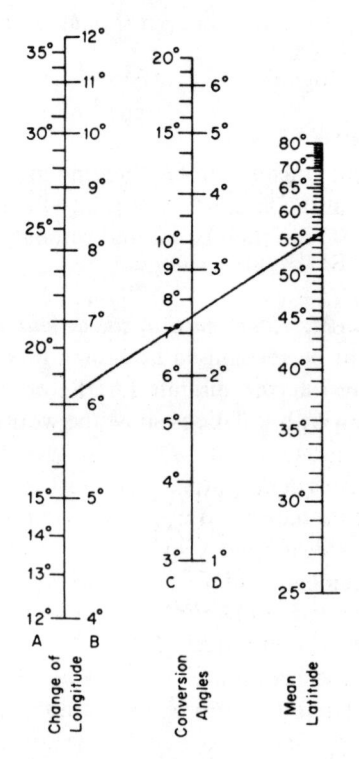

Fig. 4.1 Using the ABAC scale.

(3) Approximate factor:

lat	0	6	18	30	45	64	90
factor	0	0.1	0.2	0.3	0.4	0.5	

Example
DR position 5715N 0010E, NDB 5522N 0300W
Approximate mean lat 56°N, approximate ch long 3°
On calculator: $0.5 \times 3 \times 56 \sin = \underline{1.2°}$
On ABAC (Fig. 4.1): 3° ch long off the scale so use 6° and divide answer by 2 = $\underline{1.2°}$
Using factors: from the table, factor for 55° lat is 0.4°,
CA = $0.4 \times$ ch long (3) = $\underline{1.2°}$

Applying CA
CA should always be applied to the GC bearing measured to bring it nearer to the equator. For example, in the above example, if the aircraft had been on a heading of 330° (T) and a bearing of 267° had been obtained on the RBI of an NDB:

Brg (rel)	267
Hdg (T)	330
	597
	−360
GC Brg(T)	237
CA	− 1
RL Brg(T)	236
	−180
Plot	056 (T)

Figure 4.2 demonstrates the principle – the dotted GC shown is, of course, not a true representation. With a CA of only 1°, it would have been difficult to distinguish between the GC and the RL if they had been drawn in accurately. The diagram does demonstrate the correct sense of CA application, i.e. in this case it should be subtracted from 237° to bring the bearing nearer to 180°. If, in Fig. 4.2, the ground station was a VOR or VDF, the GC measured would have been 055° and it would have been necessary to add the 1° CA to obtain the RL of 056° to plot. Notice the application is still towards the equator (180° in Northern latitudes).

Consider now a Southern hemisphere case as shown in Fig. 4.3. The GC bearing measured at the aircraft position is 093° and the CA approximately 2° (4 × 0.4 = 1.6) and so applying the correction towards the equator gives an RL bearing of 091°. The reciprocal of 271° (T) is then plotted from the NDB.

48 *Plotting and Flight Planning*

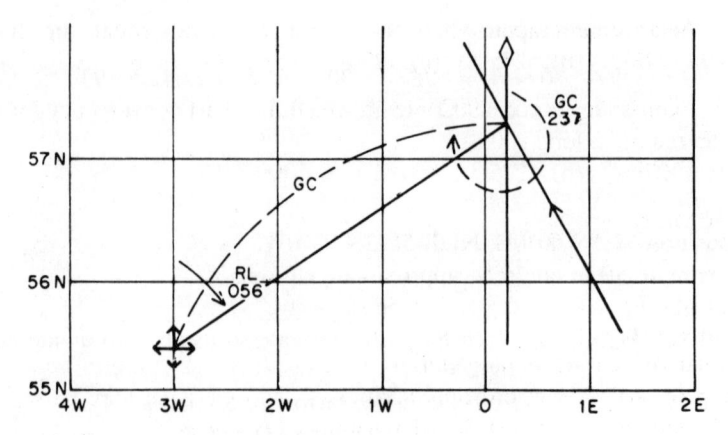

Fig. 4.2 Applying conversion angle – Northern hemisphere.

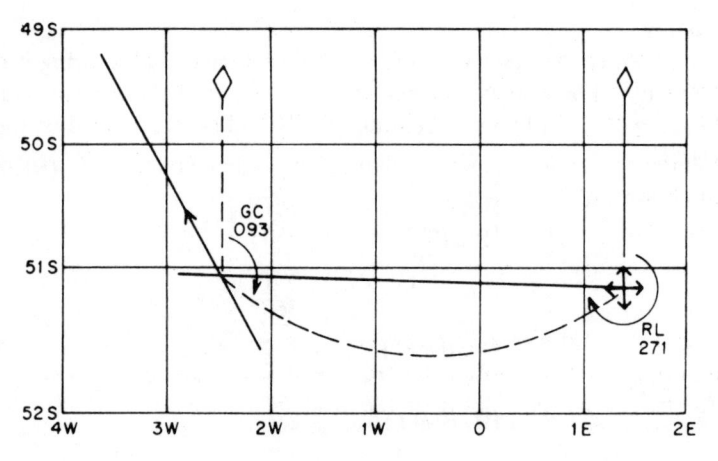

Fig. 4.3 Applying conversion angle – Southern hemisphere.

Examination questions
It is not likely that examination plotting on a Mercator will be required unless it happens to be in the equatorial region. In this case, plotting is extremely simple as no angular corrections to bearings are required and a scale ruler can be used for distance measurement. The practice questions given here, therefore, will deal merely with the resolution of bearings to plot and not the actual chart work.

Questions 1–3
An aircraft is in DR position 60°N 05°E where the magnetic variation is 3°E. An RMI reading on an NDB at 60°N 20°E where variation is 5°E is obtained of 080°. Give the bearing to plot from the true meridian at the NDB on the following:

Plotting on other Charts 49

(1) A Polar Stereographic where the chart convergency equals the ch long:
   (a) 278   (b) 275   (c) 270   (d) 280

(2) A Lambert's Conformal Conic on which the chart convergency for every degree of ch long is 0.8°:
   (a) 278   (b) 275   (c) 270   (d) 277

(3) A Mercator:
   (a) 278   (b) 275   (c) 270   (d) 272

Questions 4–6
The relative bearing of an NDB is measured as 235° by an aircraft on a heading of 065° (M) where the variations is 4°W. The ch long between the aircraft and the NDB is 11° and the mean latitude is 67°S. Give the true bearing to plot from the NDB on the following charts:

(4) Mercator:
   (a) 111   (b) 119   (c) 121   (d) 129

(5) Polar Stereographic where chart convergency = ch long:
   (a) 135   (b) 127   (c) 113   (d) 105

(6) Lambert's Conformal where chart convergency equals 0.75° per degree of ch long:
   (a) 108   (b) 116   (c) 124   (d) 132

Questions 7–9
An aircraft is in DR position 65°N 34°W where the variation is 30°W. RMI reading on a VOR in position 65°N 23°W where variation is 28°W, is 123°. Give the true bearing to plot from the VOR beacon on each of the following charts:

(7) Mercator chart:
   (a) 268   (b) 270   (c) 278   (d) 280

(8) Polar Stereographic chart:
   (a) 264   (b) 273   (c) 275   (d) 286

(9) Lambert's chart on which chart convergency is 0.85° per degree of ch long:
   (a) 266   (b) 273   (c) 275   (d) 284

Chapter 5
GRID NAVIGATION

Here we will touch only on the practical plotting on a grid chart, as the theory of the system is discussed fully in *Ground Studies for Pilots Volume 3*. The use of the grid chart for air navigation is the easiest thing in the world, overprinted on any chart with converging meridians.

A reference meridian is paralleled across the chart in an outstanding colour, and this grid line is used to measure angles, ignoring the meridians, to obtain, for example, a Tr (G). Also dotted across the chart are the grid variation isogonals, called lines of grivation (Griv). Before you mutter any imprecations, the happy word is that Tr (G) ± griv = Tr (M) and the sign of grivation is treated as for variation. Similarly for a heading, of course, so that you at once have the Hdg (M) to steer, and all problems of angular measurement on a chart with converging meridians are avoided.

A Hdg (G) will in fact differ from the Hdg (T) at any meridian by the convergence between that meridian and the reference meridian. This convergence has been applied algebraically to the variation to give grivation so that:

$$\text{Hdg (G)} \pm \text{griv} = \text{Hdg (T)} \pm \text{variation}.$$

When working on the chart, then, all angles (including WV) can be used quite satisfactorily in grid.

Have a check on the following run down, on a bit of the gridded Lambert's Chart, North Atlantic (see Fig. 5.1): the reference meridian on this one is in fact the Greenwich meridian, and n for the sheet is given as 0.748819, another way of saying 0.75. Convergence thus becomes for the North Atlantic Lambert:

$$\text{ch long} \times 0.75$$

A 5000N 4000W to B 5500N 5000W

(1) Measured from the 45W meridian: Mean GC Track 310
RL Track 310

Convergence = ch long × n
= 10 × 0.75
= 8°

This gives the initial GC Tr of 314 (RL 310 + $\frac{1}{2}$ convergence) and final GC Tr of 306 (RL 310 − $\frac{1}{2}$ convergence)

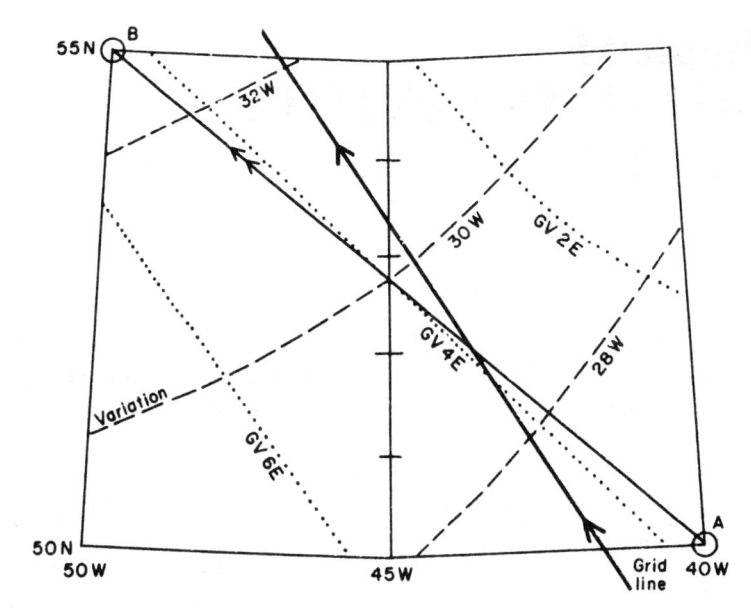

Fig. 5.1 Using a gridded chart.

(2) Now the mean GC Track of 310, keeping to the 45W meridian, would be 340 (M). The grid track there is 344 (G), grivation there is 4E giving a Tr of 340 (M), no different from the basic solution. The grid can be used overall, holding the a/c on the mean GC, avoiding the complications of the converging meridians.

There must be no mixing, of course; all the information in grid will evolve the correct navigational information. Take this example, on the computer:

Conventionally: Mean GC Tr 310 (T), TAS 300 kt
WV 250/40
∴ Hdg 303(T), Var 30W
= Hdg 333(M) and GS 280 kt
Grid: Tr 344(G), TAS 300 kt
WV 284/40(G)
∴ Hdg 337(G), Griv 4E
= Hdg 333(M) and GS 280 kt

The relationship between Tr (T) and Tr (G) is the value of the convergence of the reference meridian or grid line and the longitude in question; in this case, just a straight 45 × 0.75 = 34°, as the grid line is the Greenwich Meridian.

Chapter 6
RADIO NAVIGATION CHARTS

The main producers of these are British Airways (AERAD) and Jeppesen. When one becomes familiar with one of these systems, it is not too difficult to transfer to using the other system. Every pilot has his own preference – usually for the first charts they learnt to use! Each has certain advantages and disadvantages but there is no clear winner. Both companies are constantly seeking to improve their products and ensure that the competition does not establish an unassailable advantage.

In this chapter, the AERAD charts will be used and it is quite important to obtain a recent edition of EUR 1/2 on which to follow out the examples quoted. Of course, it is possible that you will come across some discrepancies and, after careful checking to ensure that you are not reading the chart incorrectly, you should believe your more up-to-date edition. To maintain a high level of reliability, charts are republished several times a year with often only very slight changes. It is, however, very dangerous to use out-of-date charts for operational purposes. Once a new edition of a chart is received, the previous one should be destroyed or clearly marked to show that it is no longer valid.

These charts are invaluable sources of information, not only on Radio Aids but also on all aspects of controlled airspace, restricted areas and radio communications. The charts are only part of the complete systems which incorporate manuals or supplements full of essential information regarding general aspects of aircraft operation plus local area, instrument approach charts, aerodrome plans and charts detailing standard instrument departures (SID) and standard terminal approach routes (STAR). The complete system package will be accepted as an integral part of the aircraft Operations Manual (OM) which every public transport aircraft has to carry.

AERAD charts are mostly on Lambert's Projection and sometimes this will be noted in a corner as LCO (Lambert's Conical Orthomorphic) together with the scale. Different series of charts have different colour conventions.

EUR 1/2

The following information is to be found in black:

Airway centrelines	Graticule figures
Radio facilities	Bearings and radials
Control zone boundaries	CTR, TMA, ATZ limits
FIR and ASR boundaries	Aerodromes listed in the Supplement

Under the blue colour look for the variation (isogonal) lines – the dates that these are valid are noted under the titles of the chart but they may be assumed to be accurate enough when using the current chart even if the chart and isogonal dates do not agree. Various types of restricted areas are also shown, aerodromes not listed in the Supplement, training and military areas, water features, safe clearance altitudes for latitude and longitude blocks.

Now to learn to recognise things on the chart:

(1) Controlled airspace

Airspace left uncoloured on the chart (and this applies to other specification charts) – that is, all airspace *shown in white* – is controlled airspace. The rules regarding a flight in controlled airspace are fully dealt with in our companion volume *Aviation Law for Pilots*.

(2) Airway

Airway centre line is shown in thick black line, with the name of the airway in the centre. In Fig. 6.1 it is ALPHA 47. Immediately on top of the airway name is the distance figure. This is the distance between two reporting points, compulsory or on request, the triangles at start and finish in Fig. 6.1. In this case the distance is 40 nm (all distances are in nautical miles) between Daventry and Lichfield. Daventry is shown as on request by an open triangle and Lichfield as a compulsory reporting point by a solid triangle. Facilities as shown in Fig. 6.2 are often superimposed upon the triangles.

Be careful when extracting distances. Distance breakdown occurs between reporting points and can happen between a reporting point and a sector point (X) on the route. If you have time, open up your dividers between two points and check the figure against the nautical mile (nm) scale (and not, please not, against kilometre (km)) given on top of the chart. If after a rough check your distance agrees reasonably with the printed distance, take *printed distance*. If you have made a careful check and the printed distance agrees within 2–3 miles, take the printed distance.

However, the printers do make mistakes and if your measured distance disagrees with the printed distance beyond the above limits, take the measured distance, but do point out in your answers in an examination why you are using measured distance.

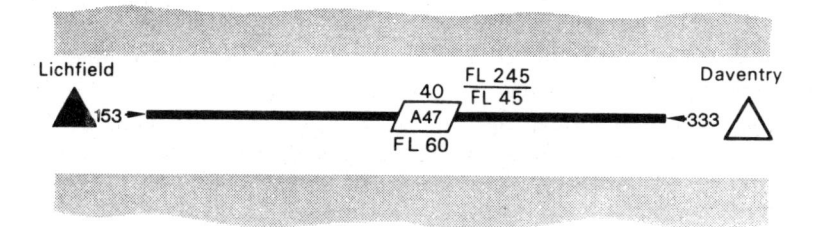

Fig. 6.1   Airway A47.

Tracks

Track angles are given at the beginning, immediately after the facility/reporting point. These tracks are *Magnetic*. In fact, no tracks, headings, bearings or radials on this (or any other) AERAD chart are True – they are all Magnetic. A one-way airway would have the track shown on one end only: the airway designation box indicates that the airway is one way, thus:

R12>

on the route from Clacton to Amsterdam.

Minimum flight level

The minimum flight level available on that particular sector of the airway is given immediately below the Airway designation: FL 60 in Fig. 6.1. This is the lowest level you can apply and get clearance for flight on this sector.

However it is usual for ATC to allocate either ODD or EVEN FLs – usually in accordance with the semi-circular rules (see *Aviation Law for Pilots*) but this is not necessarily so. AERADs (and Jeppesen) indicate by using either O> and E> or ODD and EVEN when the FLs differ from what would be expected. Alternatively, the minimum flight limit may be defined in terms of both, FL and altitude, e.g.

FL 50
(min alt 4500)

This simply means that FL 50 is available for flight provided it at least equates 4500 ft on QNH.

Airway vertical limits

Airway vertical limits must not be confused with minimum flight levels. These vertical limits legally define the controlled airspace forming an airway, CTR, TMA, etc. In our illustration the airway out from Daventry stretches from FL 45 (the base of the airway) to FL 245 (the ceiling of the Airway–Upper ATS routes start at FL 250). If these limits were to change, a pecked line at right angles to the airway centre line would indicate where the change takes place, and the ceiling and base limits would be printed on each side of this dividing line. This lowering of the base does not affect the minimum flight level available for flight on the sector.

The easiest way to distinguish between the two is: where a FL or altitude figure stands on its own on the chart it is the lowest limit at which the flight can be made; where FL or Alt appear in the form of a fraction, then those are the vertical limits imposed.

It may be mentioned that the base of an airway, or TMA need not be in terms of FL, it may be given as altitude as well, e.g. the vertical limits of ROMEO 123 SW of Brookmans Park are

$$\frac{FL\ 245}{3500}$$

Lastly, in the UK there is at least a 500 ft clearance between the base of the airway and the lowest clearance allocated by ATC on the airway.

Safe clearance altitude
The method of showing this along the airway in thousands of feet (3.3 = 3300 ft) is being replaced by the area system. Every 'box' of latitude and longitude on the chart will contain figures in large blue type:

$$3_4$$

indicating a safe clearance altitude for the 'box' of 3400 ft. The figure incorporates the following clearances:

Terrain up to	(1000 ft)	5	10	15	20	over 20
Clearance	(1000 ft)	1	1.5	2	2.5	3.0

It should be emphasised that a professional pilot is required to use the clearances laid down in his Company's OM which might exceed these.

That's just about all as far as airway symbols are concerned. We must warn you that the layout shown above (Fig. 6.1) is the ideal layout. In congested areas, information may be scattered all over the place.

(3) Now for the remaining symbols that you will see on the chart.

Reporting points
Small triangles, as shown above at Daventry and Lichfield. A full black triangle (complete block) is a *compulsory* reporting point and you *must* report there unless the current official advice is to do otherwise. A hollow black triangle is an 'on request' reporting point where ATC may request you to report.

Facilities

NDBs
Those tiny black flags above NDB symbols (but some distance away) are not indicative of holes at the local golf course. The flag direction is the direction of MN at the NDB below it. The flag to the west of the vertical line indicates westerly variation. In Fig. 6.2, the variation is easterly.

VORs
The direction of MN is indicated by a line with a flag at its top, from the 000° radial. The convention regarding easterly/westerly variation applies.

Note that a VOR on test has a special symbol (circle without calibration points) whereas an NDB on test has no separate symbol. In practice, an NDB is not inserted on the chart until it becomes fully operational.

56   *Plotting and Flight Planning*

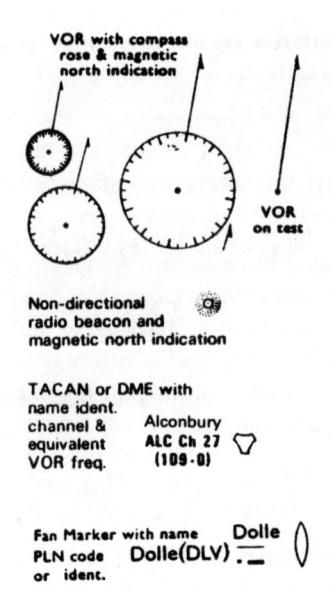

Fig. 6.2   Radio facilities.

TCAN/DME
Although ICAO has separated the two, a single symbol is used on AERADs to indicate both. The separation is achieved in the information box, see below.

Fan marker
Some of them are still left. You require a 75 MHz receiver to get the signals.

Facility frequencies
Against each facility symbol, the call sign and frequencies of the radio facilities are given. SND 362.5 for example is SOUTHEND NDB on frequency 362.5 kHz, call sign SND. In no time flat after some experience you will recognise VORs, NDBs, TACANs and so on, just from the frequencies given. On actual airways, the information is enclosed in a box. SND has no official route going through it.

Another point to note is that the callsign SND is in quotes, as is practically every other NDB in the UK. This indicates that the emission is NON A2A (or A2 as it used to be called). As explained in volume 1, the signals of this type can be heard without switching to BFO or CW on the ADF. Omission of the quotes indicates that the emission is NON A1A (or A1) for which it will be necessary to switch to CW/BFO to hear the callsign. NDBs of this latter type will still be found in many parts of the world.

As for DME and TACAN let us take a look at the following frequencies noted on the chart:

Pole Hill	Coningsby	Camelot
POL 112.1	CGY Ch 48	CMT 113.5
Ch 58 (DME)	(111.1)	CMZ Ch 82 (DME)

You will find the first and second of these on Fig. 6.6. Pole Hill is a typical airways VOR/DME using the standard frequency pairing. Tuning the VOR to 112.1 MHz will automatically set the DME to Channel 58 and the pilot will have a continuous read-out of bearing to and distance from Pole Hill. Coningsby is a military TACAN from which ranges can be obtained by tuning the VOR to 111.1 MHz and so automatically selecting Channel 48 on the DME. Bearings will not, however, be obtainable. Camelot is typical of a DME which is not co-located with the VOR. This is indicated by the DME having a different callsign ending in Z. In such cases they are fairly close together (say 1 nm apart) and frequency paired so that they can be used en route to obtain bearing and distance fixes.

Control Zones (CTRs), Control Areas, Military ATZs
CTRs are shown as white areas outlined by a black pecked line, Control and Terminal Manoeuvring Areas are surrounded by a thicker grey line. MATZ are shown as white areas outlined with a black pecked line. The vertical limits are shown:

Honington	Scampton	Ramstein (see Fig. 6.8)
(Mil) CTR	(Mil) ATZ	TMA A
$\dfrac{4000}{g}$	$\dfrac{3460}{g}$	$\dfrac{FL\ 245}{1000\,g}$

g = ground or above ground level; unqualified numbers are altitudes.

Altimeter setting regions (ASRs)
These are shown by longish pecked lines in black, the lines defining the boundaries. The names of the regions appear somewhere along the pecked lines, and when you cross this line, you should change your altimeter setting to the QNH value of the region you are entering if you wish to check for terrain clearance. For normal en-route flying, the standard altimeter setting of 1013 mb will be used.

FIR boundaries (Fig. 6.3)
The name of the FIR, its ICAO four-letter code, and the upper limit of the FIR which in each case is FL 245 is given. It is worth mentioning that the FIR does not have to be a straight line. FIR boundaries quite often coincide with national frontiers. On Fig. 6.8 find and note the shape of the boundary between the PARIS and FRANKFURT FIRs.

58 *Plotting and Flight Planning*

Fig. 6.3 FIR boundaries.

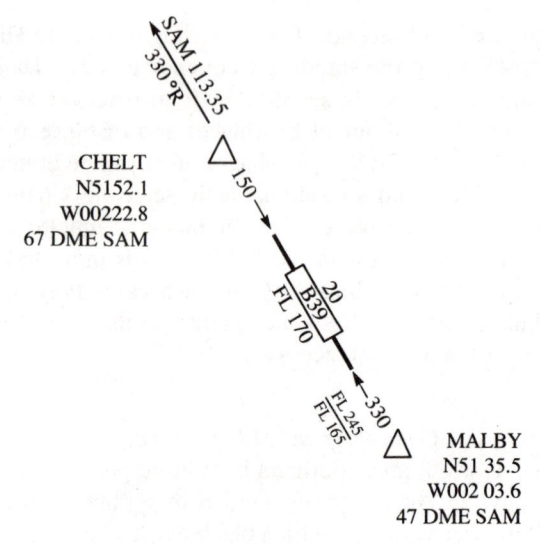

Fig. 6.4 Radial 330 from SAM.

Bearings and radials
These generally define reporting points, where they are not co-located with radio facilities; in the main they are on-request points. There are a few left, but now they are invariably radials, as illustrated in Fig. 6.4. If you do come across an odd NDB bearing, follow the line down to the NDB itself where the bearing figure is inserted.

In Fig. 6.4 note that the two reporting points MALBY and CHELT are defined by the radial 330 from SAM from which they are distant respectively 47 and 67 nm and, as SAM is off the chart, its callsign and frequency is given. Note also the ICAO practice of using five-figure identifiers for reporting points which are not located at a facility (i.e. CHELT).

Advisory routes (ADRs)
An advisory route (Class F airspace) is shown as a black line with white 'tramlines' 5 nm away on each side to indicate the route boundaries. The designators for ADRs always end in the letter D, e.g. W928D (Whiskey 928 Delta) from BLACA to IOM VOR. Being uncontrolled airspace, the FLs used will be quadrantal and it will be noted on this route across the Irish Sea that the minimum FL available is 55 and, of course, this would only be used

Radio Navigation Charts 59

going from BLACA to the Isle of Man (2nd quadrant). Check in *Aviation Law for Pilots* for more details on these rules.

Direct track
You will find, out of Ottringham, for example, a series of routes over the North Sea simply designated by a rectangle containing the letters DT for direct track:

$$\boxed{\text{DT}}$$

These are commonly used routes over the uncongested areas. The distances have been calculated by AERAD themselves, and they are therefore unofficial as it were, but they like to be helpful.

Danger areas
Danger areas should be checked before flight; the chart shows permanent danger/restricted areas as a continuous blue line; temporary ones (that is, those activated by Notam) are shown by small pecked lines. Prohibited areas are filled in with tiny blue dots.

On the last fold on each side of the chart you will find the airspace restriction panel which sorts out danger and restricted areas (which otherwise look alike on the chart: continuous line if permanent or during published hours, broken if temporary) and give pertinent details about those and prohibited areas. It is necessary that you are able to decode printers' shorthand. Here are a few examples, taken from 'France'.

R1 820–2600 g M Eveng–Sat Morng HN
R1 is the ident of the Area, and the area concerned is a restricted area (R). Limits 820–2600 g imply the figures are on QFE (above the ground), and it is restricted to night hours M–F only. Quite a biggie, this one, if you trace it round.

R77 FL60 Permanent
Here the limit is from ground or sea whichever happens to occupy the area up to FL 60 (on 1013.2 setting).

D43 FL 30–55 HJ (VMC) HN and Notified
This is a danger area (D), limits are obvious but under the remarks column we have been given times of operation: daylight hours if VMC, at night or when notified in Notam.

If the limit was given, say, as 1000–FL 55, it means both limits on 1013.2. 1000 above ground is given as 1000 g. Other abbreviations used are:

Unltd – unlimited
Wkd – weekdays, Monday to Saturday (inc.)
M   – Monday
Tu   – Tuesday, and so on

HJ – daylight hours (proof of the mapmakers' deep knowledge of the French tongue)
HN – night
agl – above ground level
(S) – Summer
(W) – Winter.

TMA boundaries
These are perhaps the most difficult ones to spot. Main boundary and all subdivisions of the TMA within it are shown by white areas (controlled airspace) bounded by thickish grey lines. What makes it difficult to trace is the fact that these boundaries generally run along the outer boundaries of airways – just where the white colour finishes and the grey starts – and the lines seem to merge with the background grey. However, with a little practice you will soon be able to keep it in sight. Try Scottish TMA for a starter on your own copy of EUR 1.

Isogonals
These are shown as blue lines. The date and annual rate of change are shown just under the chart title EUR 1. For practical purposes it can be accepted that the isogonals are accurate enough, as long as the chart that you are using is itself in date, although the magnetic information is several years adrift.

(4) Miscellaneous
Authorised routes (which are neither airways nor ADRs) are shown as ATS routes by thin black lines, with track and arrow at both ends if the route is two-way. If the route is one-way, the route line ends with an arrow. See routes in the area north of 54N and around 02 10W, north of Pole Hill (N53 44.6 W002 06.1) on EUR 1 in CUMBRIA (Fig. 6.5).

Airway frequencies
For UK and Germany, frequencies for use on the airways are no longer shown on the chart. If required, they will be found in the appropriate AERAD Supplement.

On EUR 2 you will notice that countries on the continent sectorise the territory into convenient communication sectors, and the frequency for use in a particular sector is given in a prominent (so they say) place inside the sector (boxed in a parallelogram).

Paris Ctl	Brussels Ctl
(NW of Paris)	(W of Brussels)
128.2	128.8 128.45

Paris Control and Brussels Control are the callsigns.

More frequencies are listed on the front fold of the chart – CTR, FIS, and so forth. Have a look at them.

Radio Navigation Charts 61

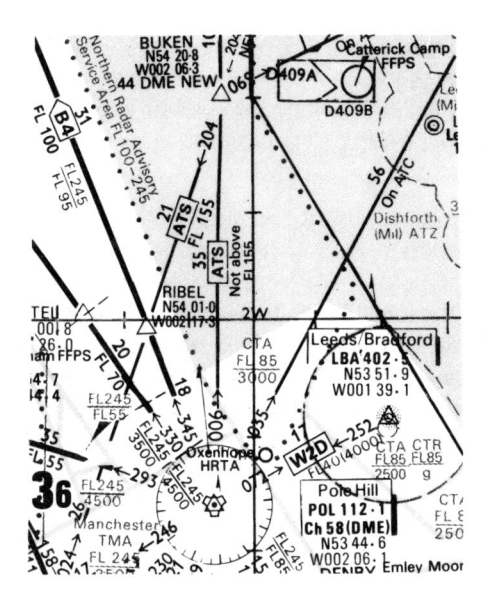

Fig. 6.5 ATS routes.

Flight levels
Generally semi-circular rules apply on airways, and AERAD inserts ODD and EVEN when necessary on the airways (e.g. A25 at Dean Cross) although these are sometimes left out in cluttered areas. In the absence of these, fly odd thousands when Tr(M) lies between 000–179; fly evens when Tr(M) between 180–359. This is, however, only a general rule and many exceptions occur (perhaps you remember that rules of quadrantal and semi-circular flying do not apply in controlled airspace in IFR: you fly the level given to you).

Information not on EUR 1/2
Any information on routes at FL 250 and above is contained on high level charts such as H203 and H112.

Information on holding (holding point, pattern, time and min. alt.) is contained in a panel on 'area charts'.

The remaining symbols on EUR 1/2 are

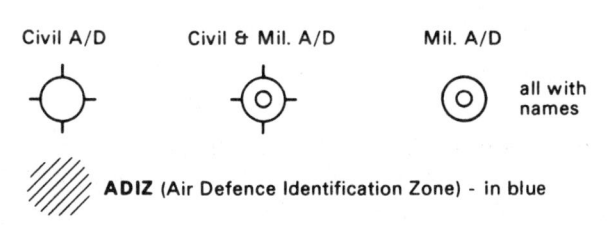

Civil A/D   Civil & Mil. A/D   Mil. A/D

all with names

ADIZ (Air Defence Identification Zone) - in blue

Notes on airway flying

(1) To stress the point again, distances are given between compulsory or on-request reporting points, the solid or open black triangles, most of the time, also between intersection or turning points marked with a cross, so watch it.

(2) A report is not necessarily required on crossing a boundary from one Flight Information Region (FIR) to another, but you must be aware you have crossed it for your subsequent reports. The parallel of latitude 55N from 0500E to 0530W is marked with a pecked line indicating such a boundary, and the name of the appropriate FIR region set on either side of it, London & Scottish. Three boundaries meet on the 0530W meridian at 5355N, for example, easy to recognise here, but on B29 on 294M out of Nicky near Brussels the boundary is a winding river which is crossed four times in about 30 nm.

(3) A report is made only to the Air Traffic Control Centre (ATCC) of the FIR in which the aircraft is flying: thus, a report in the London FIR is to London airways.

(4) The message content is crisp and its form invariable, once communication has been established (Scottish airways, this is Golf Alpha Sierra Tango on 124.9, do you read?). 'Scottish airways, this is Golf Alpha Sierra Tango, Lichfield 27, Flight Level 80, estimate Oldham 39, over'. That's all. Who you are, where you are, your Flight Level, ETA next point, over, and memorise the form.

Let us consider a stage of a flight from HEATHROW to PRESTWICK via Bravo 4 from the time of passing over BROOKMANS PARK (5145N 0006W) part of which is shown in Fig. 6.6 from EUR 1.

BROOKMANS PARK is a non-compulsory reporting point with a VOR/DME, callsign BPK and frequency 117.5 Channel 122. The route is clearly Westbound (334M) and so in the absence of any contra-indication, we will fly at an EVEN FL. The lowest acceptable is shown on the chart as 110 and so we will choose FL 120. We will be flying under the instructions of London Control and in accordance with the clearance they issued in response to the flight plan we would have submitted before take-off.

BEDFO is the next reporting point (on request only), it is 33 nm from BPK on a Tr 334(M). If arrival here is to be confirmed, the most accurate cross-check would be using DAVENTRY VOR/DME, QDM 270, range 20 nm (dividers or a suitable ruler will be needed to check this). These readings should be obtained simply by tuning 116.4 MHz on the VOR and checking the c/s DTY is being received before accepting the readings.

Another question that may be posed concerns the readings that would be expected on the BPK VOR. If the aircraft is fitted with an RMI, the answer is very simple. The head of the needle would indicate the QDM back to BPK, i.e. 154, or conversely the tail of the needle would indicate the QDR 334 – always presuming that you are accurately on track! If the aircraft is only

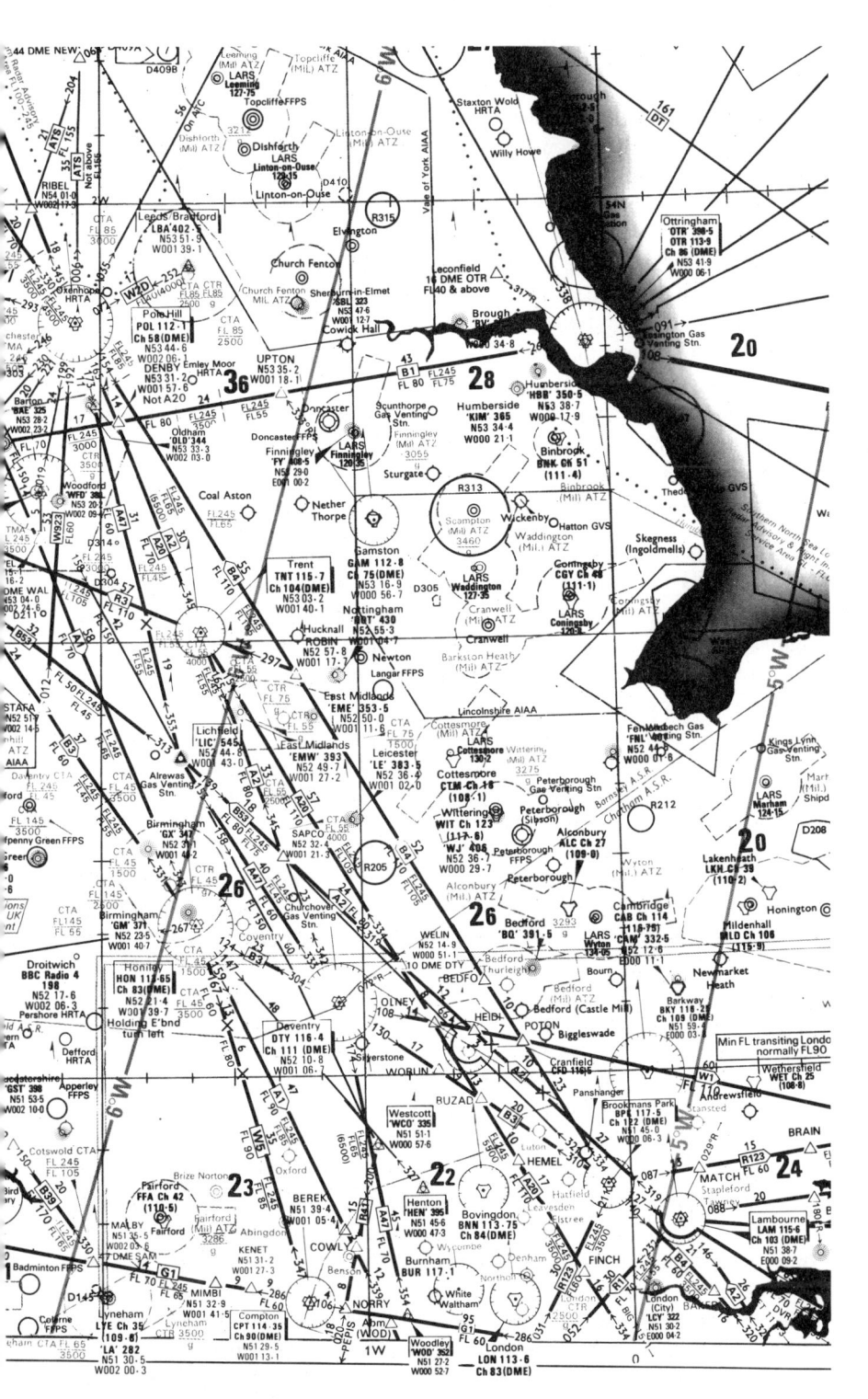

Fig. 6.6 Section of AERAD chart EUR 1.

fitted with a RBI the tail of the needle should indicate the actual drift being experienced, i.e. 10°S would show as 010°(rel) or 10°P as 350°(rel).

The next significant reporting point is POLE HILL VOR/DME. Flying at FL 120 the reception range of VHF signals will be approximately $12.5\sqrt{(120)} = 137$ nm approximately. Referring to the chart, the total distance from BPK to POL is $33 + 52 + 55 = 140$ nm. It follows that POL could be used for most of the flight to give positive checks on the aircraft's position in terms of QDM and distance to go.

How clear are we of high ground? Flying on an airway in the UK always guarantees a clearance of at least 1500 ft above the highest obstruction within 15 nm of the centreline of the airway but apart from this, we can check the minimum clearance altitudes for the 1° lat/1° long 'boxes' along the route. These give altitudes of 2200, 2600 and 3600 ft as far as POL.

Shortly before arriving at POL, the new Tr(M) required from POL of 345(M) would be selected for automatic flight or, if flying manually, it would be set on the omni-bearing selector (OBS). Arrival at POL would be indicated by the DME reading about 2 nm – at 12 000 ft, the aircraft would be about this distance above the ground beacon. Having passed POL, the VOR indications will reverse. On the RMI, the head of the needle will now show QDM 165° and on the L/R indicator, the word FROM will appear in the window of the indicator instead of TO.

A word about other controlled airspace on this route. The route starts in the London TMA, passes over the Bedford (Mil)ATZ, the Daventry CTA (not apparent on the chart) and the Nottingham (E Midlands) CTR (g to FL 75) and then goes through the Manchester TMA (up to FL 245). The actual positions of entry and exit are not easily identified on this involved area of the chart but this need not concern the pilot too much. Having been cleared to fly on Bravo 4, he will be instructed when to change from one controller to another. Although it cannot be deduced from this chart, an aircraft flying below FL 155 will be controlled by Manchester from abeam Birmingham (about 5225N) until Shapp (5430N) and then it comes under Scottish Control. To find out the details, if interested, it is necessary to either consult the AERAD Supplement or the COM section of the *UK Air Pilot*.

From Pole Hill until reaching the next significant point in the flight, MARGO, the total distance is 62 nm. There are VOR/DMEs at each end of the stage POLE HILL to TALLA on B4 and from our previous assessment, they should both be within range for the whole stage. Navigation, therefore, should be quite simple. If fitted with twin VOR/DME, it will be possible to have a constant display of both TMG and Tr required as well as distance gone and distance to go. The DMEs fitted in many light aircraft, have a simple arrangement whereby, when locked on to a DME ahead of the aircraft, both the GS and time to go can be displayed. In this case, Talla would be providing the means for a constant up-date of the ETA.

A point about this route to be noted is that the box surrounding the airway identifier or designator B4 is arrowed to indicate that this route is only normally available for traffic in the north-westerly direction. It is an interesting exercise to try to work out the route to follow for the reverse flight.

From MARGO, instead of flying along B4, the most direct path that could be followed would be the ATS route to Turnberry. The track is shown as 305°(M) and distance 78 nm (23 + 55).

If clearance was given for this route, how would it be navigated? Even if the aircraft only had the very basic navigation aid 'fit' required for airways flight, navigation of this route would be quite simple. The arrival at MARGO would be identified by the readings on the Talla VOR/DME of 345°M/52 nm. Prior to this, assuming another VOR/DME available on the aircraft, TRN VOR should have been tuned in and identified and a Tr(M) to steer of 305° selected. On arrival at MARGO, it would then simply be a matter of turning to make good the new Tr. In practice, the turn would probably have been started just before arriving at MARGO so as to turn smoothly on to the new track. (Refer to inset map in top left hand corner of EUR 1.)

A large scale area chart is available for busy areas shown on these charts by black double-lined rectangles: London area is an example. Also, each airfield has its approach charts. Area charts are simply blown up charts of the areas shown on the AERADs in a 'picture frame'. Further information is given to ease the pilot's load when in a busy area, calling for prompt attention to control instructions. There is no change in symbols, etc., but holding points and patterns, communication frequencies for the various airports when departing therefrom or arriving thereto, special charts for specific aerodromes with their departure/arrival routes are clearly shown.

Approach charts simply blow up the facilities at a particular aerodrome, and give every detail about them.

High altitude charts, labelled with an H, such as H203/4, are similar to the types we have been studying. They are for flight at or above FL 250, and since greater speeds are involved, a smaller scale is used so giving a larger ground area on each chart.

Tracks, distances, bearings, frequencies: all these change from time to time, changes incorporated every 28 days by UKAIP AIRAC amendments. So, if any of the above information does not match your chart, do not worry, so long as you understand what we are trying to convey.

Before leaving the topic, it is convenient to run over transition altitude (TA), transition level and transition layer. On take-off and landing, climb and descent, they are quite distinct.

The TA is the altitude (QNH-based) in the vicinity of an aerodrome below which the vertical position of an aircraft is controlled using altitude (QNH-based). Transition level is the lowest FL available for use which is physically (not necessarily numerically) above the TA. For example, taking-off at an aerodrome where QNH is 1000 mb and TA is 4000 ft, the pilot will use an altimeter setting of 1000 mb when complying with ATC instructions regarding the altitudes at which to fly. On reaching altitude 4000 ft, he will reset his altimeter sub-scale to 1013 mb and so increase the indicated altitude by

66 Plotting and Flight Planning

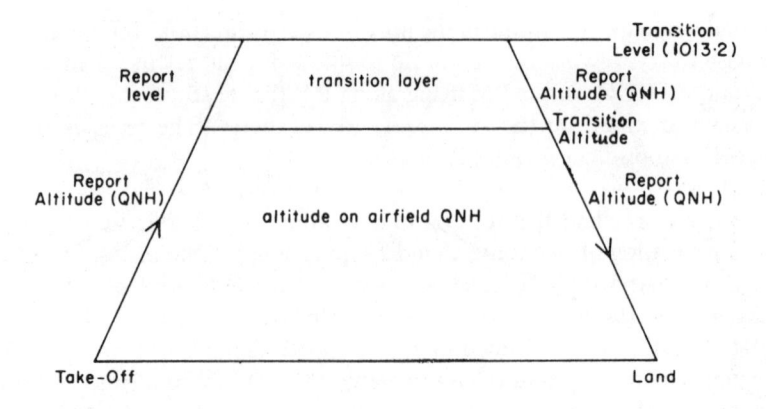

Fig. 6.7 Flight levels and altitudes.

approximately 13 × 30 = 390 ft to 4390 ft. It is likely that the first FL available will be 50 (5000 ft on an altimeter set to 1013 mb) and this will be the transition level. When at the end of a flight an aircraft approaching this aerodrome is cleared from an FL to an altitude during its descent, the current QNH will be given. On leaving its present FL, the pilot will change his altimeter setting to the QNH unless further FL passing reports are required. Once below the transition level altitudes will always be used. The transition level is the very latest level at which the change from the standard setting of 1013 mb to QNH will be made (Fig. 6.7).

The AERAD charts are of course constantly being brought up to date, and the operational use of the very latest issue is imperative.

Now try this exercise, using Fig. 6.8 and then any available EUR 2 for the latter part of the flight.

You are planning an airways flight from STUTTGART (4842N 0913E) to REIMS (4919N 0403E) via R11, R7 and R110. You join the airway R11 at TANGO reporting point and leave at MONTMEDY VOR. You are cleared to fly direct between GTQ and LUXIE. TAS 280 kt. You are equipped with twin ADFs, VORs and DMEs. Descend from MONTMEDY VOR.

Questions

(1) In the absence of any other information, are you expected to fly at ODD flight levels or EVEN flight levels?

(2) Give a complete list of the compulsory reporting points.

(3) State TANGO NDB's frequency, ident and type of emission.

(4) Is there any facility at TANGO from which you could receive range information? If so, state how you would use it.

(5) About half-way between TANGO and SUL, a grey line running North/South cuts your track on the chart. What purpose does this line serve?

Radio Navigation Charts 67

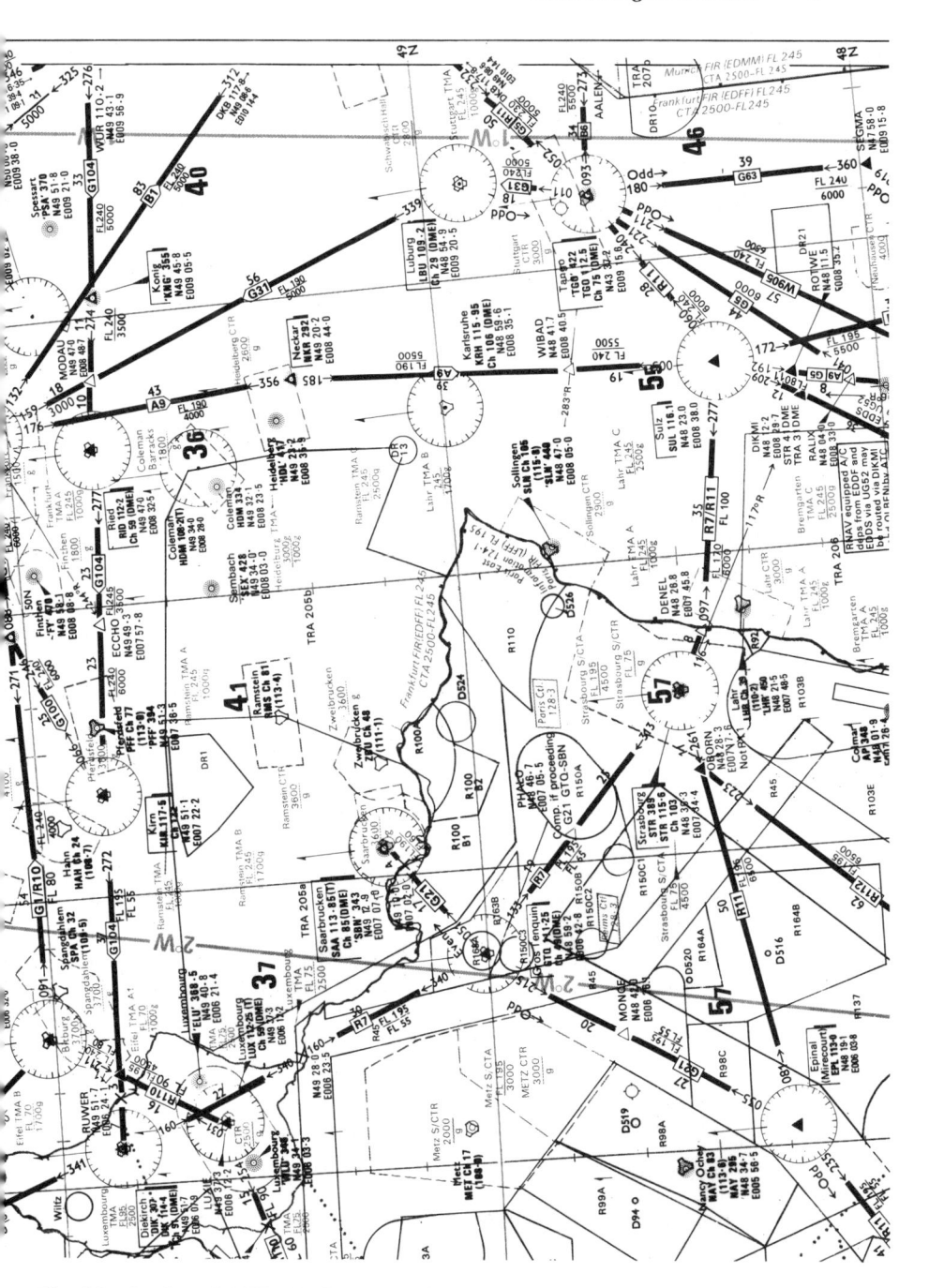

Fig. 6.8 Section of AERAD chart EUR 2.

68 Plotting and Flight Planning

(6) Arriving at the ETA for SUL reporting point, how would you check that you were at SUL if the facility there was not operating?

(7) Between SUL and STRASBOURG
    (a) what is your track?
    (b) what is the distance?
    (c) below the airway centre line, this information is given:

$$\frac{FL\ 170}{6000}$$

Give the meaning of each item.

18 nm from STRASBOURG, you cross a broken black line on the chart and 10 nm later an open triangle.

(8) What is the broken black line for?

(9) What does the open triangle signify?

(10) Just before crossing the broken black line, in whose TMA are you flying?

(11) Are you flying in any CTR at this time?

(12) How would you know from the DME when you are overhead STRASBOURG?

You leave STRASBOURG VOR at 1000 on heading 322°(M) for GROS TENQUIN. Your VORs are tuned to STR and GTQ beacons and your ADF to STR NDB. TAS is 280 kt.

(13) If you are on track, what readings do you expect on the RMI for the VOR beacons and on the RBI for the ADF?

You arrive over GROS TENQUIN at 1011.

(14) What WV was experienced on this leg?

You are cleared to fly direct from GROS TENQUIN to LUX VOR.

(15) What is your ETA at LUX?

(16) How would your VORs and ADFs be tuned on this leg?

You are overhead LUX at 1022, FL180.

(17) Assuming that the WV remains unchanged, give your full position report at 1022.

(18) What information would you expect to receive in return?

(19) When at MONTMEDY VOR, to whom would you pass your position report and request permission to leave the airway and proceed to REIMS? On what frequency?

Radio Navigation Charts

(20) Are you now in PARIS TMA?

(21) On your last leg to REIMS, while descending what is your minimum clearance altitude?

(22) What navigation facilities are available at REIMS which you could use?

(23) Between GROS TENQUIN and LUXEMBOURG, the route is subject to some kind of restricted airspace. What can you tell about it?

(24) Why is Germany shown with a white background whereas France, Belgium and Luxembourg have areas of grey?

(25) Does any of the flight pass through BRUSSELS FIR? If so, where did you enter and leave?

Answers
(1) EVEN

(2) TGO; SUL; STR; GTQ; LUXIE; MMD.

(3) 422 kHz TGO NON A2A

(4) DME. Tune VOR to 112.5 MHz.

(5) Stuttgart TMA boundary.

(6) Use TGO 240 Radial 28 nm range.

(7) (a) Tr 277(M) becoming 296(M)

  (b) 43 nm

  (c) Upper & lower limits of airway.

(8) Lahr CTR boundary.

(9) Non-compulsory reporting point at FIR boundary.

(10) Lahr TMA sector A.

(11) No. Too high. The CTR upper limit is 3000 ft.

(12) The DME will read the aircraft FL (i.e. if at FL 120, it will read 2 nm).

(13) On RMI heads of needles – 313(M) and 133(M). RBI for 9P drift reads 171.

(14) 006/60 kt. (From Hdg 322 Tr 313 GS 44 in 11 min = 240 kt)

(15) ETA 1022. (From WV 006/60; TK 333; TAS 280 kt. So GS = 230 kt. 42 nm = 11 min)

(16) VOR1 LUX 112.25; VOR2 GTQ 111.25; ADF WLU 348.

70   *Plotting and Flight Planning*

(17) Brussels Control – My ident – LUXIE 22 – Estimate MONTMEDY 31. (Using GS 297 kt Distance 44 nm)

(18) None.

(19) Paris Control on 128.1 MHz.

(20) No.

(21) 3000 ft, to give 1000 ft clearance.

(22) REM VOR and DME 112.3 MHz.

(23) R163A and R163B: Restricted areas up to 4000 ft. Summer Mon-Fri 0700–1500. Winter + 1 hr. Restricted area R45 800 ft agl–2500 ft agl Summer Mon, Tues, Thurs 0730-1500. Winter +1 hr.

(24) Grey is used for areas outside controlled airspace (Classes F and G).

(25) The flight enters Brussels FIR at the sector point 30 nm from GTQ and leaves at the sector point 15 nm from LUXIE en route to MMD.

Chapter 7
RELATIVE MOTION

Relative motion

This is defined as the motion of one body relative to another. Mathematically it is the vector difference between the velocities of two bodies. To obtain a vector difference it is necessary to add vectorially one vector to the other vector reversed. The resultant will be the vector difference.

Single track relative motion

To begin, we will consider the simplest case of relative motion when the two bodies are both moving along the same track either in the same or opposite directions. The easiest way to understand these problems is to take an actual example and explain each step of the procedure to be followed to reach a solution.

Example 1 – The overtaking case

Aircraft X is leaving A at 1015 at GS 300 kt. Y is also due to leave A at 1045 along the same track but at GS 400 kt. When will Y overtake X and when will the two aircraft be within 60 nm of each other?

Solution

(1) In any relative motion problem always start by drawing a diagram and then establish the relative positions of the two aircraft at the *earliest time when they are both in motion*. The relative motion calculation starts from this moment (Fig. 7.1). In this case the earliest time would be 1045 and so X has moved by 30 min of GS along the track at 300 kt, a distance of 150 nm.

(2) Establish the distance to close (d to c). Obviously in this case at 1045 it will be 150 nm. Imagine yourself as the pilot of aircraft Y looking ahead (perhaps with the help of radar) and seeing the aircraft that you intend overtaking 150 nm away.

(3) The closing speed (CS) at which you will be overtaking the aircraft will be the difference of the two speeds (relative velocity equals the vector difference of the two velocities) which is 100 kt.

72   *Plotting and Flight Planning*

```
1015                                          1045
X  [•]·········30 min @ 300 kt = 150 nm········[•] GS 300 kt ⟶

A  ⊙— — — — — — — — — — — — — — — — — — — —

Y  [•] GS 400 kt ⟶
1045
```

Fig. 7.1   Aircraft overtaking.

(4) The time to close (t to c) is derived from the distance to close at the closing speed. 150 nm @ 100 kt = 90 min. So the time of overtaking will be 1045 + 1 hr 30 min = <u>1215</u>.

(5) The solution can always be checked by calculating where the two aircraft will be at the overtaking time.
X will have flown 1015–1215 = 2 hr @ 300 kt = 600 nm from A
Y will have flown 1045–1215 = 1 hr 30 min @ 400 kt = 600 nm from A

(6) The two aircraft will be 60 nm apart when aircraft Y has closed a distance of 150 − 60 = 90 nm. Time to close at 100 kt will be 54 min. Aircraft will first be within 60 nm at 1045 + 54 = <u>1139</u>.

(7) They will remain within 60 nm until Y is 60 nm ahead of X. In other words, Y will have travelled a relative distance of 120 nm from 60 nm behind to 60 nm ahead. At the relative speed of 100 kt, this will take 1 hr 12 min and so ETA for 60 nm beyond will be 1139 + 1 hr 12 min = <u>1251</u>.

Example 2 – The meeting case
The distance from P to Q is 700 nm. An aircraft leaves P at 1200 flying at a GS of 300 kt towards Q. Another aircraft leaves Q at 1300 flying towards P at 180 kt. When and where will they meet?

Solution
(1) Diagram first, showing the respective positions of the aircraft at 1300 (Fig. 7.2).

(2) At the first time when they are both in motion, the distance to close is 400 nm (see Fig. 7.2).

(3) Speed of closing 300 + 180 = 480 kt.

(4) Time to close 400 @ 480 kt = 50 min. So ETA of meeting is 1300 + 50 min = <u>1350</u>.

(5) At 1350, aircraft from P will have flown 1 hr 50 min at 300 kt = <u>550 nm</u> or aircraft from Q will have flown 50 min at 180 kt = <u>150 nm</u> from Q. Check 550 + 150 = 700 nm (total distance PQ).

Relative Motion 73

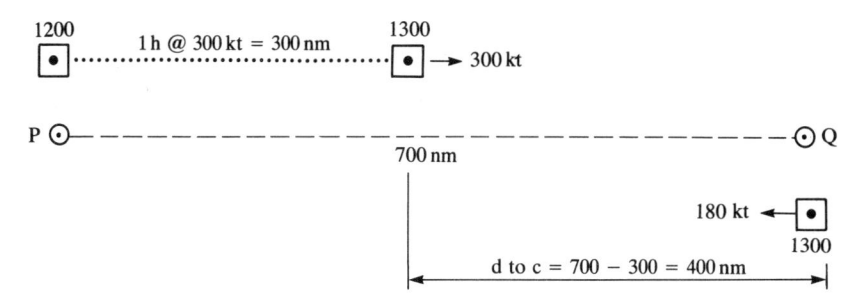

```
1200      1 h @ 300 kt = 300 nm    1300
 ■ ·········································  ■ → 300 kt


P ⊙ — — — — — — — — — — — — — — — — — — — — — — — — ⊙ Q
                        700 nm
                           │
                           │                    180 kt ← ■
                           │                               1300
                           │  d to c = 700 – 300 = 400 nm
                           ├────────────────────────────────┤
```

Fig. 7.2 Aircraft meeting.

The effect of wind on relative velocity problems

If both aircraft involved are in the same air mass, the effect of the wind can be ignored as *far as the relative motion part of the problem is concerned*. It is a similar situation to two people playing table tennis on a moving ship. However, if it is required to know the position of the aircraft in relation to the ground, the effect of wind must be considered. Consider how the previous problem would be affected if the speeds quoted were TAS and there was a wind of 60 kt blowing along the track from Q to P.

Solution (Fig. 7.3)

(1) At 1300, d to c = 460 nm

(2) CS = 240 + 240 = 480 kt (relative speed unaffected)

(3) t to c = 460 @ 480 = 57.5 min

(4) ETA of meeting 1300 + 57.5 min = <u>1357.5</u>

(5) At 1357.5 aircraft from P will have flown 1 hr 57.5 min @ 240 kt = <u>470 nm from P</u>

(6) Check – at 1357.5 aircraft from Q will have flown 57.5 min @ 240 kt = <u>230 nm from Q</u>. 230 + 470 = 700 (total distance PQ).

What has changed the problem is the positioning of the two aircraft before the relative motion commenced. If both aircraft had started at the same time, the wind would not have affected the meeting time but would have moved the meeting position downwind.

The changing speed problem

As presented, this is not a relative velocity problem and it can be solved by conventional algebra although it may get you involved in rather large numbers. A simpler solution is to convert it into a relative motion problem involving, in the speed reduction case, overtaking an imaginary slower aircraft that is scheduled to arrive at the destination at the required time. When your

74 *Plotting and Flight Planning*

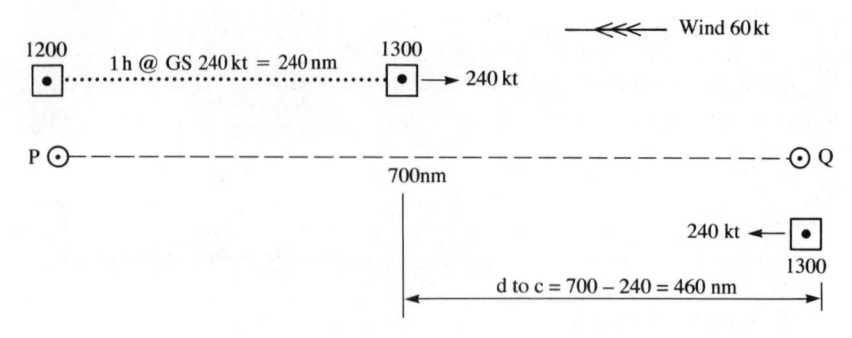

Fig. 7.3 Wind effect on solution of relative velocity problems.

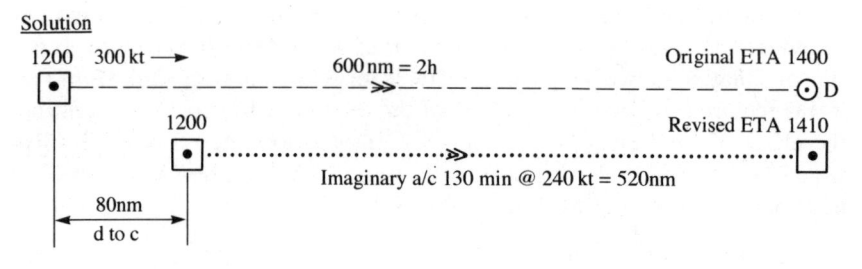

Fig. 7.4 Aircraft changing speed.

aircraft overtakes this imaginary aircraft, it will be necessary to reduce speed to that of the slower aircraft so as to achieve the desired ETA.

Example 3 – The changing speed problem
At 1200 an aircraft is flying at a GS 300 kt and is 600 nm from its destination D. It is required to delay arrival by 10 min and this will be done by reducing speed to 240 kt. What is the latest time that this adjustment can be made? (See Fig. 7.4).

Solution
(1) At 1200 d to c = 80 nm
(2) CS is 300 − 240 = 60 kt
(3) t to c = 80 @ 60 kt = 80 min
(4) ETA of overtaking 1200 + 1 hr 20 min = <u>1320</u>
    At 1320 aircraft will need to reduce speed to 240 kt so as to arrive at destination at 1410.

Relative motion between aircraft on different tracks

These problems are all solved vectorially either by scale drawing or by trigonometrical calculation. Squared paper will be provided and, even if you prefer a calculated solution, use should be made of this to prepare a reasonable sketch of the problem.

The following points are extremely important:

(1) It is always necessary, before commencing the relative velocity calculation, to establish the geographical positions of the two aircraft when they are both in motion. We did just the same in the single track problems.

(2) On the sketch there will be two diagrams to be drawn usually to different scales:
  - speed (vector) scale (knots)
  - distance scale (nm)

(3) The speed scale diagram will be representing the velocities of the two aircraft and their vector difference which will be the relative velocity between them. The distance scale diagram will be the geographical diagram representing the actual physical movements of the two aircraft.

General method of solution

The sequence of working will vary between problems but in general it should be noted:

- Always establish the geographical position of the two aircraft at the earliest time when they are both in motion. Use the distance scale for this.

- The speed scale will be used to draw the vector representing the velocity of one aircraft and to this will be added vectorially the vector reversed of the other aircraft's velocity. The remaining side of the triangle created will represent the vector difference between the two velocities which will be the relative motion between the two aircraft. This vector is only a convenient method of representing the direction and magnitude of the relative motion – *it does not represent the geographical motion of either aircraft.*

Typical general relative velocity problem

Example 4

Position Y is 44 nm due East of position X. At 1010, aircraft B left Y on a track of 335°(T) GS 150 kt and at 1015, aircraft A left X on a track of 041°(T) GS 200 kt.

(1) When will the aircraft first be within 15 nm of each other?

76 *Plotting and Flight Planning*

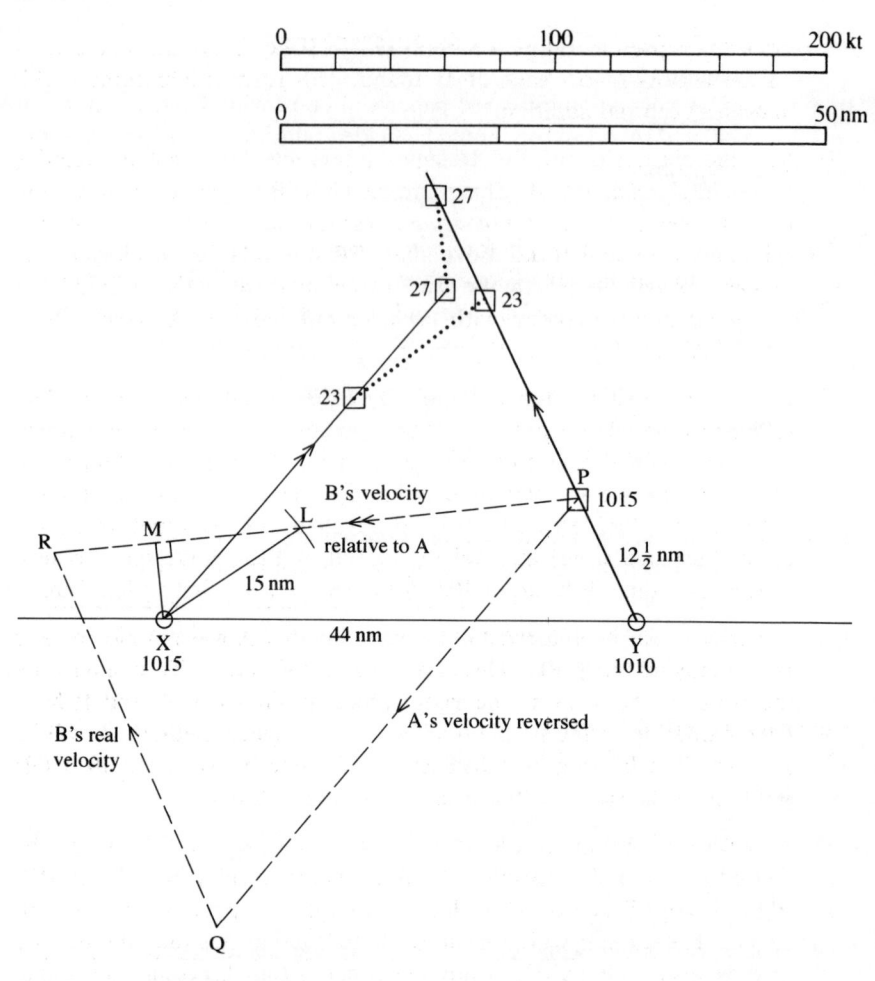

Fig. 7.5 Determining relative velocity.

(2) When will the aircraft be nearest to each other and what will the bearing and distance of B from A at this time?

Solution (Fig. 7.5)
(1) Both aircraft will be in motion at 1015 and so B's position is found at this time (P) using a track plot and the distance scale (nm).
(2) Consider the pilot in aircraft A. He will see B moving under the influence of two simultaneous velocities – B's real motion and the effect of his own motion reversed. The diagram to establish this relative motion could be drawn anywhere. In Fig. 7.5 the drawing has been commenced at P and from here PQ has been drawn to represent A's velocity reversed (vector scale 221° 200 kt). From Q the vector QR is

drawn to represent B's real motion (335° 150 kt). Note that the arrows on the vectors follow each other round. This is most important as this indicates vectorial addition.

(3) RP, the third side of the triangle, represents the resultant relative motion of *B relative to A*. This represents how B is *apparently* moving to the observer in A. *B is not actually moving along PR* but, if A was stationary at X and B did move along PR, the relative positions of the two aircraft will be exactly the same at any moment as they would be in the geographical diagram with both aircraft moving. A radar PPI in aircraft A would give exactly the same presentation in either case.

(4) It is easier to solve, either graphically or by calculation, any problem relating to the relative positions of the two aircraft on the vector diagram PQR than on the geographical diagram. To find when B is within 15 nm of A, draw an arc with centre X and radius 15 nm (distance scale) to cut PR at L. If B had left P at 1015 and travelled to L, it would have gone 26 nm (distance scale) at a relative speed of PR (196 kt speed scale). This gives a time of 8 min or 1023 for when they are first within 5 nm.

(5) The answer has been arrived at by assuming that A was not moving and B was moving along PR. This is not the real situation. To demonstrate the truth of the answer, the geographical positions of A and B have been plotted in, using simple track and groundspeed methods. It will be seen that the bearing and distance at this time between the 1023 DR positions is the same as that measured between X and L.

(6) If B was moving along PR while A was stationary at X, it would be nearest to A at point M which is where a perpendicular from A cuts PR. PM is 40 nm (distance scale) which at the relative speed of 196 kt equals 12 min. The aircraft will be nearest at 1027 and at this time the bearing and distance will be 353°/8 nm these being the direction and length (distance scale) of XM.

(7) In the diagram, the DR positions at 1027 have been plotted to confirm the bearing and distance obtained.

The meeting case (interception)
In Fig. 7.6, two aircraft X and Y are due to meet at 05 min. Their respective positions at minute intervals are shown before and after their meeting. It will be seen that the lines joining the two aircraft are always in the same direction. This is referred to as the line of constant bearing (LCB). For two aircraft to meet, an LCB must be maintained and the aircraft must be converging. Aircraft flying on diverging tracks or parallel tracks can also maintain LCBs.

The direction of the LCB represents the direction of the relative motion between the two aircraft and the rate at which its length is changing is the relative speed. In a potential collision situation, a pilot will see the other aircraft moving towards him along the LCB at the relative speed.

78   *Plotting and Flight Planning*

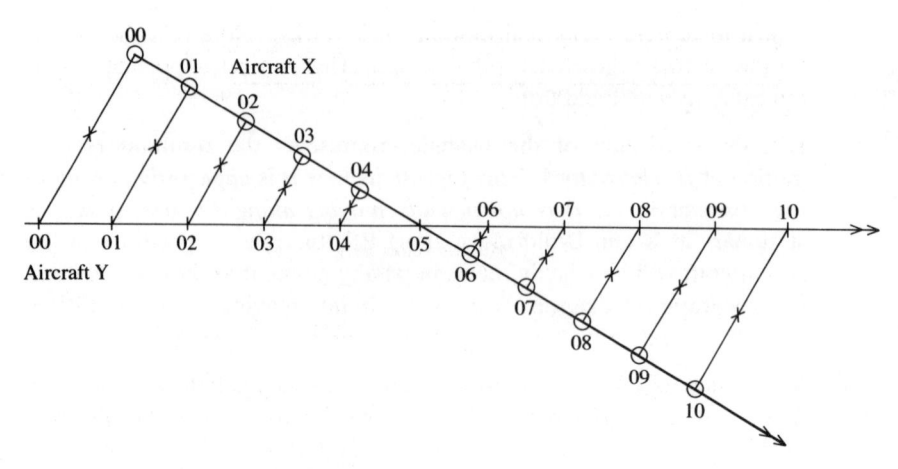

Fig. 7.6   Line of constant bearing.

Conditions for aircraft to meet

For converging aircraft to meet at a point, it will be necessary for the relative motion between the two aircraft to be along the direction of the LCB. The direction of the LCB can easily be established by taking the bearing of one aircraft from the other at the beginning of the problem. For example in the case shown in Fig. 7.6, it would be the direction of the line joining the two 00 positions (030°).

Example 5 – A meeting problem

At 1025, Aircraft A with a TAS of 180 kt and a heading of 010°(T) observes aircraft B on a relative bearing of 030° at a range of 50 nm. If B with a TAS of 240 kt is on a collision course, what is:

(1) B's true heading?

(2) the relative velocity of B with respect to A?

(3) the time at which the aircraft would meet?

Solution (see Fig. 7.7)

The direction of 030°(rel) to A or 030° + 010°(T) = 040°(T) must be the LCB that must be maintained and the relative motion between A and B must be in this direction. In the relative motion triangle, one side (A's speed and direction) is known, together with the magnitude of another side (B's speed) and the direction of the third side (LCB direction) so the triangle can be solved. The drawing sequence is as follows:

(1) Plot in the positions of A and B at the beginning of the problem (use distance scale).

Relative Motion

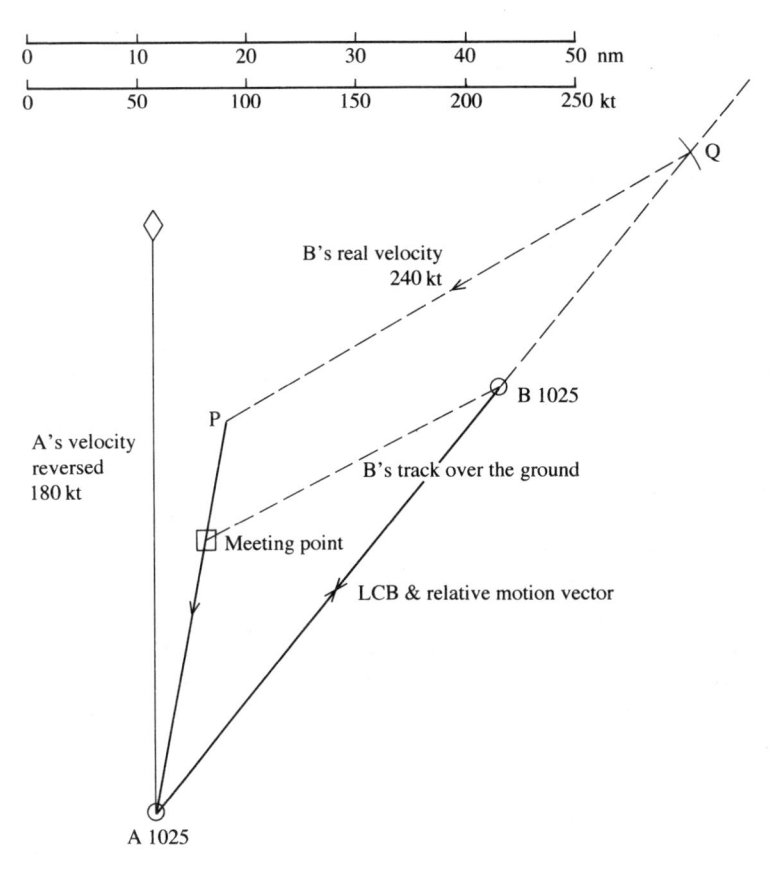

Fig. 7.7 Determining an interception.

(2) Draw PA to represent A's motion reversed (speed scale).

(3) With centre P and radius 240 kt (B's speed at speed scale) cut off at Q along the line AB extended if necessary.

(4) The required relative velocity triangle is APQ and B's heading (QP) can be measured as 240°(T).

(5) The relative velocity of B to A is given by QA – 220°(T)/382 kt.

(6) The distance to close is 50 nm and at a speed of 382 kt the time to close will be 8 min. Estimated time of interception (ETI) will be 1025 + 8 min = 1033.

Point of No Alternate (PNA)

An aircraft is on a flight where there are no nearby destination alternates. The aircraft has not got sufficient fuel to reach the destination and then still be able to divert to the distant alternate which has been passed, some way off track, on the flight. It is necessary for the Captain to know the latest point along the track from which it would still be able to make a safe diversion to the alternate.

Trial and error solution for the PNA

There are many methods of solving this problem. One method that can, in experienced hands, be very successful is a trial and error solution. An estimate is made as to a likely PNA position and then a check is carried out to find the time required to reach the estimated PNA and then to divert to the alternate. The total time required is then compared with the safe endurance available.

Even if the result does not agree, it is probable that a further estimate will prove to be reasonably accurate.

Relative motion solution for the PNA

Here, we will describe a rather more scientific method which is based on relative motion. It is not proposed to give a detailed explanation of the theory but having worked through some examples you may begin to see that we are simply flying away from an imaginary moving base and after a time altering heading to intercept it. The imaginary moving base is moving from the departure point to the alternate in exactly the time of the safe endurance to be used in the PNA problem.

Example 6

A flight is to be made from A to X, track 090°(T), TAS 200 kt WV 045°T/40 kt Distance 500 nm. The safe endurance is 3 hours. The alternate is situated 315°T/150 nm from X. Find the time and distance from A to the PNA.

Solution (Fig. 7.8)
(1) It is suggested that the lettering used in the diagram is always employed when using this method. Even if the diagrams that evolve look different, the lettering will always be a safe guide to what each line represents.

(2) On a piece of squared paper plot in A, X and the alternate B using the data given and a suitable scale (say 1 cm = 20 nm).

(3) Measure the distance AB (407 nm) and note it on the diagram. Using the safe endurance (180 min) calculate the speed of the moving base (407 nm in 180 min = 136 kt) and note this also.

(4) Using a suitable vector scale (say 1 cm = 20 kt) lay in a wind vector AC blowing away from A (225° and 2 cm).

(5) With centre C and radius TAS 200 kt (10 cm vector scale) describe an arc to cut outward track AX at D. ADC is the vector triangle for the outward flight and AD measured at 8.5 cm equals the outward GS of 170 kt (vector scale). Note this value on the diagram.

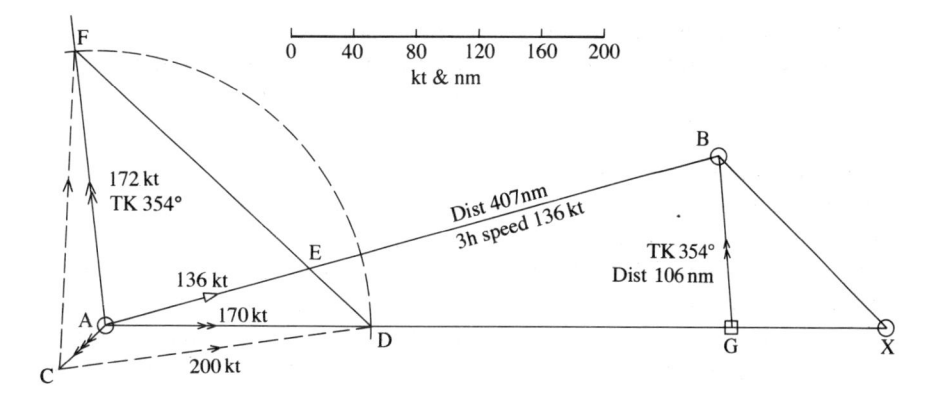

Fig. 7.8 Point of no alternate.

(6) From A measure off the speed of the moving base 136 kt (6.8 cm) to obtain point E. DE represents the LCB between the aircraft and the moving base.

(7) Extend DE so as to cut the TAS circle at F. AF will represent the track required to reintercept the moving base at a GS of 172 kt (8.6 cm). The direction of this track is 354°.

(8) Plotting a track of 354° into the alternate B gives a PNA at point G.

(9) The distance AG to the PNA (G) is 401 nm and with the outward GS of 170 kt, this gives a time of $141\frac{1}{2}$ min.

(10) Checking with the distance GB 106 nm and GS AF 172 kt, the time to reach the alternate from the PNA is 37 min. This gives a total time for the operation of $178\frac{1}{2}$ min which is $1\frac{1}{2}$ min less than the safe endurance. 1 min per hour of endurance is an acceptable error but, if an adjustment was required, it can be made by intelligent guesswork. In this case, for example, moving the PNA further along track will hardly affect the distance GB and so a more accurate PNA time would probably be 143 min.

Variations on the PNA problem

The PNA can be posed in two other ways:

(1) *The initial heading is given* instead of the track. In this case, commence by plotting the wind vector AC and then draw from C a line in the direction of the initial true heading to cut the airspeed circle at D. Then proceed as before.

(2) *A destination/alternate Critical Point is required*. This will be the point where the flying times to the destination and the alternate are the same. In this case having obtained the outward GS (AD in Fig. 7.8),

82 Plotting and Flight Planning

calculate the flying time from A to the destination. Use this flying time as the safe endurance for the problem. In this way the ETA at the alternate, having diverted at the PNA, should correspond with the ETA at the destination.

Practice questions

The following examples can all be done at a reasonable scale on sheets of A4 metric graph paper. Answers should be obtained within an accuracy of 1 minute per 1 hour of endurance.

(1) *Destination given*
    A flight is to be made from A to X, track 090°(T), WV 045°T/40 kt, TAS 200 kt, distance 500 nm. The safe endurance is 3 hr. The alternate B is situated 315°T/150 nm from X.
    Calculate the time and distance from A to reach the PNA.

(2) *Heading given*
    An aircraft sets heading from P 060°(T), TAS 300 kt, safe endurance 2 hr. The alternate Q is 000°T/200 nm from P. WV 310°/60 kt.
    Calculate the time and distance from P to the PNA.

(3) *Track given*
    An aircraft sets heading from X to maintain a track of 135°(T), TAS 250 kt, WV 040°T/35 kt. The safe endurance is 2 hr 15 min. The alternate Z is 170°/150 nm from X.
    Calculate the time and distance from X to the PNA.

(4) *Critical point*
    An aircraft is on a flight from L to M, distance 450 nm, track 148°(T), TAS 350 kt, WV 100°T/75 kt. The alternate N is situated 172°T/300 nm from L. Calculate the time and distance from L to the CP between M and N.

Answers
(1) 398 nm $140\tfrac{1}{2}$ min
(2) 217 nm   50 min
(3) 332 nm   80 min
(4) 344 nm   70 min.

Part 3
FLIGHT PLANNING

Chapter 8
PRINCIPLES OF FLIGHT PLANNING

Introduction

Before flight in the commercial business of carrying passengers or cargo for hire or reward, a very comprehensive flight plan must be made, giving the Hdgs(M) to steer, the time on each leg, the fuel to be consumed, the height to fly, the alternates available, and any other detail useful for the trip. It is a plan, a guide, and its main purpose is safety, ensuring primarily that sufficient fuel is uplifted plus a bit extra for mother. In the air, amendments to Hdgs and times will be made, with a continuous check on fuel consumption and weather ahead, by actual navigation.

The first prerequisite on arrival at the field is to obtain the latest Met. information for the route, and for all the aerodromes likely to be used; forecast WV and temperatures at pertinent heights will be given, and from these, the flight plan can be filled in. This done, adequate fuel can be ordered and other matters such as range, point of no return can be duly entered. The complete plan will be reported to ATC, so that in the air a full surveillance of the aircraft's progress will be kept.

A couple of lines of a flight plan might look like the example in Table 8.1.

Having gaped at that lot for a moment or two (and perhaps checked the TAS, times, Hdgs on your computer), you will appreciate that here is most of the information required for the trip and on the trip; but of course, temperatures, WVs are forecast, fuel consumption may not go according to the book, ETAs will invariably change, but the plan is there.

You will have remarked that fuel consumption has decreased slightly on the second leg: as the weight of the aircraft decreases with fuel being burned off, so there is less weight to heave through the air, and consumption will be reduced. It is commonsense that as an aircraft gets lighter, with the fuel being consumed, its performance will improve assuming that there is no significant wind change. By an improved performance, we mean a smaller value for the ratio of fuel flow to TAS. This is usually expressed as nm/kg, often referred to as the economy figure. Modern turbo-jet aircraft are usually operated at a constant Mach No. – in fact on some routes it is an ATC requirement that this is done. Usually the Captain has very little choice in the speeds at which he may operate. As set out in the OM for a modern tri-jet it is:

Plotting and Flight Planning

Table 8.1

STAGE		Press height ft ×1000	RAS kt	Temp °C	TAS kt	WV	Tr (T)	Hdg (T)	Var	Hdg (M)	Dist nm	GS kt	Time min	ETA	Fuel flow kg/h	Fuel kg
From	To														
ALICE SPRINGS	Abm OODNA	31	264	−45	423	270/60	149	156	5E	151	237	450	32	0447	3900	2080
Abm OODNA	LEIGH	31	264	−46	423	260/60	149	156	6E	150	231	442	31	0518	3860	2000

Note: On Computers such as Airtour CRP 5, when the TAS calculated from RAS using pressure altitude and temperature exceeds 300 kt, a further correction has to be made using the window on the slide rule marked comp. corr. (compressibility correction) – see handbook for the computer. Neglecting this correction would give a TAS 10 kt too high in this case.

High speed (HS) cruise
Flying at Mach 0.85 subject to not exceeding the engine limitations.

Long range (LR) cruise
Flying at Mach 0.82.

In both cases, of course, the economy will improve as the aircraft gets lighter.

Apart from the speed selected and the wind, over which we have no control, the other factor having a marked effect on the economy is FL. Generally speaking with modern turbo-jets it is best to fly as high as is possible and permitted. This should be done even to the extent of increasing level as the aircraft gets lighter. Maximum economy would be achieved by a gradual upward drift throughout cruising flight. This cruise–climb technique is used by supersonic aircraft but in the more crowded levels, ATC prefer constant level cruising.

It is possible, that at intervals, an aircraft may be permitted to 'step up' to the next available FL (usually 4000 ft higher). This is only likely every three to four hours even with the biggest modern aircraft.

It is quite often stated that air temperature affects operating economy. This is not, in general, of practical significance. Cruising at constant Mach No., a higher temperature produces a higher TAS at the expense of more engine power and so higher fuel flows. Practical tests show that the two effects tend to balance out producing no significant change in the overall economy (kg/nm). The higher TAS will, of course, give a slightly better flight time.

The principles of flight planning
In the very first place, with the information available before flight, the problem is one of work with the computer to resolve this information into the essentials for the flight itself. After this, as the pilot considers fuel, it is aircraft weight which is the governing factor; this weight decreases dramatically as the trip progresses with the high rate of fuel consumption, and a mean consumption or a mean TAS *per sector* must be deduced. Aircraft manufacturers set out this data in the aircraft manual, and for a 'weight at start' of a leg will, for the altitude and temperature, proffer a consumption for the next hour, or even for only the next half-hour, as we shall see. Such data sheets are used in the ATPL exam, but in CPL the knowledge of principles is introduced, and the averages of consumption or TAS must be calculated.

Let us consider first a flight plan for a voyage where the TAS is reasonably constant, or in other words, is given, but the fuel consumption varies as the aircraft's weight reduces.

A snippet from the data:

88 Plotting and Flight Planning

Consumption (kg/h) at varying weights (kg)			
70 000	65 000	60 000	55 000
4 200	4 000	3 900	3 800

Take-off wt (TOW): 68 500 kg
Climb: Mean TAS 340 kt, time 38 min, fuel used 3900 kg

The body of the flight plan – RAS, GS, times, distance covered on the climb and descent, ETAs, can be completed straight off. The weight at start is 68 500 kg, so at the top of climb, having used 3900 kg, it will be 64 600 kg for the commencement of level flight. We need the mean weight on the next leg in order to estimate as closely as possible the average consumption on it. Assume for ease of example that the leg will take one hour; from the table above, after half an hour, about 2000 kg will have been burnt off, giving a weight in mid-leg of 62 600 kg; using this figure to enter the table, a mean consumption will be extracted of 3950 kg, rounded off to avoid pedantic digits.

To proceed, the weight at start of the next leg is 60 650 kg (having flown for one hour at a consumption of 3950 kg/h from a start of 64 600 kg): say the leg will take 40 min. After 20 min at 3910 kg/h – and do not strain here, visual and mental calculation is enough – 1300 kg will be burnt off and the mean weight may be taken to be 59 350 kg. This weight from the tables gives a consumption of 3890 kg/h, which is entered on the plan, and in 40 min will use 2590 kg, giving a weight at start of the next sector of 58 060 kg. And so on.

A flight plan with a constant consumption but varying TAS is somewhat more involved; the plan must be done line by line, and the estimation of weights to find a mean TAS has its hazards, since no *times* on the legs are available.

A snippet from the data:

Consumption	Mean Weight (kg) v TAS (kt)			
kg/h	79 000	77 000	74 000	72 000
2400	300	308	319	326

Weight at commencement of climb: 81 000 kg
Climb: Mean TAS 235 kt, time 48 min, fuel used 2250 kg

The climb leg can be solved for GS, time, distance and the rest, and the weight at start of level flight is 78 750 kg.

The best technique is to commence by estimating an approximate economy (kg/nm) figure. In this case, using conveniently rounded off figures of

2400 kg/h and 300 kt, the economy figure would be 8 kg/nm in still air. If the next stage was 190 nm, the appropriate fuel used for *half* the stage would be 4 × 190 = 760 kg. The mean weight would, therefore, be 78 750 − 760 = approx 78 000 kg.

Use this weight to extract the TAS from the table = 304 kt and complete the leg of the flight plan. The actual fuel used will be 1560 kg. Check. The weight at start of next leg is 77 190 kg, whence to continue the exercise.

On finishing the final line to destination, the fuel used from departure to destination can be totted up, often called 'burn off', and the weight over the destination field calculated; this weight, less any fuel used for final descent and landing, will give the anticipated landing weight.

In calculating the fuel or TAS for the alternate from the data given, it is sufficient to use the weight at destination as a leader into the requirements for the leg.

The fuel to destination plus alternate fuel plus contingency fuel plus taxi, take-off, circuit, landing plus any other reserves or percentages will give the total fuel required for the trip; from this figure, the payload can be worked out, and this is what keeps us in business.

All this, the type of flight plan in qualifying exams for pilot licences, may have astounded you in its vagaries and guesswork; have no fear, it is but a presentation of the *principles* of the stuff to be student pilot: the manuals are of course much more precise, full of information garnered from tests and checks carried out with care and accuracy, but still on mean weights as shown, though for a specified period of time. We will move on to this practical matter at once.

Presentation of data

Every aircraft type produces a Cruise Control Manual, wherein all information at all heights at all temperatures for each specific purpose is shown, either graphically or tabulated, the latter by far the more popular. Climb, short range diversion, level cruise by appropriate methods, four-engines, three-engines, two-engines, level cruise; in fact anything that the pilot requires for his aircraft for his route, presented succinctly, for rapid production of the flight plan with the station manager breathing down his neck to get him away, the fuel wallah palpitating for the fuel requirements, the load people agitating for pay load particulars. You won't get the aircraft type on your licence till you've mastered the manual, but for examination purposes, the CAA has produced some Data Sheets set out along the accepted lines. Data Sheets 33 are part of your equipment, so we'll refer to them constantly and work out a flight plan sample.

The performance of an aircraft is dependent on pressure and temperature which in turn determine air density. The pressure is conveniently expressed as the pressure altitude, i.e. the altimeter reading with 1013 mb on the sub-scale. The temperature is normally described by the temperature deviation which is:

90 Plotting and Flight Planning

correct outside air temperature (COAT) − standard temperature

The standard temperature is the standard used for each particular FL in the preparation of the tables. In Data Sheets 33, these standard temperatures are detailed in Table 33F. This table differs from that used in most tables which generally use an approximation to the International Standard Atmosphere (ISA). The first step in working out a flight plan is to deduce the temperature deviation for each stage. When extracting performance for any part of the flight, it is important to check that the table being used is for the appropriate temperature deviation range as shown at the top of the table.

Let us now plough gently through the following flight plan, assisted by Data Sheets 33. See Tables 8.2 and 8.3. Remember the penalties are heavy for serious arithmetical inaccuracies in the exam as well as in the air: − you would feel a real charlie to find in mid trip that you'd uplifted 1000 kg too little fuel.

Information is as follows:

A flight is to be made from ROME TO ACCRA. LAGOS is the terminal alternate. Route details are given on the proforma.

Loading: Weight at start of take-off is 130 000 kg.
Climb: Climb on track from 1000 ft over ROME to FL 340 (Table 33A).
Cruise: Cruise at the levels given in the flight plan (Table 33C).
Descent: Descend on Track to arrive over ACCRA at 1000 ft (Table 33E).
Alternate: Use Table 33G. Assume diversion is commenced 1000 ft over ACCRA and ends at 1000 ft over LAGOS.
Fuel: Sufficient for take-off and climb to 1000 ft over ROME, plus:
Sufficient for flight from ROME to ACCRA and to alternate LAGOS, plus:
800 kg for circuit and landing, plus:
9000 kg reserve.

Complete the flight plan.
What weight of fuel is required?

Before starting, note that computer work is reduced by drift and wind component tables (pages 24 and 25 of the Data Sheet). The TAS is regarded broadly to give sufficient accuracy for flight planning purposes: a set is provided for each aircraft, with its mean cruising speed, mean climb and mean diversion speed. Here we have two tables, 480 kt and 380 kt; the wind speed is set out across the top, with the angle between wind direction and Track down the side. Thus, a drift and wind component can be read off, though the port or starboard bit must be determined. Thus, Tr 180(T), WV 290/70, your expected TAS 486 kt − angle is 110° down the side, against WS 70, drift is 8, component +20; use GS 506 kt, and with a southerly Tr with rough westerly wind, drift is clearly port. The appropriate table can be used to press on with the flight plan.

Principles of Flight Planning 91

Table 8.2

Flight Plan

STAGE		Flight Level	Temp. Dev °C	WIND		Track °(T)	Drift	Heading °(T)	TAS kt	Wind comp. kt	GS kt	Distance nm	Time min	Fuel flow kg/h	Wt at start kg	Fuel required kg
From	To			Direction	Speed kt											
TAKE OFF FUEL																
ROME	Top of climb	↗	−3	040	20	170						↗ 244		↕ —		
Top of climb	PALERMO	340	+2	340	50	170						331				
PALERMO	IDRIS	350	+4	290	70	180						490				
IDRIS	GHAT	350	+4	310	50	198						824				
GHAT	NIAMY	350	+8	280	80	213										
NIAMY	Top of descent	350	+12	210	15	197						↗ 487				
Top of descent	ACCRA	↘	—	200	10	197					—	217		—		
ACCRA	LAGOS	↗	—	200	20	075								—		

92 *Plotting and Flight Planning*

Table 8.3

Flight Plan

STAGE From	STAGE To	Flight Level	Temp. Dev °C	WIND Direction	WIND Speed kt	Track °(T)	Drift	Heading °(T)	TAS kt	Wind comp. kt	GS kt	Distance nm	Time min	Fuel flow kg/h	Wt at start 1000 kg	Fuel required kg
TAKE OFF FUEL																1 0 0 0
ROME	Top of climb	↗	−3	040	20	170	2S	168	379	+14	393	131	02 20	↓ —	130.0 129.0	4 4 0 0
Top of climb	PALERMO	340*	+2	340	50	170	1P	171	488	+49	537	244 113	12½	7050	124.6	1 4 7 0
PALERMO	IDRIS	350*	+4	290	70	180	8P	188	486	+20	506	331	39¼	6900	123.1	5*0* 4 5 4 0
IDRIS	GHAT	350	+4	310	50	198	6P	204	486	+17	503	490	58¼	6710	118.5	6 5 5 0
GHAT	NIAMY	350	+8	280	80	213	9P	222	486	−36	450	824	110	6430	112.0	1 1 7 9 0
NIAMY	Top of descent	350	+12	210	15	197	0	197	494	−15	479	394	49½	6115	100.2	5 0 5 0
Top of descent	ACCRA	↘	—	200	10	197	0	197	369	−10	359	487 93	15½	—	95.1	7 0 0 0
																3 5 5 0
ACCRA	LAGOS	↗↘	—	200	20	075	2P	077	—	+12	—	217	35	—	94.4	3 7 3 0

* Step

Principles of Flight Planning

Aircraft weights

It is necessary to keep a running record of the aircraft weight. We will keep the record in thousands of kg (tonnes (t)) to an accuracy of 1 decimal place (i.e. 100 kg). This will be quite accurate enough for entering the performance tables. Fuel amounts will be calculated to the nearest 10 kg. We start our weight record by putting the take-off weight, 130.0 t, on the first line in the weight column. Turn to Table 33A on page 4 (temp devn −5 to −1°C). Footnote 2 gives us our first line entries – time and fuel to 1000 ft, 2 min and 1000 kg. Subtracting 1 t from 130.0 gives the weight at the start of the main climb, 129.0, and this is entered on the ROME to TOC line in the weight column.

Climb

Table 33A is now entered with the take-off weight and the FL 340 for the first cruise stage. This is a surprising FL because under the semi-circular rules 340 is not generally used. Against the figure for 34 000 TAS 379 kt is read being the mean TAS for the climb, and along the same line under 130 000 kg, read off the fuel required and the minutes to reach 34 000 ft – 4400 kg and 20 min. Write these in the plan and subtract 4.4 t from 129 to get the weight, 124.6, for the start of cruise. Using your calculator obtain the distance gone on the climb (20 min at 379 kt), 131 nm, and subtracting from the total stage length to PALERMO from ROME obtain the balance of the distance to go in cruising flight.

Level

All the time the temp dev and FL must be watched: there is absolutely no reason why one shouldn't move from one page to another. And as an *obiter dictum*: flight level is the same thing as pressure height. Here we go to Table 33C, Standard 0 to +9°C. The top line is separated into individual hours of cruise, and the side has again pressure height and mean TAS: if you started at 137 000 kg, at 34 000 ft and flew at that pressure height, provided the temperature did not go outside the limits for the table, one could go steadily along the line. In this case, our weight at start is 124 600 kg, at 34 000 ft, TAS is straight 488 kt, but we must interpolate for fuel flow between the column:

$$129 : 7300 \text{ and } 122 : 6900$$

The columnar weight difference is 7000 kg for a consumption difference of 400 kg

So: $124\,600 - 122\,000 = 2600$

$\dfrac{2600}{7000} \times 400$ gives 150 kg to the nearest 10 kg

∴ consumption for 124 600 kg initial weight is $6900 + 150 = 7050$ kg

which enter, and complete the PALERMO line, and be careful where you enter the fuel required of 1470 kg (that's what you made it, I hope). The biggest boobs in flight planning are invariably arithmetical, cocking up a thousand with a hundred digit.

Proceed now with a start weight of 123 100 kg to IDRIS, checking the temp dev, OK, keep the same page: but the pressure height is now 35 000 ft. From the notes on page 2 of the Data Sheets, an en-route climb of 4000 ft is ignored for time, but add 200 kg to fuel used: to be perfect then, we need to throw in 50 kg to the fuel required on the IDRIS leg for a 1000 ft climb. From Table 33C, TAS 486 kt, and 6900 kg is accurate enough for 123 100 kg weight at start. Complete the line, and you'll find $39\frac{1}{2}$ min gives you 4550 kg required, +50 kg, a round 4600. Weight at start for GHAT 118 500 kg. Into the Tables again, check the temp dev, OK. Interpolate as before, between 123:6900 kg and 116:6600 kg for a consumption at 118 500 kg aircraft weight.

$$\frac{2500}{7000} \times 300 = \frac{750}{7} = 110 \,\text{kg}$$

to be added to the 116 000 weight consumption = 6710 kg, and the TAS is still 486 kt.

Complete the GHAT and NIAMY lines. We now must deal with the descent line to find time and distance covered before we can find out how far along the Tr NIAMY–ACCRA to fly before commencing the descent. This is Table 33E, and is as plain as a pikestaff: as we're leaving 35 000 ft, TAS is 369 kt, fuel used 700 kg, time $15\frac{1}{2}$ min. Complete the descent line, enter distances for the level and descent bits, and now to finish off NIAMY–TOD: the temp dev is +12°C, so with a weight at start of 100 190 kg on the table marked 'Standard +10°C to +14°C', enter at 35 000 ft, TAS 494 kt, interpolate for 100 000 kg between 103:6200 and 96:6000, giving 115 kg to add to 6000, giving 6115 kg consumption. Finish off so far: add the burn off fuel requirements from departure to destination and above all check that your weight at ACCRA + this figure = 130 000 kg.

The alternate must now be dealt with, Table 33G. The explanatory notes are reasonably clear: enter the tables for your conditions, and then make corrections. We're at 1000 ft, will climb to 35 000 ft and descend to arrive over LAGOS at 1000 ft. From drift and wind component table for TAS 380 kt, extract drift 2P, wind component +12, enter 33G and with a spot of visual interpolation: 35 min, 3620 kg. Corrections are: none for height, weight is 94 400 kg ∴ add 3%, 108 kg say 110, used 3730 kg. The corrections are all straightforward, and they are set out for you: no need to learn them by heart; it is automatic to check them, though, in every flight plan.

All that needs be done now is to tot up the fuel on board (FOB) requirements, as demanded by the question, or by the station officer on the route. It is wise to set it out as on a fuel chit.

Principles of Flight Planning 95

Burn off	35 550
Alternate	3 730
Circuit and Landing	800
Reserve	9 000
FOB	49 080 kg

This makes it easy to deduce the landing weight at ACCRA, for example: you will use the 800 kg for circuit and landing, but still have alternate and reserve fuel in the tanks, so landing weight = 130 000 − 36 350 = 93 650 kg.

Divers problems in flight planning (Data Sheets 33)

The quite practical type of problem that involves a trip of a certain distance, part at low altitude (29 000 ft or below), part at high, hold and descent, is straightforward once you know your way around the Data Sheets. The information presented to you in an examination or in the Briefing Room must be complete enough for an answer to be arrived at, and there should be no difficulty, for example, in working out a descent before solving the time and fuel for cruise: there's nothing new in that. Table 33E for descent couldn't really be easier. I'm not trying to offend your intelligence in reminding you that a hold is a hold, where a ground speed is unnecessary: in the artificial atmosphere of the exam room, it is easy to start hunting for the absurd like 'how far have I gone on the hold leg'.

Table 33D gives the low level cruise information, and do, oh do, notice the footnote about the mean weight of 100 000 kg. A mean weight of 135 000 kg increases the consumption at 15 000 ft at ISA +7, by 705 kg/h. The table otherwise is self explanatory, calling for only the simplest interpolation.

A climb from 15 000 ft to 34 000 ft in Table 33A demands a simple subtraction of fuel at 15 000 ft for the weight at start of climb from the fuel at 34 000 ft, but a visual interpolation is required at bottom and top for intermediate weights. Keeping ISA +7, with a weight of 133 840 kg at 15 000 ft to start the climb to 34 000 ft, the table says –

		135 000 kg		130 000 kg	
Press Height	Mean TAS	Fuel kg	Time min	Fuel kg	Time min
34 000	387	5800	31	5300	28
15 000	324	2100	9	2000	9

Fuel at 15 000 ft for 133 840 kg aircraft weight is 2080 kg
Fuel at 34 000 ft for 133 840 kg aircraft weight is 5700 kg
Fuel used for this climb, then, is 3620 kg, and such a round-off figure is quite adequate, as is the similarly subtractive time of 22 min.

The mean TAS for this climb demands an entry into the graph labelled for

96   Plotting and Flight Planning

the exercise as Table 33B: enter with top of climb height across to the appropriate start of climb height curve, drop to the reference line, and then parallel up or down as far as the temp dev axis, and read off the mean TAS. Our example above gives 418 kt. Interpolation of the bottom of climb curve is visually done. Don't make a large theoretical chore of any of this: the table, anyway, gives an example, which is worth a moment's study.

Descent is plain sailing (Table 33E) just read off TAS, fuel used and time taken from altitude to 1000 ft: if the bottom of descent is not 1000 ft, subtract one fuel from t'other, ditto time; add the two TAS and subtract 290. Hold is taken at the altitude on Table 33D, and the fuel calculated for the time of hold.

Try this, using Data Sheets No. 33

An aircraft is to fly from A to B, a distance of 950 nm on a Tr of 250(T). Take-off weight is 140 000 kg, and the aircraft will successively:

(a) Climb from 1000 ft to 15 000 ft, and then cruise at this level for 25 min (Table 33D).

(b) Climb from 15 000 ft to 34 000 ft and cruise at this level until a descent is made to arrive over B at 6000 ft.

(c) Hold at 6000 ft over B for 30 min (Table 33D) and then descend over B to 1000 ft.

Details of these stages, temp dev and WV are given below.

Complete the flight plan, giving the total fuel required and the total time.

STAGE Press Alt	Temp Dev	WV	TAS	Wind Component	GS	Dist	Time min	Fuel Flow kg/h	Start Weight kg	Fuel kg
Take-off & climb to 1000 ft	—	—	—	—	—	—	—			
1000–15 000 ft	+3	200/40							—	
Level 15 000 ft	+6	240/50					25			
15 000–34 000 ft	+6	260/60							—	
Level 34 000 ft	+8	290/70								
34 000–6000 ft	—	230/50							—	
Hold at 6000 ft	+6	—		—	—	—	30			
6000–1000 ft	—	—		—	—	—	—			
						950				

Answer: 24 000 kg; 3 h 2 min (±200 kg ± 2 min)

Principles of Flight Planning

The following problem is really an exercise in figure manipulation and logical method, but it has a very practical role, for often the *weight of the aircraft at destination* is the limiting factor.

Using Data Sheets 33, a flight is to be made from A to B, distance 1150 nm, to arrive over B at 6000 ft at weight 98 000 kg.

Climb
On Track from 1000 ft over A to FL 340 (Temp dev +6°, hwc 30 kt).

Cruise
Four-engine level cruise at 0.86 Mach at FL 340 (Temp dev +6°, hwc 55 kt).

Descent
On Track to arrive over B at 6000 ft (head wind component 25 kt).
Give the time and fuel required for:

- Climb from 1000 ft
- Cruise
- Descent

Solution
Descent first, from Table 33E:
TAS (367 + 300) − 290 = 377 kt:
∴ GS is 352 kt. Time given 12 min, so distance 70 nm:
Fuel given 600 kg:
Weight at start of descent is therefore 98 600 kg.
Level next, Table 33C, temp dev +6°C:
TAS 488 kt ∴ GS 433 kt.
The aircraft's weight is going to finish the cruise sector at 98 600 kg; in the Table, from 102 000 to 98 600 kg gives fuel 3400 kg.
At noted consumption of 6200 kg/h, this takes 33 min:

$$33 \text{ min at GS 433 kt gives distance 238 nm}$$

The preceding hour uses 6400 kg and distance 433 nm.
A mental check indicates that there may be little cruise distance left, so take a summary:
After the climb *and* an undetermined period of cruise, the all-up-weight (AUW) is:

$$98\,000 + 600 + 3400 + 6400 = 108\,400 \text{ kg}$$

Similarly, the distance *gone* is:

$$1150 - (70 + 238 + 433) = 409 \text{ nm}$$

To enter the climb table, the TOW is required, so this must at this stage be estimated as accurately as possible. A glance at the appropriate page of Table

33A suggests a 22 min climb at a TOW of 115 000 kg, fuel used 4300 kg; the climb GS 357 kt for this time means 131 nm will be covered on the climb, and 278 nm is left for the very first cruise bit. Continuing with this procedure, enter the level cruise Table, read off the consumption 6700 kg/h, calculate the time to do 278 nm at GS 433 kt; thus, $38\frac{1}{2}$ min and fuel used 4300 kg. The approximate TOW is:

$$108\,400 + 4300 + 4300 = 117\,000\,\text{kg},$$

and although the climb table gives fuel and time from 1000 ft which is just what the question demands, the top line is classified as TOW and 1000 kg must be included in the TOW figure for the initial take-off climb. Entering the table then with 118 000 kg:

Climb takes 23 min, uses 4500 kg, distance 137 nm. Level flight starts at 112 500 kg all-up-weight (the initial climb fuel of 1000 kg being allowed for), and so this portion will take 38 min to fly the 272 nm at GS 433 kt, at fuel consumption 6600 kg/h = 4200 kg. There is an element of meaning-off the extracted figures from the entered figures in the tables for intermediate weights, but there is no need for pedantic precision.

The answers are:

- Climb: 23 min, fuel 4500 kg
- Cruise: 2 h 11 min, fuel 14 000 kg
- Descent: 12 min, fuel 600 kg

Diversion and hold

Another practical problem in this paper is a diversion arranged for you somewhere in the closing stages of a trip. As the examiner wants to know if you are really familiar with the tables, he will divert you half way down the descent, and give you a hold. At one fell swoop, he's got you in every table in the book, and a good thing too. Since a diversion is assumed to be demanded after a shot at landing which has proved out of the question, diversion tables have overshoot, climb to a suitable level, reserve fuel all included in the figures; to peel off on the way down and head for the alternate field must require suitable corrections to these figures. In Data Sheets 33 these corrections are clearly shown, but in Sheets 34 they are not, and circumstances will decide which of the more thumbed tables are appropriate in the latter case, not forgetting the low level cruise set.

Perhaps it's opportune to take a look at Data Sheets 34; these are geared for heavier aircraft, but are similar in format, and mainly self-explanatory, though watch the footnotes as before. Interpolations for fuel consumption between stated weights are definitely only to the nearest 100 kg, and the low level cruise table is the one to use if holding.

An aircraft cruising at 0.83 indicated Mach at FL 350 is on Tr to destination B which is 640 nm distant. Aircraft weight is 238 500 kg, temp dev +7°C, hwc 40 kt.

Principles of Flight Planning 99

Later, descent on Tr is commenced, hwc 20 kt.

(a) Give the time and fuel required for:
- Cruise
- Descent

The aircraft arrives at B, but diverts after an overshoot to D, 156 nm distant, twc 30 kt, temp dev +8°C.

(b) Give the aircraft weight at commencement of diversion.

(c) Determine time, flight level, and fuel required for diversion. The aircraft holds over D at FL 160 for 17 min, temp dev +14° (Table 34D).

(d) Give the fuel required for holding.

Descent 15 min, 2000 kg, TAS 378 kt, from Table 34E
∴ GS 358 kt, distance run 90 nm.
Cruise which will be for 550 nm
TAS 484 kt, ∴ GS 444 kt, time $75\frac{1}{2}$ min
AUW 238 500 kg

Enter Table 34C, temp devn 0 to +9°C (page 10) at the FL 350 and guestimate a fuel flow for the stage of 9400 kg/h. The fact that it is just over an hour is not significant.
Cruise fuel = $75\frac{1}{2}$ min at 9400 kg/h = 11 830 kg
Answer (a) $75\frac{1}{2}$ min 11 830 kg, 15 min 2000 kg

Now for the diversion; fuel used to B is 14 000 kg, and the aircraft weight after overshoot is 238 500 − 14 000 = 224 500 kg.

Entering Table 34B, interpolate for 156 nm and a 30 kt tailwind, read fuel 13 900 kg, FL 220, time 31 min. The start of diversion weight is 30 500 kg less than tabulated, so footnote correction (a) must be applied; this is 6% of 13 900, subtractive, 800 kg, = 13 100 kg.

Answer (b) 224 500 kg, (c) 31 min, FL 220, 13 100 kg.

For the hold, TAS 434 kt is extracted from the Table 34D, but the fuel flow must be checked against aircraft weight as per the footnote. Diversion started at 224 500 kg AUW, and 13 100 kg was to be used; this figure contains 7500 kg reserve, and the aircraft has descended only to FL 160. Of the actual fuel required, 5600 kg (13100 − 7500), the amount unused at the hold point would be the descent from FL 160 to landing, a figure of 1800 kg from the descent table. A round estimate of what fuel has in fact been burnt off would be 3800 kg, and the AUW at holding 220 700 kg. Thus, the noted consumption of 12 500 kg in the Table is satisfactory, and the correction element is not applicable.

Answer (d) 17 min at 12 500 kg/h = 3550 kg.

This example has put you into the diversion table, but if the descent had been broken off, say, at FL 180, whence to proceed direct to the alternate, then the calculations must be made from the descent, climb and cruise tables, starting from the AUW at the time of break off; since the diversion table showed that FL 220 would be climbed to, then from FL 180 a climb to around FL 340 would be possible and advisable.

Just to make sure you're not betting on avoiding a question on three-engine operation, take a look at Table 34G in Data Sheets 34 for such a problem as the following.

An aircraft en route to K goes on three engines at 1307.
Descent will be made on Tr. Details are:

    Distance   926 nm
    Cruise wind comp   −33 kt
    Descent wind comp −36 kt
    FL   310
    Temp dev   +8°C
    Aircraft weight at 1307 is 235 700 kg
    Fuel in tanks at 1307 is 41 300 kg

(a) Give ETA K

(b) How much fuel remaining on landing?

Descent first: TAS 358 kt, fuel 1900 kg, time 14 min
                 ∴ GS 322 kt, distance 75 nm, and cruise distance is then 851 nm.

AUW 235 700 kg, mean TAS 451 kt, 9700 kg/h at first, from the appropriate section of Table 34G. (Mean weight will be about 230 000 kg in first hour)

∴ GS 418 kt, time 2 h 2 min

Fuel	first hour	9 700 kg
	next 62 min	9 500 kg (use consumption 9200 kg/h)
	Cruise fuel	19 200 kg
	+Descent fuel	1 900 kg
	Total used	21 100 kg

This total subtracted from fuel available at 1307 gives 20 200 kg left on landing.

ETA 1307 + 2 h 2 min cruise + 14 min descent = 1523 hrs
Answer (a) ETA K 1523, (b) 20 200 kg.

Quite straightforward, providing you have familiarity. As a rider, the three-engine cruise in our favourite Data Sheets 33, Table 33H, is set out page by page for temp dev from standard, giving TAS at height and consumption per hour for a given weight at start: descent would call for normal descent Table 33E. Take a look at it right now or you'll be sorry.

To sum up for the flight plan itself, and such matters just discussed, you will need to do some of the published exam papers to get up some reasonable speed with accuracy: there is no need to be pedantic about fuel consumption. For instance, the tables themselves are not precise to a couple of hundred kilos – a weight of 101 100 kg gives a consumption 6400 kg/h and the following hour the AUW at start is 95 000 kg. There is a lot of averaging out, and though precision is always to be aimed for, it must be reasonable. You will find too the drift and wind component table at the end of the book helps speed things along, using the appropriate table for the climb or level: all that computer work is avoided. The failing point in flight planning is pure arithmetical error, frequently induced by examination neurosis.

Flight planning examinations are now in the multi-choice format. If you find it difficult to envisage how this can be done you should obtain *CAP 505* or *CAP 511* (see Appendix 3). You will find that it is still necessary to complete a flight plan as a preliminary to answering a series of objective questions.

Chapter 9
CHOICE OF ROUTE AND AREA NAVIGATION

On an airline running scheduled services, it would appear at first sight that the Captain has precious little say: certainly the majority of local trips around the UK to the European continent are fixed on an airways route at pre-arranged altitudes, and fortunately for pilot morale, however much they may appear to resemble a taxi service, the vagaries of weather and the need to practise all types of let-downs are ever present. On long routes, despite the firm establishment of various different tracks across the water or desert, the Captain must study the overall weather picture at selected heights and pick the best route for speed, the best height for his particular aircraft under the conditions, never forgetting passenger comfort (or animal comfort if he's carrying a load of monkeys), viewing the whole thing with an eye on fuel consumption and safety at all times. This takes some expertise to do briskly and surely, and while there is nothing worse than the type who hums and ha's muttering 'ye canna be too careful', it is positively better than the impulsive one who decides too quickly and pours his 100 ton flying cigar into turbulent weather away from operating navigation aids.

The scheduled services are but a part of the airline picture: any number of firms specialise in charter operations, and the majority are prepared to do charters, hiring aircraft if necessary from their competitors. Immediately, the profit motive could incite the Captain to take undue risks, especially if he is recently promoted to command and is anxious to make a name for himself as a good company man. Happily, by the time he is ready for such elevation, he has learnt more sense, apart from the legislative exercises he has had to undergo.

In such operations, the route and height are his decision: he will have in good time pondered the variables, and be ready at the briefing with a selection of possible routes from which to make a quick and safe choice; in fact, he may already have decided from his bedside after listening to the met man and the operations chap, so that on arrival at the field the flight plan is prepared and he needs only to check and corroborate that the latest information confirms his previous telephone briefing.

The procedure hardly varies; knowing his aircraft's heights for optimum operation, power- and fuel-wise, he will view a route first which will give him the best time track, examine it for trappy forecasts of turbulence or icing; for navaids en route; for active danger areas notified for the time on the Notams; for ATC restrictions and requirements; for safe clearance of topographical obstacles. Can he get over the highest mountains en route at the weight he will be at the time he gets there? Not only over them, but well over them? The broad decision now taken, he must at once examine the forecast weather at destination and departure field and at suitable alternates; not only alternates at his destination, but at the departure point, in case of return. Is there an en-route aerodrome available for landing if the destination clamps, thereby avoiding a possible diversion to some destination alternate when fuel is getting low, and the destination alternate is suffering from the same foul weather as the destination itself? Is a chosen alternate not only far enough away from the clamped destination to be reached comfortably with the fuel aboard, forecast OK for weather, but also politically OK for the passengers and crew to be allowed through immigration in the case of a long wait? Is the required type of fuel available there? Are the take-off and landing conditions restrictive? Are the necessary services available there at the possible arrival time? The world is scattered with airfields which do not fill all these requirements, only useful in case of *force majeure*.

The next check is on TOW and landing conditions: at expected TOW will the met conditions allow a safe unstick? With that TOW, less the expected fuel consumption from departure to destination (burn off + oil and water used, + extra required for climb, taxi, T/O, circuit and landing), is the maximum landing weight greater than the maximum allowed for the aircraft or by the airfield itself? If so, will the fuel uplift be reduced to allow a safe operation? Or should the payload be reduced?

He can now address himself to cruise control and fuel: long range or high speed cruise, depending on whether fuel conservation is more important than speed, or whether speed is possible with no fuel problems. All aircraft manufacturers produce their tables, and a little experience of their operation makes the decision more or less immediate. With the burn off + fuel required for alternate (latter usually at Long Range Cruise) he now considers his reserves, bearing in mind all the previous factors mentioned. A Route Contingency reserve is usually laid down by the Company, a percentage of burn off, with a maximum amount: this allows for the hard trip when actual winds are more adverse than forecast or for any of those happenings which are part of the flying game, such as being ordered to fly at an unsatisfactory altitude for the aircraft, or to move off flight planned track for any reason, weather or traffic. The amount of contingency fuel is normally determined by the route: over country plentifully supplied with good airfields, the percentage of burn off would not be so large as that over the oceans or deserts. A similar percentage is usually applied to the alternate fuel, and for the same reasons. An emergency reserve is frequently added for Mother, plus a goodly quantity for stand off, climb out, and taxi, the amount depending on the aircraft, and the complexity of the traffic at destination. It is almost normal in dodgy weather to have a stack of twenty aircraft at a place like NEW YORK, and plaintive cries from pilots that fuel is low and precedence is required are viewed very palely indeed from the other poor devils holding at precise altitudes for hours on end.

104 Plotting and Flight Planning

The only likely major difference to this type of routine will be if the destination is an island set solitary-like in the silver sea, a hearty distance from another aerodrome. Then, once having passed the PNR, or the latest time to divert to a suitable field on the beam of Tr, and a landing at destination becomes obligatory, an island reserve is substituted for alternate fuel, reserve fuel, and stand off fuel, to permit a long hold.

Add the lot up, and that's the load sheet fuel: an endurance is worked out from this from a graph or a rule of thumb average to give the maximum time the aircraft can be airborne.

Sundry wrinkles will become apparent, nearly all allowed for in the Aircraft Type Manual. The total FOB may include a quantity of unusable fuel in the tanks: the only interest in this for the operation is that it's part of the weight. Climb, taxi, take-off fuel will be laid down in the Manual, and included on the flight plan; en-route climb and allowances for it will be considered in the body of the flight plan from an appropriate table or graph; fuel for heaters, de-icers and so on are similarly allowed for. One pretty point often overlooked especially on shortish sectors is to jug up to the gills with fuel where the price is cheap, or to take the minimum consonant with safety where it is high: this will endear you to the commercial side of the company, for the savings can be appreciable. However, companies will usually lay down very precise rules as to when excess fuel is to be loaded.

Area Navigation (RNAV)

Traditionally, air navigation for commercial flights evolved from the use of point-source aids such as described in volume 1, initially with radio-ranges and NDBs, later to be followed by VORs, DMEs etc. These point-source aids led to the current ATS route structure which is particularly complex in the European/Mediterranean region and which is inherently inflexible. Unfortunately too, the present route structure offers little scope for expanding traffic capacity, options available to pilots or improving on the current levels of efficiency which already impose high workloads on air traffic controllers and pilots alike, especially in terminal areas. Also it has to be borne in mind that aircraft using airways vary considerably in their age, their performance and the degree of sophistication of their on-board equipment, leading to varying standards of navigation, even though they are meeting the internationally-agreed mandatory minimum requirements for airways flying. Even the national ATS systems in adjoining countries may differ in operating concepts and procedures within the internationally-agreed parameters, all adding to the difficulties encountered when trying to improve route capacity and all-round efficiency, at the same time as trying to offer pilots a practical choice of routes when flight planning.

For the closing years of the 1990s it is believed that the development of Area Navigation (RNAV) will overcome the present deficiencies and enable ATS systems to accommodate the increasing need for operators to enjoy a greater route flexibility and traffic capacity, handled safely and efficiently. So what is RNAV? In ICAO Annex 11, RNAV is defined as a method of navigation which permits aircraft operation on any desired flight path within the coverage of station-referenced navigation aids, or within the limits of the capability of self-contained aids, or a combination of these. Thus RNAV may, in general terms, be considered as any system of navigation which is capable of maintaining track and time to a specified degree of accuracy without having to overfly a point-source aid.

The advantages of adopting the RNAV principle over the present fixed route system stem from the introduction which will then be possible of more direct routeing so reducing flight distances, times and fuel required. It could lead to increasing existing or new route capacities by enabling the use of dual or parallel routes, reduced separation horizontally and vertically between routes and of the basic volume of protected airspace. It will allow pilots and operators to exercise greater freedom of choice while also giving ATC greater flexibility.

All this however depends upon the time when virtually all aircraft are equipped to the necessary RNAV standard – hopefully well within this decade. It is recognised that there will be difficulties to be overcome during the transitional stage because there will still be aircraft operating wholly dependent on over-flying point-source navigation aids. In Europe, time scales are being established and initially RNAV will be used within the existing ATS route system. Then it is envisaged that as most aircraft come to meet the approved minimum equipment standards, there will be 'Fixed RNAV Routes' (published permanent ATS routes which can only be flight-planned by aircraft with the appropriate RNAV capability), 'Contingency RNAV Routes' (published ATS routes usable by RNAV capability aircraft during specific time-limited periods) and 'Random RNAV Routes' (unpublished routes which can be flight-planned within certain designated RNAV areas) which will be options open to pilots.

Within the RNAV concept itself, there are two recognised levels of accuracy of operation – Basic RNAV (B-RNAV) of which the accuracy is comparable with that of aircraft operating the present system on routes defined by VOR/DME, and Precision RNAV (P-RNAV) which requires a track-keeping accuracy of 0.5 nm standard deviation or better. Already many UK-registered aircraft are fitted with RNAV capability equipment and as the phases of introduction are implemented, so in the UK the Air Navigation Order (ANO) will be amended to lay down the rules for approval of RNAV equipment, its installation and maintenance together with the operational procedures to be used. The current position is laid down in Articles 39, 39A, 39B of the ANO and expanded in a yellow (Ops/ATS) Aeronautical Information Circular. The intention is that carriage of RNAV equipment will be mandatory from 1st January 1998 within the airspace of ECAC member states. By then, the pilot's choice of route will have been usefully extended, even in heavily-trafficked areas, if his aircraft is RNAV fitted.

Chapter 10
WEIGHT CALCULATION

Being in an international business the pilot is constantly plagued with units different from the ones he's been brought up on, and despite efforts to bring them all to one acceptable type world-wide, there's always the nation which won't conform or won't agree. In general, kilograms are becoming the accepted weight unit, though the pilot will find pounds aplenty on the trips. Volume should thus be in litres, and this comes hard to many, used to Imperial gallons. The US gallon is only about 4/5 of the Imperial gallon, so there's another snag. It is quite unnecessary to memorise the conversion units, they're all on the computer anyway or in the Flight Manual, but when dealing with large figures, you should have an approximate idea of the relationship in order to get the number of noughts correct.

> 1 kilogram is 2.2 lb
> 1 litre is about 1/5th Imperial gallon
> 1 litre is about 1/3rd of a US gallon

The weight of fuel varies with temperature and air pressure: the conversion from volume occupied (i.e. litres or gallons) to weight (kg or lb) is found by knowing the fuel's specific gravity at the time of loading. An engineer will have used his hydrometer to find this, and the sum is simple. It must of course be entered on the load sheet; on the flight plan, weight is the only concern.

The specific gravity is simply the relation of the weight of fuel at the time for a given volume to the weight of water for the same volume (the water being under standard conditions of temperature and pressure) (see Fig. 10.1).

The circular slide rule works all this out for you, and you will see that kg to lb is straightforward, but you cannot convert litres to kg, gals to lb, or any variant of these without knowing the sg – the errors can be considerable, and there must be no guesswork at all.

The precautions to be observed with respect to maximum TOW and maximum landing weight after obtaining total fuel requirements have already been mentioned; the fuel requirements, although calculated with precision, are the minimum requirements for safe operation, for there would be no point in lugging excess fuel around; thence, the payload carried must be such that these maxima are not exceeded, and off-loading passengers or freight is a serious decision in a commercial concern. But just as maxima are laid down

Weight Calculation 107

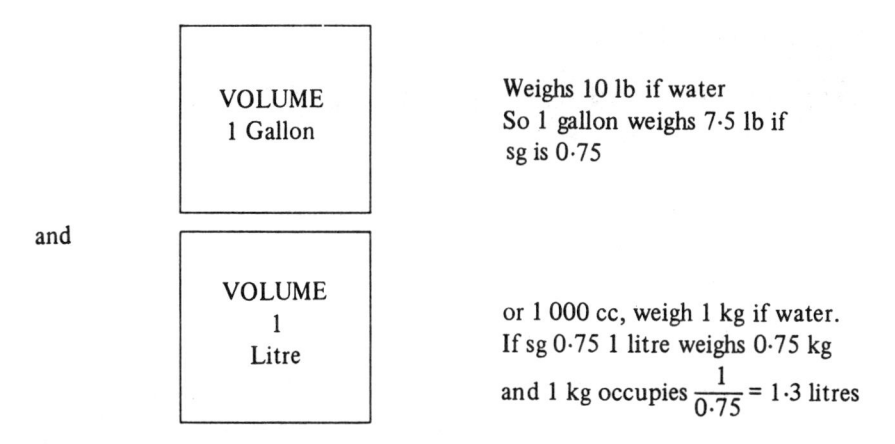

| VOLUME 1 Gallon | Weighs 10 lb if water
So 1 gallon weighs 7·5 lb if sg is 0·75 |

and

| VOLUME 1 Litre | or 1 000 cc, weigh 1 kg if water.
If sg 0·75 1 litre weighs 0·75 kg
and 1 kg occupies $\frac{1}{0\cdot 75}$ = 1·3 litres |

Fig. 10.1 Specific gravity.

for aircraft weight, so for *each flight* there must be a maximum payload that can be carried.

Consider the following example:

>Maximum TOW 250 000 kg
>Maximum ldg wt 190 000 kg
>Weight without fuel or payload 170 000 kg
>FOB 23 535 kg
>Fuel required from departure to destination 16 535 kg

The point to start with is max ldg wt 190 000 kg. The only difference between this imperative maximum and the actual TOW is the fuel used up from departure to destination, the burn off.

>So 190 000 kg
>   16 535 kg
>   206 535 kg   is the TOW

This is well below the maximum TOW, but dare not be exceeded, for if it was, the aircraft would be above maximum landing weight at the destination and would be forced to chunter around simply to use fuel and get the weight down.

The weight without fuel or payload, 170 000 kg, may now be added to the total fuel on board to give 193 535 kg, the weight without payload. Then 206 535 − 193 535 = 13 000 kg payload, pretty poor for such a heavy aircraft, but when going to spots like Iceland, calling for much fuel for an alternate in Scotland, such a case can frequently happen.

Another example:
Maximum TOW 47 300 kg
Weight less fuel and payload 33 400 kg
Fuel required from departure to destination 9775 kg

Reserve fuel (assume unused) 1985 kg
What is maximum payload that can be carried?
47 300 − 33 400 = 13 900 kg = fuel + payload.
FOB is 9775 + 1985 = 11 760 kg
∴ playload is 2140 kg

All the problems boil down to either of these types, and in practice the Station Duty Officer has a simple form to resolve them. The burn off may include not only the fuel used from departure to destination but also oil and water.

A further example:

Regulated landing weight (RLW)	52 618 kg	Max TOW under forecast
Burn off	18 240	conditions 72 575
	70 858 kg	
Max permissible TOW	70 858 kg	
Estimated weight, no fuel (empty tank weight)	42 628	(including traffic load)
Max fuel uplift	28 230 kg	
Flight plan fuel	28 230 kg	
Excess available	NIL	
Loadsheet fuel	28 230 kg	
+ taxi and etc.	500	
This is the fuel in your tanks	28 730 kg	TOW 70 858 kg

And you will see that the restricting factor on this trip was ldg wt, and the fuel uplifted exactly the flight plan requirement.

Zero fuel weight (ZFW)

There is one further restriction – the Maximum Zero Fuel Weight (MZFW). Modern aircraft carry most, if not all, of their fuel in the wings. If the tanks are empty, there will be a maximum permissible weight for the aircraft including all its contents (equipment, crew, passengers and cargo). Exceeding this weight would put an unacceptable load on the aircraft structure. To check that all three restrictions are complied with, the following procedure, illustrated by an example, is recommended.

Example 1

RTOW 167 t (tonne = 1000 kg)
RLW   139.55 t
MZFW 132 t

Aircraft weight without fuel and payload 90 t (often called the aircraft prepared for service (APS) weight)

Reserve fuel   3 t
Flight time   3 h 33 min

Weight Calculation

Diversion time 51 min
Fuel flow throughout 2.5 t/hr

What is the maximum permissible TOW and payload?

Solution

TOW (t)			RLW (t)			ZFW (t)		Burn off	8.875 t
			139.55			132		Diversion	2.125 t
	Burn off	8.88		Total FOB	14		Reserve	3.000 t
167			148.43			146		Total	14.000 t

Max permissible TOW is lowest of the three figures = <u>146 t</u>
APS weight 90
Total FOB 14   104 t

maximum payload   42 t

Example 2

APS weight 40.00 t
RLW 49.55 t
RTOW 65.00 t
MZFW 48.00 t
Burn-off 12.89 t
Reserve 1.65 t

Calculate the maximum permissible TOW and payload.

Solution

TOW (t)			RLW (t)			ZFW (t)			
			49.55			48.00		Burn off	12.89
	Burn off	12.89		Total FOB	14.54		Reserve	1.65
65			62.44			62.54		Total	14.54

Maximum permissible TOW   62.44 t
APS   40.00
Total FOB   14.54   54.54 t

Maximum payload   7.9 t

Example 3
Load sheet reads:

A/c wt, no fuel, no payload	63 200 kg
Max TOW	99 000 kg
Route fuel (excluding reserve)	18 200 kg
Reserve (assume unused)	3 000 kg

If max ldg wt is 76 500 kg, and MZFW 74 000 kg, find:
 (a) TOW when maximum payload is carried.

 (b) Maximum payload.

Solution

TOW (t)	RLW (t)		ZFW (t)		
	76.5		74.0	Burn off	18.2
Burn off	18.2	Total FOB	21.2	Reserve	3
99	94.7		95.2	Total	21.2

Maximum permissible TOW	94.7 t
APS weight 63.2	
Total FOB 21.2	84.4 t
Maximum payload	10.3 t

Example 4
You are fly from P to Q where your fuel is not available, and return to P: a maximum payload is to be off-loaded at Q, and a maximum payload uplifted there. The following are the pertinent data:

Distance P to Q	610 nm
Wt, no fuel, no payload	36 500 kg
Max ldg wt	52 400 kg
Max TOW	63 000 kg
Reserve (unused)	4 000 kg
Fuel for each flight (circuit, take-off, etc.)	500 kg
Mean consumption	1 350 kg/h
Mean GS P–Q	240 kt
Mean GS Q–P	280 kt

Give (a) The fuel which must be uplifted at P.

 (b) Maximum payload which can be carried from P to Q.

 (c) Maximum payload which can be carried from Q to P.

Weight Calculation

Solution

Both flights use less fuel than MTOW − MLW, so MLW is restricting.
P–Q: 610 nm @ 240 kt = 2 h 32 min @ 1350 kg/h = 3420 kg fuel.
Q–P: 610 nm @ 280 kt = 2 h 10 min @ 1350 kg/h = 2925 kg fuel.

∴ FOB at P 3 420 kg (P–Q)
            2 925 kg (Q–P)
Reserve   4 000 kg
Circuit   1 000 kg (500 for return to P)
FUEL REQD. 11 345 kg ... (a)

P–Q

Wt, no fuel, no payload	36 500 kg	Max ldg wt	52 400 kg
FOB	+11 345 kg	Fuel used	3 420 kg
Wt, no payload	47 845 kg	Circuit	+ 500 kg
		TOW	56 320 kg
		Wt, no payload	−47 845 kg
		PAYLOAD P to Q	8 475 kg ... (b)

Q–P

Wt, no fuel, no payload	36 500 kg	Max ldg wt	52 400 kg
Q–P fuel	2 925 kg	Fuel used	2 925 kg
Reserve	4 000 kg	Circuit	+ 500 kg
Circuit	+ 500 kg	TOW	55 825 kg
Wt, no payload	43 925 kg		

∴ TOW   55 825 kg
Wt, no payload −43 925 kg
PAYLOAD Q to P 11 900 kg ... (c)

Chapter 11
POINT OF NO RETURN

PNR is the point beyond which an aircraft cannot go and still return to its departure field within its endurance.

This is entirely a fuel problem, and some reserve for holding or diversion should always be allowed for before setting about the calculation. A PNR is scarcely pertinent on trips over land well served with airfields, though a pilot will often prefer, if his destination and destination alternates are forecast en route to be below limits for his ETA, to return home rather than lob into an airfield where conditions for waiting with a crowd of passengers are miserable, expensive or politically troublesome. But over the oceans and deserts, a PNR is a must; the time to it is noted on the flight plan, and the ETA threat put in on departure: it can be amended on the way if forecast winds are diabolically different from actual, or the flight is conducted at a different height or power than planned.

The solution of the problem can be found by formula, simply solved on the computer. The distance to the PNR is the distance to be covered back if the aircraft returns, i.e. distance out = distance home. The time for this distance at GS Out plus the time for this distance at GS Home will equal your endurance time excluding reserves.

If E = total endurance in hours (excluding reserve)
T = Time to PNR in hours
O = GS Out
H = GS Home
R = Distance to the PNR

Then:

$$E = \frac{R}{O} + \frac{R}{H}$$

$$EOH = R(O + H)$$

$$R = \frac{EOH}{O + H}$$

and since

$$T = \frac{R}{O}$$

$$OT = \frac{EOH}{O + H}$$

$$T = \frac{EH}{O + H}$$

Work in minutes, if you like, as the computer work is eased; and beware of assuming that a wind component Out of +20 must give a wind component Home of −20; at lower GS, drift is greater, so check the GS out and home against Tr Out and Home. Having obtained the time to PNR, the distance can be readily found at GS Out, e.g. endurance 4 hr, excluding 45 min reserve, Tr 300(T), WV 270/40, TAS 200 kt

$$\therefore \text{GS Out 164 kt} \quad \text{GS Home 234 kt}$$
$$T = \frac{240 \times 234}{164 + 234}$$
$$= 141 \text{ min}$$
and 2 h 21 min at 164 kt = 386 nm

All straightforward and the accuracy of the result can be checked − 2 h 21 min out +386 nm at GS 234 kt or 1 h 39 min = 4 h endurance.

PNR on two or more legs

Weather systems and ATC systems seldom permit a long drag on a single track nowadays, and finding the PNR on a route where one or more changes of Tr are involved is quite simple, and rational, even with the changing flight conditions such as a return with one engine failed.

Example
Following are route details: ignore climb and descent:

	Tr(T)	*Distance*	*WV*
TAIPEH–KAGOSHIMA	042	606	260/110
KAGOSHIMA–SHIZUOKA	064	417	280/80
SHIZUOKA–TOKYO	011	61	290/50

ETD TAIPEH 1020 UTC
TAS 410 kt (four engines) 350 kt (three engines)
Fuel consumption 3000 kg/h (four engines) 2800 kg/h (three engines)
Reserve (assume unused) 45 min
FOB 15 000 kg

Question
Give distance to and ETA at the PNR assuming the return flight will be on three engines.

114 Plotting and Flight Planning

Solution

The method used is a very powerful one that can take account of any number of variables. Although it may seem a little laborious, it should be remembered that nearly half the work will have already been done when the flight plan was prepared. Briefly the technique is:

(1) Progressively check the total fuel required to go out to and back from each successive turning point.

(2) Eventually the fuel available will not be sufficient to go out to and return from a turning point. From the previous turning point decide how much fuel is available to go from there to the PNR and back to the point.

(3) Comparing this amount with the total fuel required to go out and back on the complete stage will give the ratio of distance and time out to the PNR compared with the stage distance and time out.

The importance of a systematic layout cannot be over-emphasised:

Outward flight: TAS 410 kt   Fuel consumption 3000 kg/h

	Tr °T	GS kt	Dist nm	Time min	Fuel kg
TAI–KAG	042	491	606	74	3700
KAG–SHI	064	472	417	53	2650
SHI–TOK	011	399	61	$9\frac{1}{2}$	480

Return flight: TAS 350 kt   Fuel consumption 2800 kg/h

TOK–SHI	191	354	61	$10\frac{1}{2}$	490
SHI–KAG	244	282	417	89	4150
KAG–TAI	222	257	606	$141\frac{1}{2}$	6600

Fuel analysis:

	Out	Home	Out + Home	Total
TAI–KAG	3700	6600	10300	10300
KAG–SHI	2650	4150	6800	17100
SHI–TOK	480	490	970	18070
	6830	11240		
	11240			
	18070 kg			

18070 kg { Check that this figure agrees with the running total (underlined) above.

FOB	15000 kg
Reserve 45 min @ 2800 kg/h	2100
PNR fuel	12900
Fuel TAI–KAG–TAI	10300
Fuel KAG–PNR–KAG	2600
Fuel KAG–SHI–KAG	6800

Point of No Return 115

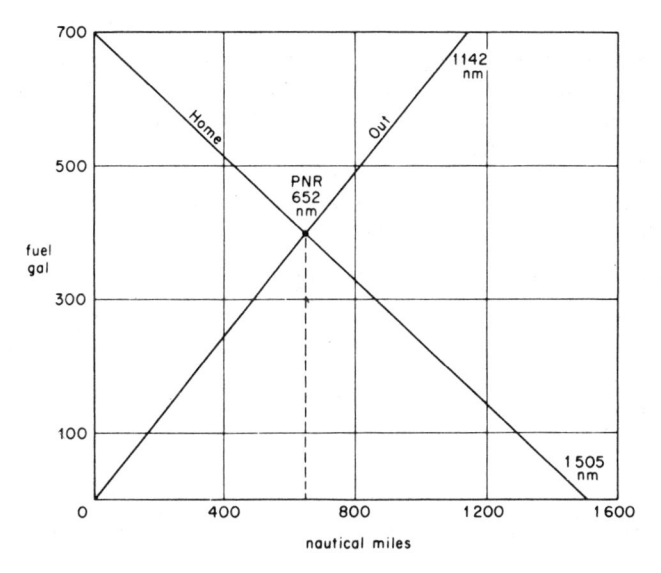

Fig. 11.1 Finding PNR.

$$\frac{2600}{6800} = \frac{d}{417} = \frac{t}{53}$$

$$d = 159\,\text{nm} \quad t = 20$$

	Dist	Time
TAI–KAG	606	74
KAG–PNR	159	20
TAI–PNR	765	94

ETA at PNR = 1020 + 1 hr 34 min = <u>1154</u>

Graphical solution
Given: FOB 750 gal, TAS 180 kt, consumption 95 gal/h
HWC 25 kt
Find the PNR, leaving 50 gal in reserve.

Steps:
(1) Endurance for 700 gal at 95 gal/h = 442 min

(2) Distance OUT for 442 min = 442 min at GS 155 kt
= 1142 nm

(3) Distance HOME for 442 min = 442 min at GS 205 kt
= 1505 nm

(4) With coordinates fuel and distance, plot these curves (Fig. 11.1).

The point of intersection is the PNR.

116 *Plotting and Flight Planning*

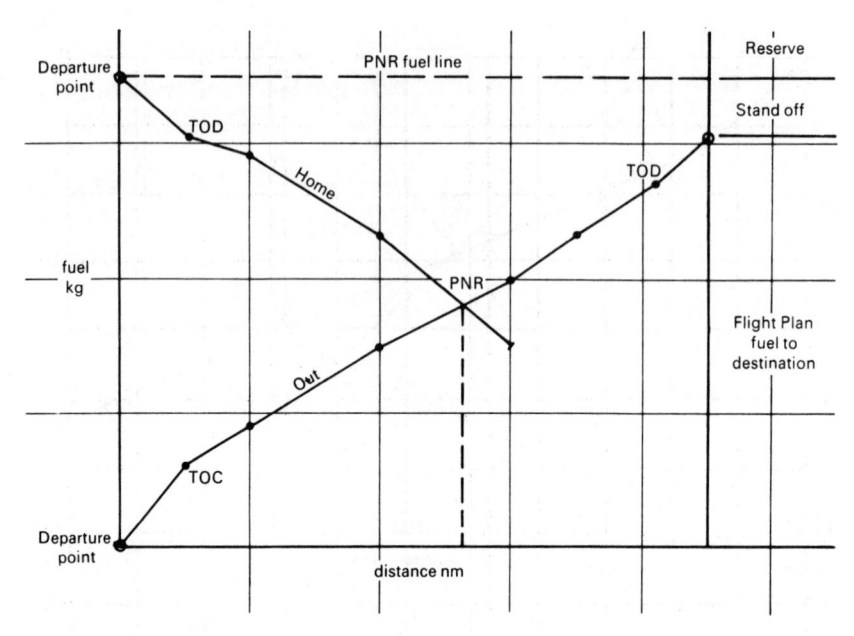

Fig. 11.2 Howgozit chart.

This can be checked correct with the formulae. On the graph, as large a scale as possible should be chosen to ensure an accurate result.

Progress charts (Howgozits)

To find a PNR graphically as part of the usual flight involving various FLs, WVs, speeds, etc., will necessitate the use of a progress chart or, as the Americans say, a Howgozit. The basic idea behind this is to present the pilot with a graphical forecast of how the fuel will be used during the flight. The graphs may be drawn upwards as in Fig. 11.2, or downwards (Fig. 11.3) starting with the total FOB and showing the fuel expected to be left at each turning point. This chart can then be used to obtain the PNR and also the CP as explained in the next Chapter.

Proceed as follows:

(1) Complete the flight plan.

(2) Plot the fuel/distance Out, starting with TOC and ending with TOD, reading the stages off the flight plan. This is in fact the chart to be used for the flight progress; as the turning or reporting points are reached, the fuel used so far is entered on the graph, and a comparison with fuel planned is at once visually apparent.

(3) Draw a line across the graph to represent the fuel available for PNR calculation; where this line meets the fuel coordinate may now be

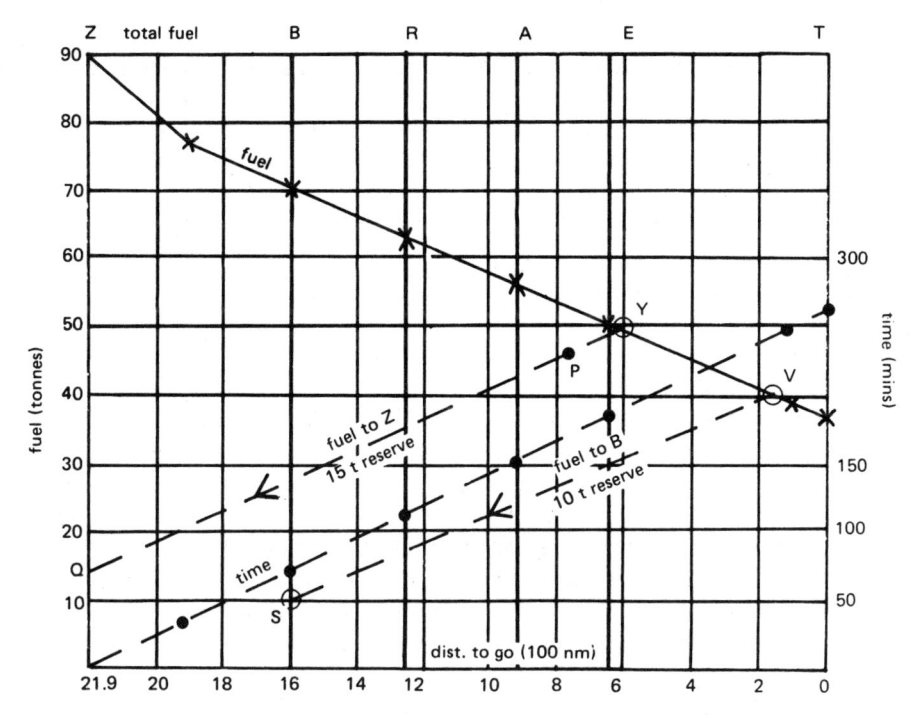

Fig. 11.3 Finding PNR on Howgozit chart.

deemed the 'departure point' whither the aircraft is returning having used the PNR fuel.

(4) From this point, work *backwards* to TOD and thenceforth in fuel used per sector, until the curves cross. Fig. 11.2.

Practical solution of PNR on progress chart

In practice, it is usual to approximate the return flight, when obtaining the PNR, assuming one speed and one consumption throughout. Here is an example for a flight from Z to T via B, R, A and E worked out for you (Fig. 11.3).

Example
Assume:

(1) Outward flight of 2190 nm taking 260 min as plotted on the chart – derived from the flight plan.

(2) Average return TAS 496 kt.

(3) Average return wind component −13 kt.

(4) Average return fuel flow 10 500 kg/h. PNR reserve is 15 000 kg.

Solution

Choose a convenient return time about $\frac{3}{4}$ of flight time – in this case choose 3 hr.

3 hr at 10 500 kg/h = 31 500 kg at GS 483 kt = 1449 nm
PNR reserve   15 000
Total return fuel   46 500

Plot 46 500 kg at 2190 − 1449 = 741 nm to go (P).
Plot 15 000 kg at 2190 nm to go (Q).
Join and extend QP to cut outward fuel graph at Y.
Y is the PNR – 600 nm to go to T.
Dropping a perpendicular down to the time line will give the time to reach the PNR from Z as 193 min.

The reasoning behind the method is as follows. At any point, for example A, the fuel to return to Z is represented by the distance from the outward fuel graph upwards (at A about 31.5 t). Similarly the distance downwards represents the fuel to return to Z with a 15 t reserve (at A about 42 t). The distance between the two graphs at any point (at A about 15 t) represents the fuel surplus to the requirement to be able to go out and still be able to return with 15 t available to Z. At Y this surplus has disappeared and so the requirement can only just be satisfied. Y is, therefore, the PNR required.

The great advantage of this technique for finding the PNR is its extreme flexibility. For example, if it was required to find the PNR for a return to B retaining a reserve of 10 t, it would be done by drawing a line through the 10 t point at B (point S) parallel to QP so that it cuts the outward fuel line at V at 170 nm to go. Time to V, 204 min.

Practical significance of the PNR

Knowledge of the PNR is useful in cases where there is some doubt about the availability of the destination and its alternates. The most likely reason for this is weather but there are a number of other reasons why airports may be closed to traffic. One that could well affect all airports in a country is political unrest. Obviously before reaching the PNR, the Captain must make his decision as to whether or not to proceed with the flight. After the PNR, he is committed to carrying on to the destination or an alternate to it.

Engine failure PNR

The common practice of assuming that the return flight from the PNR will be with one engine failed is designed to produce a PNR that is valid even if, after deciding to return at the PNR because of some emergency at the destination, the engine then fails with a resulting loss in economy on the return flight. It must be emphasised that the primary emergency is still that at the destination. If the failure of the engine was the primary emergency, it is more likely that the main point of concern would be: How soon can a safe landing be made? This is dealt with in the next Chapter.

Significance of PNR reserves

Any PNR calculated must, inevitably, be inaccurate. There are so many possible causes of error – WVs, temperature, FLs, route, aircraft performance – to mention just some of them! The safeguard is in the reserves allowed. If these are sensibly adequate, any PNR should be valid, even if the assumptions made in the calculation are not accurate. The leeway that an adequate reserve provides enables many operators to rely on PNR tables for a particular aircraft. These are entered with TOW, fuel load and estimated average wind component for the operation and a distance to the PNR can then be extracted. Errors caused by the approximations involved should be taken care of by the reserves employed.

Factors affecting the PNR

The maximum distance to the PNR will be achieved in still air conditions. In fact, a very quick approximation is to use half the still air range as the distance to the PNR. Any wind will reduce the distance for either or both of the following reasons:

(1) If there is any drift, the effective head wind component on a track is more than the effective tail wind component on the reciprocal track.

(2) The aircraft will take longer and so experience more head wind effect (time × wind component) when flying into a head wind than it will experience tail wind effect on the reciprocal track.

The other two factors are simpler to understand:

(1) Fuel available. Other things being equal, the distance to the PNR will vary directly with the fuel available: 10% more fuel available will mean 10% greater distance to the PNR if nothing else, such as wind component, changes.

(2) Aircraft performance. The better (more economical) the performance, the greater the distance.

Practical examination questions

(1) If the PNR is calculated to be 880 nm with 10 000 kg of fuel available, the distance to the PNR with 11 000 kg available, other things being equal, will be approximately:
 (a) 928 nm (b) 968 nm (c) 960 nm (d) 920 nm.

(2) On a flight an aircraft is found to be achieving GSs 10% higher than planned. Assuming all conditions remain the same, the revised distance to the PNR will be:
 (a) Less (b) More (c) Unchanged
 (d) It is impossible to say.

(3) The distance to a PNR flying directly into a 50 kt head wind is 1200 nm. The distance to the PNR with an exactly reciprocal WV will be:
 (a) Less than 1200 nm   (b) More than 1200 nm
 (c) 1200 nm   (d) It could be any value.

(4) With a TAS of 400 kt, the distance to a PNR in still air is 1200 nm. The distance (nm) with a forecast WV at 90° to the track of 40 kt will be:
 (a) 1194   (b) 1206   (c) 1140   (d) 1200.

(5) The primary emergency for which a PNR with engine failure is computed for is:
 (a) Engine failure
 (b) Emergency at the destination and its alternates
 (c) Any on-board emergency requiring a landing to be made as soon as possible
 (d) Fuel shortage.

(6) In-flight checks reveal that the fuel flows are 4% greater than expected at preflight planning. If everything else is as expected, the distance to the PNR will be:
 (a) 4% more   (b) Unchanged   (c) 2% less   (d) 4% less.

Chapter 12
CRITICAL POINT

Critical point is the point from which it would take equal time to continue to destination as to return to a suitable aerodrome.

This is not a function of fuel: there is a critical point when crossing the road or swimming a river: distance and related GS are the factors to consider and it is important to bear in mind that it is a flight plan problem initially, to prepare for some eventuality like an engine failure when an instant decision must be taken to proceed or return, the quicker being the choice as there is some concern among those present.

Again, the solution is done by simple formula, and the ETA CP entered on the flight plan; the same arguments hold as previously as to the trips on which a CP is vital.

Take a straightforward case first (Fig. 12.1).

Where D = total distance
P = the CP
X = distance to CP (in nautical miles)
O = GS Out (in knots)
H = GS Home (in knots)

Then by definition:

P to A at GS Home = P to B at GS Out

i.e.
$$\frac{X}{H} = \frac{D - X}{O}$$
$$OX = H(D - X)$$
$$OX = HD - HX$$
$$OX + HX = HD$$
$$\therefore \frac{DH}{O + H} = X, \text{ the distance to the CP.}$$

Now the CP is bursting with importance when the aircraft is acting up, usually an engine out, not in itself an emergency, but leading towards it if something else happens: an aircraft on three engines will not go as fast as on four, strangely enough, especially when fuel conservation is high priority. An operator, therefore, lays down in the manual an average three-engined and two-engined TAS at specified heights; thus, the CP data must be worked using the reduced TAS so that the equal times home

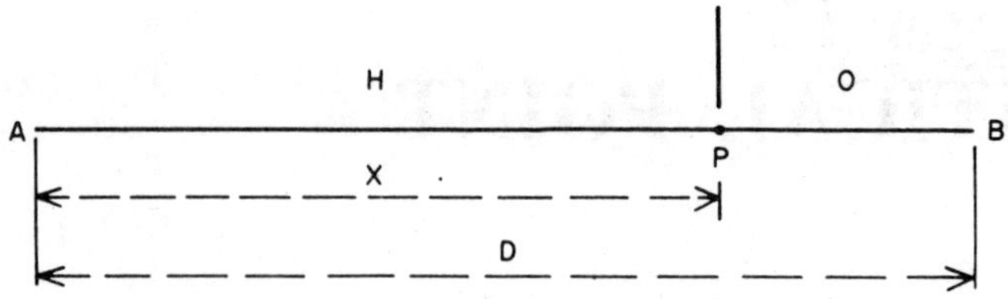

122 *Plotting and Flight Planning*

```
                    H              O
A ───────────────────────────────────── B
       X                  P
   ←─ ─ ─ ─ ─ ─ ─ ─ ─ ─ ─ ─→|
                    D
   ←─ ─ ─ ─ ─ ─ ─ ─ ─ ─ ─ ─ ─ ─→
```

Fig. 12.1 Finding CP.

and away from the CP are appropriate to the conditions should the exigency occur. In the air, once the CP is passed (and the ETA to it will be calculated at normal GS, just like a reporting point), the pilot will proceed to his destination. A separate CP at full TAS can be calculated readily, to cope with serious situations like a loose panther in the hold, or a berserk and frothing passenger which affect the safety of the aircraft and its occupants, but not its power. But in a pressurisation failure, for instance, while the power is unaffected, the CP is dependent on a TAS at a new enforced height with implications very similar to the engine failure cases. This, too, calls for a separate CP, not an arduous calculation since the action for the pressurisation failure will be laid down and the optimum height with the appropriate data is set out in the aircraft manual.

There are several pertinent possibilities, then; and bear in mind that they are just that. One or more CPs are noted on the flight plan to be referred to as though they are turning points, with their ETA. Once a CP is passed, the pilot's action is clear: if a near-emergency arises, he will aim for the destination airfield. The CP is but a preparation in case of emergency, and if that emergency happens, he has the facts before him at once.

Some samples:

(1) Track 240(T), WV 310/35, TAS 260 kt distance 530 nm
∴ GS on = 245 kt   GS Home = 270 kt

$$\text{Distance to CP} = \frac{DH}{O + H}$$

$$= \frac{530 \times 270}{245 + 270}$$

$$= 278 \text{ nm}$$

and time to CP = 278 at GS on 245 kt = 1 h 08 min

Check
278 at GS Home 270 kt   = 1 h 2 min
(530 − 278) at GS on 245 kt = 1 h 2 min

(2) What is distance to CP en route from DARWIN and MELBOURNE distance 1728 nm, cruise TAS 425 kt, 3-engine TAS 400 kt, hwc from

CP to MELBOURNE 5 kt, headwind component CP to DARWIN 20 kt?

∴ for the CP calculation: GS on = 395 kt, GS Home = 380 kt, } both at reduced TAS

$$\text{Distance to CP} = \frac{DH}{O + H}$$
$$= \frac{1728 \times 380}{395 + 380}$$
$$= 847 \text{ nm}$$

You check.

The ETA CP can then be found simply from the normal flight plan after departure; this type of problem is most frequently used in practice and, despite finding the wind components by inspection, is proved reasonably accurate: with a long trip going fairly to plan until an engine drops out, a pilot who turns back because it happens five minutes before the CP cannot be criticised for being dogmatically correct, but his employers and passengers might think him rather lacking in dash and élan.

(3) Now for the several Track CP.
TAS 200 kt engine failure TAS 160 kt

Route
BAGHDAD–BASRA   Track 115(T), Dist 170 nm WV 180/20
BASRA–KUWAIT   Track 178(T), Dist 110 nm WV 230/30
KUWAIT–BAHRAIN   Track 129(T), Dist 147 nm WV 250/15

Find ETA CP if ATD BAGHDAD is 1115.

Using the reduced TAS to obtain the GSs, calculate the onward and return times.

	Tr	GS	dist	time	
BGW–BAS	115	151	170	$67\frac{1}{2}$	
BAS–KWI	178	140	110	47	ONWARD
KWI–BAH	129	167	147	53	
BAS–BGW	295	167	170	61	
KWI–BAS	358	177	110	$37\frac{1}{2}$	RETURN
BAH–KWI	309	152	147	58	

Now prepare a diagram, as in Fig. 12.2, to show from each turning point the total time on to BAHRAIN and back to BAGHDAD. At the CP, the difference between the two totals will need to be zero. From inspection, it can be seen that a zero difference will be found between BASRA and KUWAIT. Interpolate between the time differences of −39 and $+45\frac{1}{2}$ to find the zero position:

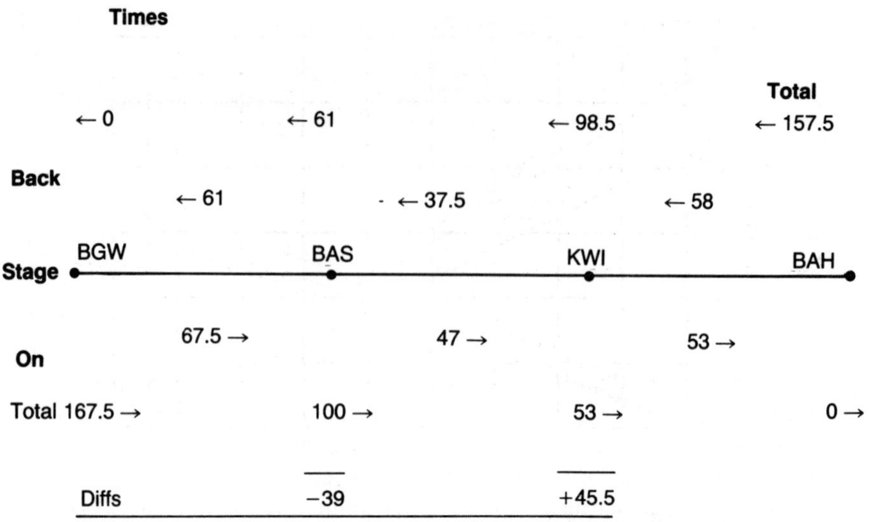

124 *Plotting and Flight Planning*

Times

```
                                                                    Total
         ← 0              ← 61                  ← 98.5              ← 157.5
Back
                  ← 61              ← 37.5              ← 58
         BGW              BAS                   KWI                 BAH
Stage  •─────────────────•────────────────────•──────────────────•
                  67.5 →            47 →                53 →
On
Total 167.5 →            100 →                 53 →                 0 →
                         ─────                 ─────
Diffs                    −39                   +45.5
```

Fig. 12.2 Critical point on multi-leg flight.

$$\frac{39}{39 + 45\frac{1}{2}} = \frac{d}{110} = \frac{t}{37} \text{ (time at full GS to go 110 nm)}$$
$$d = \underline{50} \quad t = \underline{17}$$

To find the total distance and the time from BAGHDAD (at full TAS):

	dist	time
BGW–BAS	170	$53\frac{1}{2}$ (170 nm/GS 191 kt)
BAS–CP	50	17
BGW–CP	220	$70\frac{1}{2}$

ETA CP = 1115 + 1 h $10\frac{1}{2}$ min = $1225\frac{1}{2}$.

Graphical solution
A simple graphical solution of the following problem is shown in Fig. 12.3.

Example
Flight from A to B:
distance 850 nm;   wind components: out −45 kt, back +40 kt;
full TAS 280 kt;   engine failure TAS 240 kt.
Find the CP with and without engine failure.

Critical Point 125

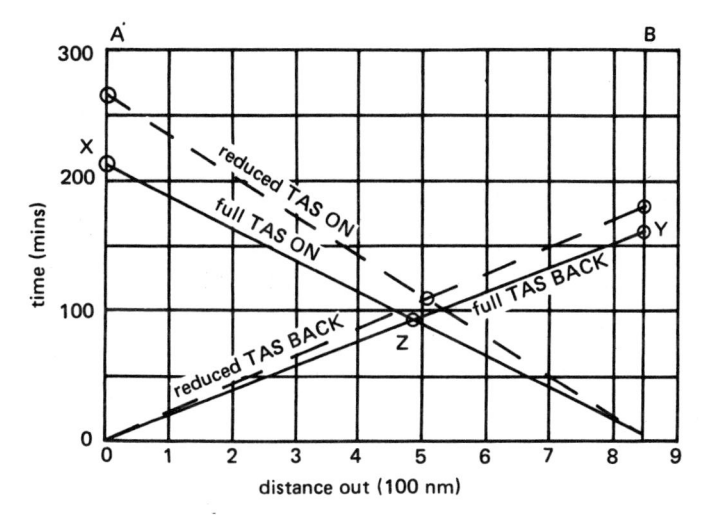

Fig. 12.3 Graphical solution of critical point.

Solution
Full TAS

	GS	dist	time
A–B	235	850	217
B–A	320	850	$159\frac{1}{2}$

At X on the vertical line through A on the graph, plot the time to go to reach B and join to the zero time point at B. Similarly, plot Y on the vertical line through B the time to go to reach A and join to the zero time point at A. The intersection of the two lines at Z gives the CP at a distance of 490 nm from A.
  Check by calculation:
Reduced TAS

	GS	dist	time
A–B	195	850	$261\frac{1}{2}$
B–A	280	850	182

Follow a similar plotting procedure as indicated by the pecked lines in Fig. 12.3 and obtain a position for the reduced TAS CP of 500 nm from A. Again check by calculation. Notice that the CP has moved upwind with the reduced TAS. It is not possible to read off the time to the CP directly from these graphs although the necessary information could be obtained from the full TAS 'ON' graph by a process of subtraction:

126   *Plotting and Flight Planning*

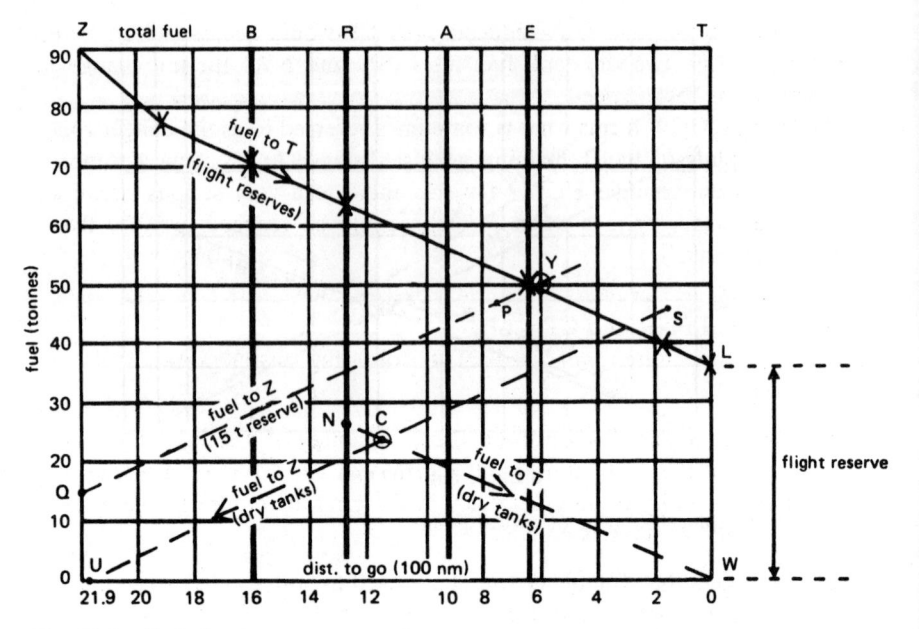

Fig. 12.4 Critical point on progress chart.

$$\begin{aligned}\text{Time on at the full TAS CP} &= 92\\ \text{Total time A to B at full TAS} &= 217\\ \text{Time to reach full TAS CP} &= 125\end{aligned}$$

To find the ETA for the reduced TAS CP is a little more complex and involves checking the distance to go on the full TAS 'ON' graph first. See if you can figure it out – check your answer by calculation.

Critical point by using progress charts

In the previous Chapter, it was seen that the PNR could be derived from the progress chart. The CP can also be obtained although, strictly speaking, it has no connection with fuel. The method is to find the point where the fuel needed to fly to the two aerodromes being considered is the same. As we are considering one particular aircraft, at the same weight and operating in a fairly consistent ambience of temperature and pressure, it would indicate that equal fuel represents equal time.

Figure 12.4 is a reproduction of Fig. 11.3 with the outward time graph omitted for the sake of clarity. To obtain the CP between Z and T, draw a line US from the zero fuel point at Z (point U) parallel to the return fuel line QPY. SU represents a return flight to Z to dry tanks (0 reserve). Similarly, draw in the line NW parallel to the outward fuel line ZYL. As ZYL is not a straight line, paralleling it is best done by using a pair of dividers, opened to the distance LW (the outward flight fuel reserve), to drop each plotting point on ZYL by the same amount. The intersection of NW and SU at 'C' will give the required full TAS CP. A reduced TAS CP would necessitate adjusting the slopes of the two dry tank fuel lines (SU and NW) for the change in economy at the lower speed.

The triangle UCW forms what is sometimes referred to as the danger zone. If in flight, plots of fuel remaining against distance to go show a trend of running into the triangle UCW, it would indicate a very serious situation. Within the danger zone neither Z nor T could be reached even by flying down to dry tanks!

Comparison of PNR and CP

These are quite often confused. The following distinctions should be understood:

(1) PNR is required when there is no possibility of a safe landing being made at the destination or its alternates. The CP is required against the possibility of an emergency in the aircraft requiring a landing to be made as soon as possible

(2) Although the symbols O and H are used in both the CP and the PNR formulae, they have different meanings:

Symbol	PNR	CP
O	Full GS out from A to PNR	Full or reduced GS FROM CP ON to B
H	Full or reduced GS Home from PNR to A	Full or reduced GS FROM CP Home to A

Careful inspection will show that in a case with varying wind components throughout the flight and/or a requirement for engine failure to be considered, there could be considerable differences between the values used for the CP and PNR calculations.

(3) PNR depends on endurance. It is quite possible, given sufficient fuel for the PNR, for the PNR to be at the destination. This just indicates that the reserves are sufficient to fly out to the destination and return without refuelling. To some isolated places or aerodromes where the price of fuel is very high, this may be a very sensible arrangement. On the other hand the CP is dependent not on fuel but on the total distance between the two bases. It will always tend to be around the mid-point area.

Relationship of CP and PNR

Having insisted on the distinctions between the CP and the PNR, let us now consider their affinity to each other. In a straightforward case with only one track, WV and TAS to consider, the 'H' and 'O' values would be identical in the two formulae and so if the CP and PNR are to coincide:

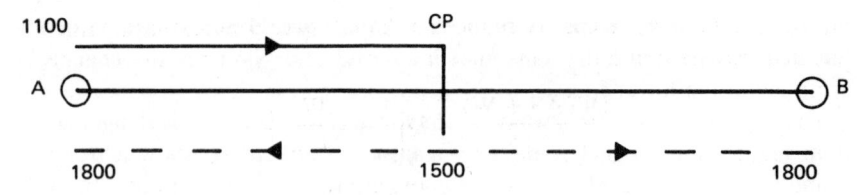

Fig. 12.5 Relationship between critical point/PNR.

$$CP = \frac{DH}{O + H} = \frac{EOH}{O + H} = PNR$$

so DH = EOH
or D = EO
or $\frac{D}{O} = E$

Distance divided by the GS out is the flight time and so when the PNR endurance equals the flight time, the PNR and CP will coincide in this simple case. However, even in a more realistic complicated case of varying wind components and performance, the relationship can still hold good. In Fig. 12.5, a flight is due to reach the CP at 1500 and the destination B at 1800. By definition, if the aircraft turned round and returned to A at the CP, the ETA back at A must be identical with the ETA at B, i.e. 1800 in this case. So, if the aircraft in this case had a PNR endurance equal to the flight time (seven hours), the CP and the PNR would be coincident. Notice that no provisos have been put in about constant wind components or performance. It is, therefore, true in all cases not involving engine failure, that the CP and PNR will be coincident if the PNR endurance equals the flight time. This implies that the PNR reserves will be the same as those being carried for the flight outward. PNR reserves will normally consist of a holding reserve and a diversion reserve, whereas the flight outward reserves will probably include a contingency reserve also. As a result the PNR will usually lie beyond the CP although, if the return diversion is much greater than the destination diversion, this may not be true.

Factors affecting the CP
In still air conditions or with a wind at 90° to track giving an equal effective hwc in both directions, the CP will be exactly half-way between the two bases being considered. The factors affecting the position of the CP are:

(1) Total distance between the two bases.

(2) The wind components – the CP will always be along track and up-wind of the mid-point.

(3) The TAS – reducing the speed will increase the significance of the wind and so cause the CP to move further along track into the wind.

Given a hwc (W) going out and an equal twc coming back, the CP formula may be written:

$$\frac{D(TAS + W)}{2TAS} = D\left[\frac{1}{2} + \frac{W}{2TAS}\right]$$

$$= \frac{D}{2} + \frac{DW}{2TAS}$$

This means that the CP will be displaced from the mid-point by a distance equal to:

$$\frac{DW}{2TAS}$$

Based on this some OMs provide a simple table for adjusting the halfway point to derive a CP. Here is a typical example:

This table gives the percentage increase of the half-way distance necessary to allow for a 10 kt hwc.

TAS	100	200	300	400	500	600
%	10	5	3.3	2.5	2.0	1.7

(note % = 1000 ÷ TAS)

Taking the first example in this Chapter, the approximate wind component was $12\frac{1}{2}$ kt (15 kt out and 10 kt back) and the TAS 260 kt. The above table suggests about 4% adjustment for a 10 kt wind at a TAS of 260 kt. This represents 5% for $12\frac{1}{2}$ kt. The total distance was 530 nm and so the half-distance is 265 nm; 5% of this is 13 nm. Adding, because it is a head wind (CP moves into wind) gives the correct distance to the CP of 278 nm.

Practical multi-choice questions

(1) The effect on the position of the CP of reducing the TAS if there is a hwc will be to:
   (a) Increase the distance
   (b) Decrease the distance
   (c) Leave the distance unchanged
   (d) Move it nearer the half-way point.

(2) In flight and flying at the planned TAS, it is found that the aircraft is achieving faster stage times than planned. Presuming the situation remains unchanged, the CP's position will be:
   (a) Unchanged
   (b) Nearer to the half-way point if tail winds were forecast
   (c) Nearer to the destination
   (d) Nearer to the departure point.

(3) A CP is calculated for a 1500 nm flight assuming a 50 kt hwc out and a 50 kt tail wind component coming back and comes to 825 nm. It is dis-

130 Plotting and Flight Planning

covered that the winds are the wrong way round. The correct distance to the CP will be:
(a) 675 nm   (b) 825 nm   (c) 750 nm   (d) Some other value.

(4) In the event of a return to the departure point, 10 000 kg of fuel should be available when back over the departure aerodrome. The flight reserves being carried are 15 000 kg, the average fuel flow is 5000 kg/h, TAS 400 kt and there is a 'dead' head wind out of 100 kt. The position of the PNR in relation to the CP will be:
   (a) 200 nm further
   (b) 250 nm further
   (c) 188 nm less
   (d) 188 nm further.

(5) Compared with still air conditions, the CP with a strong wind at 90° to track will be:
   (a) In the same position, with an earlier ETA
   (b) In the same position, with a later ETA
   (c) At greater distance, with the same ETA
   (d) At shorter distance, with the same ETA.

(6) Flying across the North Atlantic with the usual westerly winds the CP will be:
   (a) Only nearer to North America when flying eastwards
   (b) Only nearer to North America when flying westwards
   (c) Always nearer to North America
   (d) Always nearer to Europe.

(7) The effect on the CP of reducing the TAS is to:
   (a) Always increase the distance to the CP
   (b) Always reduce the distance to the CP
   (c) Always move it along the track further away from the mid-point
   (d) Have no effect in the case of zero winds or winds at 90° to track.

(8) To calculate distance and time to the CP in the case of engine failure use the:
   (a) Reduced TAS for all calculations
   (b) Reduced TAS for all the distance calculation only
   (c) Reduced TAS for GS back but full TAS for GS on
   (d) Full TAS for all calculations.

Chapter 13
FLIGHT PLANNING RE-CHECK

We have laid down the principles and methods of flight planning, but for all the pages a student will be faced with in the professional examinations, speed and accuracy are positively vital in this for satisfying the examiner. So plenty of practice is required in preparation – and there is not much time for cogitation when practically called on while flogging the routes either. Incidentally, polish up the old examination technique; allot the appropriate time to a question that its marks warrant. Divide the number of questions into the time allowed so that you can easily check if you are keeping up with the clock. Do not waste time on any unfamiliar or awkward question. Leave it and, hopefully, you will have time to return to it when you have dealt with all the easier questions.

CP/PNR invariably feature on the planning papers. When dealing with them it is important to remember that:

PNR distance *out* is the same as the distance *home*. Its position depends on the *fuel* available for its calculation.

CP *time home* is the same as the *time to* destination.

Example 1

An aircraft is to fly from A to B on a Tr of 280T distance 959 nm, mean TAS 230 kt. WV for the first 430 nm is 200/50, and 260/65 for the remaining distance. FOB is 26 500 kg, 3100 kg to be held in reserve: consumption 3400 kg/h. Give the time and distance to:

(a) PNR,

(b) CP, assuming engine failure at the CP and a reduced TAS of 190 kt.

Solution
(a) PNR Draw a diagram first, and insert what is known: a rough direction is adequate, of course (Fig. 13.1).

Tr 280T
TAS 230 kt

$$\text{Endurance} = (26\,500 - 3100)\,\text{kg} @ 3400\,\text{kg/h}$$
$$= 23\,400\,\text{kg} @ 3400\,\text{kg/h}$$
$$= 413\,\text{min}$$

132 Plotting and Flight Planning

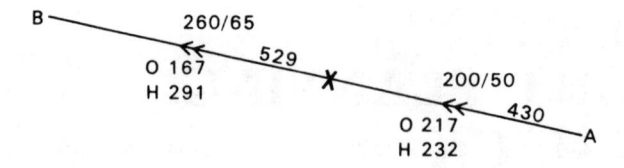

Fig. 13.1 Finding PNR and CP.

Insert on the diagram the GS for each leg evolved from the computer. Treat as two legs, and try to lose A to X in the first place.

$$\begin{aligned}
\text{A–X } out \; 430\,\text{nm @ 217 kt} &= 119\,\text{min} \\
\text{X–A } home \; 430\,\text{nm @ 232 kt} &= \underline{111\,\text{min}} \\
&\; \underline{230\,\text{min}}
\end{aligned}$$

Thus, as the total endurance is 413 min, the PNR is beyond X, and we have endurance from X of 413 − 230 = 183 min for the calculation.
Formula

$$T = \frac{EH}{O + H} \text{ from X}$$

$$T = \frac{183 \times 291}{291 + 167}\,\text{min}$$

$$= \frac{183 \times 291}{458}\,\text{min}$$

$$= 116\,\text{min or } 1\,\text{h } 56\,\text{min}$$

and at 167 kt = 324 nm from X.

Thus distance to PNR from A is (430 + 324) nm = 754 nm
Time to PNR from A is

$$\begin{aligned}
&\phantom{+324\,\text{nm @ 167 kt}\quad} 1\,\text{h } 59\,\text{min from A–X} \\
&+324\,\text{nm @ 167 kt} \quad \underline{1\,\text{h } 56\,\text{min}} \text{ from X–PNR} \\
&\phantom{+324\,\text{nm @ 167 kt}\quad} \underline{3\,\text{h } 55\,\text{min}} \text{ from A–PNR}
\end{aligned}$$

Should the time out from A–X, plus the time home from X–A come to more than the endurance of 6 hr 53 min, then the PNR is on AX, and the second leg is superfluous: the formula could be entered at once. You should be so lucky.

A quick check for correctness:

A–X	1 h 59 min
X–PNR	1 h 56 min
PNR–X (324 nm @ 291 kt)	1 h 07 min
X–A	<u>1 h 51 min</u>
	<u>6 h 53 min</u> which is our endurance.

Flight Planning Re-check 133

(b) CP (reduced TAS) (See Fig. 13.2)

	(dist)	ON GS	ON time	BACK GS	BACK time	ON (FULL TAS) GS	ON (FULL TAS) time
A–X	430	176	147	192	134	217	119
X–B	529	128	248	250	127	167	190

From Fig. 13.2, CP lies between X and B and so:

$$\frac{114}{114 + 261} = \frac{d}{529} = \frac{t}{190}$$

$$d = 161 \quad t = 58$$

	dist	time
A–X	430	119
X–CP	161	58
A–CP	591	177 = 2 h 57 min

Check

CP–B = (529 − 161) nm @ 128 kt = 368 nm @ 128 kt = 2 h 52 min
CP–X = 161 nm @ 250 kt = 38 min
X–A = 430 nm @ 192 kt = 2 h 14 min
                                  2 h 52 min

Example 2
This one is severely practical:

Given:
    Max TOW weight   61 000 kg
    Weight, no fuel, no payload 37 000 kg
    TAS   410 kt
    Distance   2 250 nm
    Consumption   2 800 kg/h
    Reserve (assume unused)   3 200 kg
    Wind component outwards   −40 kt
    Wind component back   +40 kt

Determine
  (a) Maximum payload that can be carried
  (b) Time and distance to the CP
  (c) Time and distance to the PNR

Solution
GS 370 kt, distance 2250 nm
∴ time to destination 6 h 5 min

134 *Plotting and Flight Planning*

Times

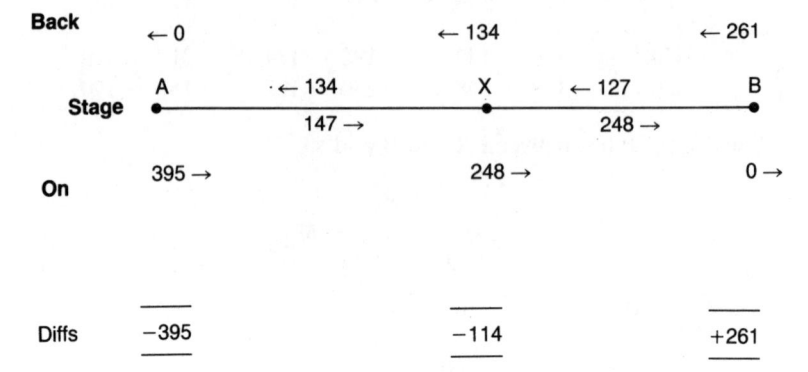

```
Back          ← 0                    ← 134              ← 261
         A       · ← 134         X        ← 127            B
Stage    ●─────────────────────●──────────────────────────●
                  147 →                    248 →
                395 →                 248 →                0 →
On

Diffs          -395                  -114                +261
```

Fig. 13.2 Finding CP with a reduced TAS.

At 2800 kg/h, fuel used = 17 035 kg, rounded off.

Empty wt	37 000 kg	Max TOW	61 000 kg
Fuel	17 035 kg	Wt, no payload	57 235 kg
Reserve	3 200 kg	PAYLOAD	3 765 kg ... (a)
Wt, no payload	57 235 kg		

CP
GS Out, 370 kt; GS Home, 450 kt

$$\text{Distance to CP} = \frac{DH}{O + H}$$
$$= \frac{2250 \times 450}{370 + 450}\text{nm}$$
$$= \frac{2250 \times 450}{820}\text{nm}$$
$$= \underline{1235\text{ nm}} \quad \ldots \text{(b)}$$

And time is 1235 nm @ GS 370 kt = 3 h 20 min ... (b)

Check
1235 nm @ 450 kt = 2 h 45 min
1015 nm @ 370 kt = 2 h 45 min

PNR

$$T = \frac{EH}{O + H}$$
$$= \frac{365 \times 450}{370 + 450}\text{min}$$

Flight Planning Re-check 135

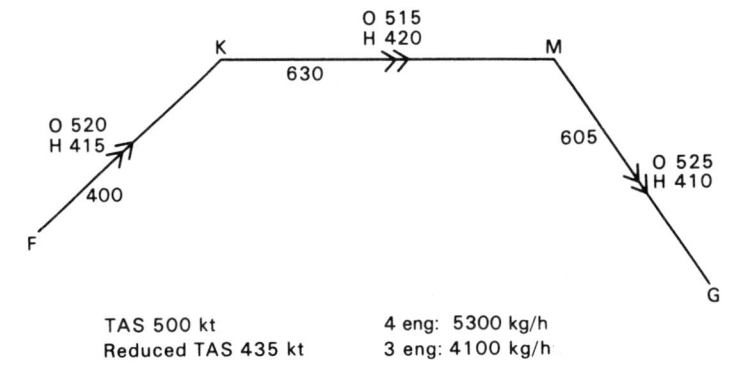

```
              O 515
              H 420
         K  ─────────▶  M
            630
O 520                          605
H 415                              O 525
   ╲                                H 410
    400
    
  F                              G

TAS 500 kt           4 eng: 5300 kg/h
Reduced TAS 435 kt   3 eng: 4100 kg/h
```

Fig. 13.3 Finding PNR on a multi-track route.

$$= \frac{164\,250}{820}\,\text{min}$$

$$T = 3\,\text{h}\,20\,\text{min} \quad \ldots (c)$$

And distance is 3 h 20 min @ 370 kt = 1233 nm ... (c)

but we did not have to do this calculation for the PNR. As the PNR endurance is the flight time, the CP and the PNR should coincide!

Example 3
This is a PNR involving a return to base on three engines on several Tracks. Practical enough, but there are pitfalls easily fallen into, if you are rushed for time.

An aircraft is to fly from F to G via K and M; the data is as follows:

Stage	Wind component (kt)	Distance (nm)
F–K	+20	400
K–M	+15	630
M–G	+25	605

Mean TAS	500 kt
Mean TAS (three engines)	435 kt
Mean fuel consumption (four engines)	5 300 kg/h
Mean fuel consumption (three engines)	4 100 kg/h
FOB (inc. reserve, 5500 kg, assume unused)	30 000 kg

Calculate the time and distance to the PNR from departure F, the return flight to F to be made on three engines.

Flight out (TAS 500 kt) (Fig. 13.3)

	Wind comp	GS	dist	time	kg/h	kg
F–K	+20	520	400	46	5300	4060
K–M	+15	515	630	73½	5300	6490
M–G	+25	525	605	69	5300	6100

Flight back (TAS 435 kt)

K–F	−20	415	400	58	4100	3960
M–K	−15	420	630	90	4100	6150
G–M	−25	410	605	$88\frac{1}{2}$	4100	6050

Fuel analysis

	Out	Back	Out + Back	Total
F–K	4060	3960	8020	8020
K–M	6490	6150	12640	20660
M–G	6100	6050	12150	32810
	16650	16160	check	
		16650		
		32810		

Total FOB	30000
PNR reserve	5500
PNR fuel	24500
Fuel K–M–K	20660
Fuel M–PNR–M	3840
Fuel M–G–M	12150

So

$$\frac{3840}{12150} = \frac{d}{605} = \frac{t}{69}$$

$$d = 191 \quad t = 22$$

	dist	time
F–M	1030	$119\frac{1}{2}$
M–PNR	191	22
F–PNR	1221	$141\frac{1}{2}$
	nm	min

∴ PNR is 400 + 630 + 191 = 1221 nm from F
and 46 + $73\frac{1}{2}$ + 22 = $141\frac{1}{2}$ min (2 h $21\frac{1}{2}$ min) from F.

Example 4

On a trip from P to R via Q, an aircraft is ordered in the event of turning back to proceed to its alternate Y via Q. TAS on four engines is 500 kt, on three engines is 420 kt.

Stage	Wind component (kt)	Distance (nm)
P–Q	−25	565
Q–R	−45	900
Q–Y	+30	240

(a) Give the time and distance from P to the three-engined CP between R and Y.

(b) FOB 38 000 kg, consumption 6300 kg/h, reserve (assume unused) 6500 kg, and the whole flight is made on four engines, what is the distance from P to PNR to Y?

Solution
(a) CP
Full TAS (500 kt)

	wind comp	GS	dist	time
P–Q	−25	475	565	71½
Q–R	−45	455	900	118

Reduced TAS (420 kt)

	wind comp	GS	ON time	w/c	Back GS	time	dist
Q–R	−45	375	144	+45	465	116	900
Q–Y				+30	450	32	240

From Fig. 13.4, CP is between Q and R.

$$\frac{112}{260} = \frac{d}{900} = \frac{t}{118}$$

$$d = 388 \quad t = 51$$

	dist	time
P–Q	565	71½
Q–CP	388	51
P–CP	953	122½

∴ Time and distance from P to CP = 2 h 2½ min, 953 nm.

(b) PNR
Flight out (TAS 500 kt)

	Wind comp	GS	dist	time	kg/h	kg
P–Q	−25	475	565	71½	6300	7 510
Q–R	−45	455	900	118	6300	12 390

Flight back (TAS 500 kt)

R–Q	+45	545	900	99	6300	10 400
Q–Y	+30	530	240	27	6300	2 840

138 *Plotting and Flight Planning*

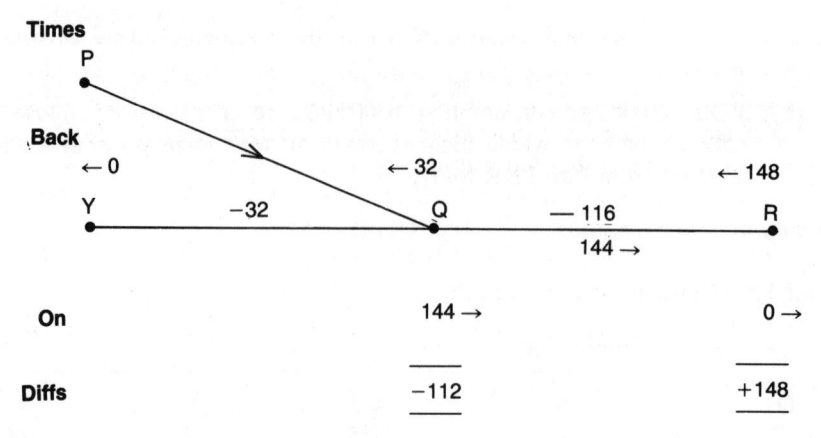

```
Times
         P
         •
 Back
         ←0              ←32                       ←148
         Y      −32      Q       −116              R
         •──────────────•────────────────────────•
                                 144→
                                 
  On                     144→                      0→
                        ─────                    ─────
 Diffs                  −112                     +148
                        ─────                    ─────
```

Fig. 13.4 Finding CP after one-engine shutdown.

Fuel analysis

	Out	Home	Out + Home	Total
P–Q	7 510	–	10 350	10 350
Q–Y	–	2 840		
Q–R	12 390	10 400	22 790	33 140
	19 900	13 240		
		19 900	check	
		33 140		

Total FOB   38 000
PNR reserve   6 500
                    ──────
PNR fuel   31 500
Fuel P–Q–Y   10 350
                    ──────
Fuel Q–PNR–Q   21 150
Fuel Q–R–Q   22 790

$$\frac{21\,150}{22\,790} = \frac{d}{900} = \frac{t}{118}$$

$$d = 835 \qquad t = 109\tfrac{1}{2}$$

	d	t
P–Q	565	71½
Q–PNR	835	109½
P–PNR	1400	181

∴ Distance from P to PNR = 1400 nm.

Example 5

There is a lot to be said for working out a full flight plan, completing it with a CP and PNR: after all, that is what would happen on the routes when you are forced to land at a field not manned by your own company's personnel.

Let us take one step-by-step with the trimmings left out:

A flight is to be made from A to D at cruise Mach 0.75: FOB 23 000 kg, reserve fuel (assume unused) 4000 kg. Ignore descent.

Complete the flight plan and calculate

(a) time and distance for PNR to A

(b) time and distance for CP between A and D.

In our print-out of the flight plan (Fig. 13.5), the data given has the column marked with an asterisk.

Solution

(1) Evolve the temperature at FL from the temperature deviation column.
    Standard temperature at FL 330 is −51°C
    (33 000 ft @ 2°C per 1000 ft =   −66°C
    Standard at sea level =   +15°C
                                     −51°C)

    ∴ A to B = −42
      B to C = −46
      C to D = −53

    Fill in the return temperature details.

(2) Evolve TAS from Mach 0.75 from computer.
    Mach index in airspeed window v ambient temperature and read speed of sound (S of S) on outer scale against 1 on the inner.
    Do you agree consecutively 593, 587, 579, 583, 593, 600?
    Then $\dfrac{\text{TAS}}{\text{S of S}}$ = Mach 0.75, or simply 593 on outer scale against 10 on inner, and read off 445 on outer against 0.75 on inner, and so on, and the TAS is as shown on the flight plan.

(3) Complete the flight plan. We have 19 000 kg usable fuel, adequate for A–D and some suitable alternate.

The PNR will be:

Fuel analysis

	Out	Home	Out + Home	Total
A–B	4 200	3 410	7 610	
B–C	3 450	2 900	6 350	13 960

FLIGHT PLAN

*STAGE From	To	Temp. °C	*Flight Level	*Temp. Dev. °C	*WIND Direction	Speed kt	*Track °(T)	Drift	Heading °(T)	TAS kt	Wind comp. kt	G/S kt	*Distance nm	Time min	*Fuel flow kg/h	Fuel required kg
A	B	−42	330	+ 9	230	60	290	7S	283	445	−35	410	430	63	4 000	4 200
B	C	−46	330	+ 5	250	70	303	8S	295	440	−49	391	365	56	3 700	3 450
C	D	−53	330	− 2	260	50	312	5S	307	434	−34	400	386	58	3 550	3 430
D	C	−50	310	− 3	270	40	132	3P	135	437	+31	468	386	49½	3 650	3 000
C	B	−42	310	+ 5	240	60	123	7P	130	445	+25	470	365	46½	3 750	2 900
B	A	−36	310	+11	220	50	110	6P	116	450	+15	465	430	55½	3 700	3 410

Fig. 13.5 Flight Plan with PNR and CP.

Flight Planning Re-check

Fuel analysis

	Out	Home	Out + Home	Total
C–D	3 430	3 000	6 430	20 390
	11 080	9 310		
		11 080	check	
		20 390		

Total FOB   23 000
PNR reserve   4 000
PNR fuel   19 000
Fuel A–C–A   13 960
Fuel C–PNR–C   5 040
Fuel C–D–C   6 430

$$\frac{5040}{6430} = \frac{b}{386} = \frac{t}{58}$$

$$d = 303 \text{ nm} \qquad t = 45\tfrac{1}{2} \text{ min}$$

	list	time
A–C	795	119
C–PNR	303	$45\tfrac{1}{2}$
A–PNR	1098	$164\tfrac{1}{2}$ = 2 h $44\tfrac{1}{2}$ min ... (a)

CP (See Fig. 13.6)
From Fig. 13.6, CP between B and C:

$$\frac{58\tfrac{1}{2}}{102\tfrac{1}{2}} = \frac{d}{365} = \frac{t}{56}$$

$$d = 208 \text{ nm} \qquad t = 32 \text{ min}$$

	dist	time
A–B	430	63
B–CP	208	32
A–CP	638	95 = 1 h 35 min ... (b)

Now a few worked examples which hurl you into the tables.

An aircraft is at FL 350 over aerodrome B: its weight is 123 000 kg, and it is cruising at Mach 0.86, mean headwind component 60 kt, temperature deviation −7°C. Fuel on board excluding reserves is 21 000 kg.

Example 6
What is the range of the aircraft which will permit it to return to overhead B at the same FL? (use Table 33C)

Times

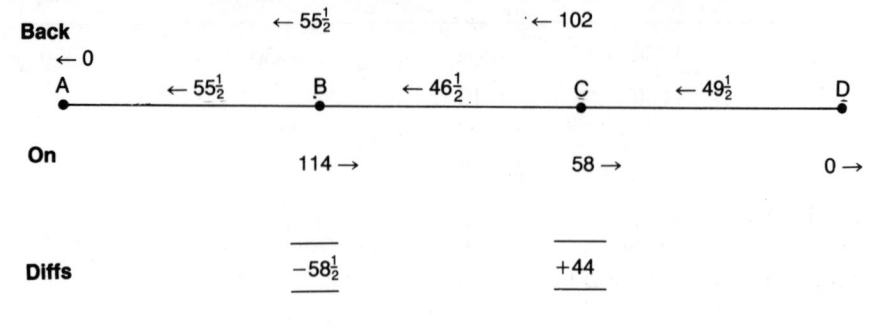

Back

```
         ←55½              ←102
  ←0
  A      ←55½    B   ←46½   C   ←49½   D
  •───────────────•──────────•──────────•
```

On   114→   58→   0→

Diffs   −58½   +44

Fig. 13.6 Finding CP.

Solution
Table 33C in the −10°C to − 1°C temperature deviation set, with a lucky 123 000 kg AUW gives

Fuel flow 6 700 for 1st hour ∴ 14 300 kg left
           6 500 for 2nd hour ∴ 7 800 kg left
           6 200 for 3rd hour ∴ 1 600 kg left
           ────────────────────
           19 400 in 3 hours

and 1600 kg at the 4th hour flow of 6000 kg/h will be used in 16 min. So endurance is 3 h 16 min.

TAS is 475 kt, so O and H can be inserted on diagram (Fig. 13.7), and the formula entered.

$$T = \frac{EH}{O + H}$$

$$= \frac{196 \times 535}{415 + 535} \text{ min}$$

$$= \frac{196 \times 535}{950} \text{ min}$$

$$= 110 \text{ min or } 1 \text{ h } 50 \text{ min}$$

and at 415 kt, the distance out is 760 nm.
A quick check will verify this.

We must try the other tables, so there follows a descent and hold job: for the holding, use Table 33D.

Example 7
An aircraft is over its destination field (elevation 3000 ft) at 30 000 ft, weight 88 000 kg, temperature deviation −3°C. The aircraft is instructed to hold at

Flight Planning Re-check 143

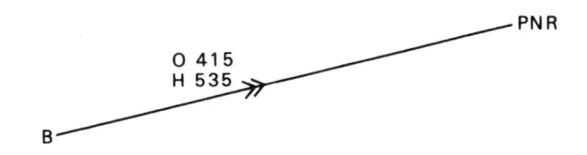

```
                                          PNR
                  O 415
                  H 535 ⟫
         B
```

Fig. 13.7 Finding aircraft range.

FL 140. Allowing fuel for circuit and landing from 1000 ft of 1000 kg, how long can it hold if fuel to be used before landing must not exceed 5000 kg?

Solution
From the descent table (Table 33E), the descent from FL 300 to FL 40 (1000 ft over the field) takes 12 min and uses 500 kg. Add to this the circuit and landing fuel of 1000 kg, then we have (5000 − 1500) kg, 3500 kg for holding.

In Table 33D, read off against pressure height and temp dev the fuel flow 6600 kg/h. But watch the footnote: $1\frac{1}{2}$% reduction in flow for every 5000 kg in *mean* weight below 100 000 kg.

The hold will start at 87 700 kg AUW, since the descent from FL 300 to FL 140 uses 300 kg, a simple substraction in Table 33E; and the hold will use 3500 kg, so the mean weight will be (87 700 − 1750) kg = 85 950 kg, call it 86 000 kg.

A decrease of 14 000 kg in weight = 4.2%, and 4.2% of 6600 kg is 277 kg (we are keeping up the pedantic work) ∴ flow is 6320 kg, rounding off the digits and 3500 kg @ 6320 kg/h = 33 min, holding.

Keep going!

Example 8
An aircraft diverts from 1000 ft overhead its destination aerodrome (elevation 4000 ft) to its alternate (elevation 2700 ft). Weight is 75 000 kg, distance is 515 nm, mean wind component −45 kt.
The diversion is made at FL 320, temp dev −8°C.

(a) What fuel is required to overhead alternate (Table 33G)?

(b) Give mean TAS for climb from FL 200 to FL 320, temp dev − 6°C (Table 33B).

Solution
(a) A spot of interpolation in Table 33G; against ground distances 510 nm and 520 nm, and in hwc columns 40 and 50.

144 Plotting and Flight Planning

515 nm at −50 reads 7485 kg, 85 min at FL 420.
515 nm at −40 reads 7355 kg, 83 min at FL 420.
So at −45, use 7420 kg, 84 min at FL 420.

Now for the corrections:

(1) Start diversion at 5000 ft   −300 kg

(2) End diversion at 3 700 ft   Nil

(3) Start diversion at 75 000 kg
so subtract 1% of fuel for each 1500 kg below 90 000 kg
10% of 7420 kg   −740 kg

(4) Cruise at FL 320 for 84 min
If at FL 350, +240 kg for 84 min
If at FL 300, + 1020 kg for 84 min
∴ 84 min at FL 320 = 1020 − ($\frac{2}{5}$ × 780) = +700 kg
                                                                                        −340 kg

∴ fuel required 7080 kg ... (a)

(b) Table 33B. Cross from 32 TOC height to the 20 000 ft curve, down to the reference line, then UP to −6°C temp dev. Read 412 kt?

The following is quite a difficult problem; we have already done one of these, but not with an entrance into the tables, nor calling for some inspired guesswork. Use Tables 34C and 34G as appropriate.

Example 9
An aircraft is to fly from PETALING to GLINKA, via KARVEL (See Fig. 13.8). Should an engine fail after overlying KARVEL, the return must be made to the alternate QUONTEK, via KARVEL.

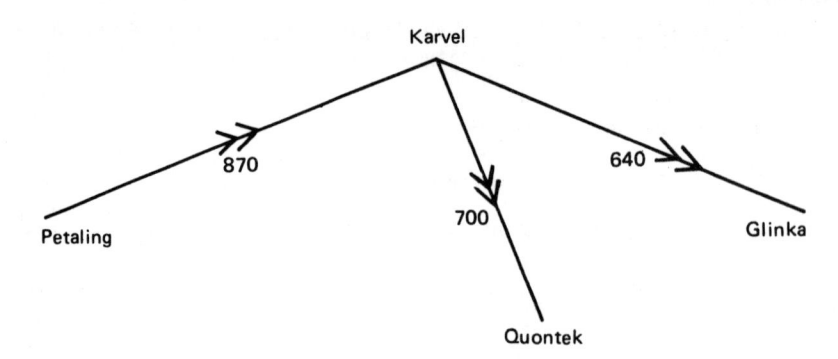

Fig. 13.8 Diversion to alternate after one-engine shutdown.

Flight Planning Re-check 145

The route details are as follows:

SECTOR	Dist (nm)	FL	Wind Component (kt)	Temp (°C)
PETALING–KARVEL	870	250	−20	−18
KARVEL–GLINKA	640	260	−30	−23
GLINKA–KARVEL	640	250	+30	−22
KARVEL–QUONTEK	700	260	−25	−23

Weight at start 280 000 kg, fuel available excluding reserves 61 000 kg: ignore climb and descent.

(a) If an engine fails after KARVEL, how far can it travel towards GLINKA before turning for QUONTEK as directed?

(b) How long after leaving PETALING will this point be reached?

Solution

Diagram first, and do not move without consulting it and the table of route details.

Here is the working for the outward and return flights. The return flight was worked backwards (i.e. upwards from the bottom line of the flight plan Table 13.1) from the known landing weight at QUONTEK, i.e. TOW less the PNR fuel weight.

Table 13.1 Flight plan for PNR

From	To	FL	Temp Dev	TAS	Wind comp	GS	d		t	Fuel Flow	Wt at Start (t)	Fuel Required
PET		250	+17	517	−20	497	870	497	60	13 900	280.0	13 900
	K	250	+17	517	−20	497		373	45	13 700	266.1	10 280
KAR		260	+14	510	−30	480	640	480	60	12 900	255.8	12 900
	G	260	+14	510	−30	480		160	20	12 700	242.9	4 230
GLIN		250	+13	444	+30	474	640	173	22	10 900		4 000
	K	250	+13	437	+30	467		467	60	10 500	246.3	10 500
KAR		260	+14	436	−25	411	700	297	43½	10 000	235.8	7 250
	Q	260	+14	428	−25	403		403	60	9 500	228.5	9 500

TOW 280 t − PNR fuel 61 t = 219.0

146 *Plotting and Flight Planning*

Fuel analysis

	Out	Home	Out + Home	Total
PET–KAR	24 180	–		
KAR–QUON	–	16 750	40 930	40 930
KAR–GLIN	17 130	14 500	31 630	72 560
	41 310	31 250		
		41 310	check	
		72 560		

PNR fuel   61 000
Fuel P–K–Q   40 930
Fuel K–PNR–K   20 070
Fuel K–G–K   31 630

$$\frac{20\,070}{31\,630} = \frac{d}{640} = \frac{t}{80}$$

$$d = 406 \qquad t = 51$$

K–PNR   406 nm ... (a)

	t
P–K	105
K–PNR	51
P–PNR	156 min = <u>2 h 36 min</u> ... (b)

Chapter 14
CRUISE CONTROLS, FUEL RESERVES AND EROPS

Introduction
In this Chapter we look at a number of things which have a great bearing on the fuel to be loaded before a flight can be safely undertaken.

Methods of cruise control
The Operations Manual (OM) will lay down the various methods by which the aircraft can be operated. It is not the purpose here to go into all the theory of cruise control but just to draw attention to the various methods that may be encountered and to appreciate the effect that the different techniques will have on the aircraft performance throughout the flight.

Table 14.1 gives some methods which will be frequently employed together with the changes encountered during flight as fuel is used and the aircraft gets lighter.

In each case the economy of operation (kg/nm) will improve as the aircraft gets lighter. It is fairly obvious that less work will need to be done to move a lighter aircraft a given distance and so less energy and less fuel will be required.

Stepped cruise
To get the best possible range out of a modern jet aircraft the ideal method would be to do a cruise-climb. In this, the aircraft is taken up to the maximum possible level where the ideal airspeed for economy can be achieved using the engines at their maximum continuous power settings. As the aircraft gets lighter with fuel used, the aircraft is permitted gradually to increase altitude while still maintaining the power settings and the required best speed. This technique is not popular with ATC and only very high flying (supersonic) aircraft are likely to be found using this method. An approximation to this method is for the aircraft to fly as high as possible at the beginning of cruise and then, when the aircraft weight reduces sufficiently to be able to operate at the next available flight level, stepping up to that level. Table 14.2 shows typical economy figures for a modern jet aircraft flying at a constant Mach No. Notice how the economy improves both as the aircraft gets lighter and as the aircraft flies higher. The absence of figures indicates that the operational ceiling for this speed has been exceeded.

If at the beginning of cruise the aircraft was weighing 205 t the maximum

148 *Plotting and Flight Planning*

Table 14.1 Methods of cruise control

	Power	Fuel flow	Airspeed	Economy
Constant FL constant power	constant	constant	increases	improves
Constant FL constant speed	decrease	decrease	constant	improves
Constant FL maximum range	decrease	decrease	decrease	improves

Table 14.2 Economy figures (kg/nm) for flight at constant Mach No: M 0.82

weight (t)	FL							
	250	270	290	310	330	350	370	390
205	19.47	18.74	18.23	17.86	—	—	—	—
200	19.23	18.50	17.92	17.50	17.63	—	—	—
195	19.00	18.22	17.61	17.17	17.03	—	—	—
190	18.80	17.98	17.32	16.86	16.57	—	—	—
185	18.60	17.74	17.05	16.55	16.19	16.48	—	—
180	18.40	17.51	16.79	16.24	15.84	15.84	—	—
175	18.21	17.29	16.54	15.95	15.52	15.30	—	—
170	18.00	17.09	16.30	15.66	15.22	14.90	15.35	—
165	17.78	16.89	16.07	15.40	14.90	14.54	14.63	—
160	17.56	16.71	15.85	15.16	14.60	14.22	14.04	—
155	17.33	16.49	15.65	14.92	14.32	13.91	13.63	—
150	17.11	16.27	15.46	14.69	14.07	13.60	13.27	13.37

FL available would be 310 but, if the aircraft was required to fly at ODD FL, it would have to operate at FL 290. This aircraft uses fuel at about 8 t/h and so in less than an hour it would be down to 200 t and so could request a 'step' clearance to FL 330. The table indicates that this is achievable at 200 t. The next FL would probably be 370 and this requires the weight to be down to 170 t. Another 30 t of fuel used would take about 4 h. A computer generated flight plan would quite probably plan the flight to allow for these steps to be made. Note how the economy would have improved even if flying at one level and then note how much better it is when the steps are carried out.

Choosing the best level for economy

The only certain method to select the best level for economy is to check the actual economy figures by dividing the fuel flows by the speeds. If TAS is used it will only be valid for still air but using GS, allowance will be made for the wind effect. In practice with modern aircraft, changing from the best still air FL to improve the economy is only likely to be effective if the vertical

Cruise Controls, Fuel Reserves and EROPs 149

Table 14.3 Figures for operating for best range

FL		\multicolumn{8}{c}{Weight (t)}							
		110	105	100	95	90	85	80	75
410	kg/h						3230	3000	2850
	TAS						458	458	458
	kg/nm						7.05	6.55	6.25
390	kg/h				3600	3350	3140	2970	2850
	TAS				458	458	458	458	457
	kg/nm				7.86	7.31	6.86	6.48	6.24
370	kg/h	4280	3950	3690	3480	3290	3130	2970	2810
	TAS	460	459	459	459	458	458	455	449
	kg/nm	9.30	8.61	8.04	7.58	7.18	6.83	6.53	6.26
350	kg/h	4050	3830	3640	3480	3320	3160	2990	2820
	TAS	463	462	461	460	459	455	447	439
	kg/nm	8.75	8.29	7.90	7.57	7.23	6.95	6.69	6.42
330	kg/h	4010	3850	3680	3520	3400	3180	3010	2830
	TAS	465	464	462	460	455	447	438	427
	kg/nm	8.62	8.30	7.96	7.65	7.47	7.11	6.87	6.62
310	kg/h	4050	3890	3730	3550	3380	3200	3010	2840
	TAS	468	465	460	453	446	437	426	416
	kg/nm	8.65	8.36	8.11	7.84	7.58	7.32	7.06	6.83

Table 14.4 Preserving contingency fuel

	\multicolumn{4}{c}{FL}			
	370	350	330	310
kg/h	4280	4050	4010	4050
TAS	456	460	465	468
still air (kg/nm)	9.39	8.80	8.62*	8.65
wind comp	−20	−35	−50	−40
GS	436	425	415	428
wind (kg/nm)	9.82	9.53	9.66	9.46*

*indicates best FL economy

wind shear gives something like a 5 kt, or greater, more favourable component. In Table 14.3 typical figures are given for the operating of a modern aircraft for best range. To make the table more useful, the still air economy figures have been inserted. Table 14.4 shows the effect on the economy figures when the aircraft is at a weight of 110 t and consideration might be given to moving away from FL 330 – the best still air level. It will be seen that with a considerable wind shear of 5 kt/1000 ft, there would be some advantage in flying at FL 310. Of course it is quite possible that this might not be available.

Effect of temperature on time and fuel

Flight planning tables are often provided for different temperature deviation conditions. Quite often, however, the tables are only provided for ISA conditions with possibly correction provided for other conditions. In practice with modern jet aircraft, temperature has little effect on the fuel required for a particular flight but will have some effect on the time required. Flying at a constant Mach No., a higher temperature will result in a higher TAS but to achieve the higher speed more power will be required with a consequent rise in fuel flow. The percentage increases will usually just about balance each other out.

In tables for a typical modern aircraft that are presented only for ISA conditions, a correction suggested for 10° rise in temperature would be to increase the TAS by 10 kt (this assumes the same Mach No. is maintained) and the fuel flow by 3%. If the aircraft was flying at about 450 kt, a 10 kt increase would represent a speed rise of 2.2% so in still air the result would be a cruise flight time reduction of 2.2% or just over a minute per hour and a fuel required increase of 0.8% (3 − 2.2).

The following figures have been extracted from the Data Sheets 34 for a large four-jet aircraft at a given FL, weight and Mach No.:

temperature deviation	−15°C	−5°C	+5°C	+12°C
Fuel flow kg/h	8200	8370	8600	8750
TAS kt	459	470	482	489
Economy kg/nm	17.86	17.81	17.84	17.89

The economy variation is not significant. The slight differences are quite likely to be due to the fact that the speeds and fuel flows have all been rounded off and are not the exact values.

The effect of wind on range

Quite obviously, wind affects the ranges that can be achieved. No matter how fast the aircraft is, a 50 kt hwc over a five hour flight will require an additional 250 nm of air distance to be flown in addition to the route distance. If an aircraft is being operated at its most economical speed for still air conditions, it is possible that flying faster into a head wind might be slightly beneficial to the economy. The shorter flight time would mean that the total head wind effect experienced during the flight would be less and this could more than compensate for the slightly poorer economy caused by increasing the speed. No general rule can be given for this – checking the resultant economy figures (kg/h ÷ GS) for different speeds would indicate if there was any advantage to be gained.

Fuel reserves
Any usable fuel on board the aircraft that is not required for the actual flight from starting the engines to engines off at the destination will be regarded as the fuel reserves for the flight. Sometimes some of this fuel is only being 'tankered' if the company policy is to load as much fuel as possible at certain aerodromes and as little as possible at others. The reason for carrying the fuel is of no significance in fuel calculations – if it is on board obviously it can be used.

The law regarding fuel
The law simply requires that the aircraft captain should be satisfied that sufficient fuel is being carried so that the flight and all foreseeable contingencies can be accommodated. For Public Transport operations, however, the flight must be conducted in accordance with the OM which has been approved by the authority (the CAA in the UK). The OM will lay down the operator's fuel policy. The fuel to be carried may be given either as 'block' fuel figures for particular operations or in the form of a formula which can be applied to any operation.

The CAA publishes a guide as to what will be acceptable in the OM (*CAP 360 – Air Operators' Certificates*). It says that it should be planned to arrive overhead the destination with sufficient fuel to:

(1) make an approach to land

(2) carry out a missed approach

(3) fly to an alternate aerodrome

(4) hold at the alternate and then carry out an approach and landing for:

    (a) 45 min for propeller-driven aircraft

    (b) 30 min at 1500 ft in ISA conditions for jets

(5) allow for contingencies that cause more fuel to be required.

Holding fuel – 'island' reserve
When no suitable alternate is available because the aerodrome of intended landing is geographically isolated, items (2), (3) and (4) in the previous paragraph may be replaced by a holding reserve related to the statistical data on local weather conditions. The minimum acceptable will be two hours at normal cruise consumption.

In Fig. 14.1, the aircraft could only reach B and divert to C if all the contingency reserve was used. In practice, a Point of No Alternate (PNA) would be calculated so that the aircraft would take eight hours to reach C if a diversion was initiated at the PNA. This would leave a reserve of one hour for contingencies.

152   *Plotting and Flight Planning*

```
                        Flight 6h              PNA
      A O— — — — — — —>>— — — — — — — —O— — —O B
                                           ⤸
   Flt fuel        6h                Diversion 3h
   Island reserve  2h        C O
   Contingency     1h
```

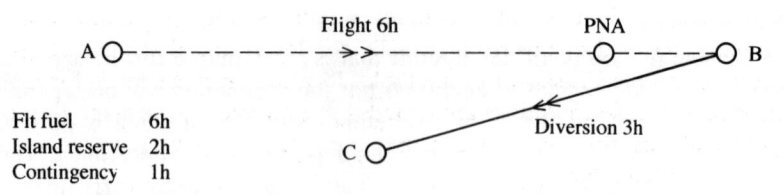

Fig. 14.1 Preserving contingency fuel.

Contingency reserve

This need not be shown as a separate quantity if, as is sometimes done, an adequate safety reserve is built into the tabulated figures. Typical contingencies that this reserve should provide for are:

- forecast wind errors
- navigation errors
- ATC restrictions on altitude and route
- power plant failure
- weather causing route or altitude variations
- inaccuracy of tabulated data.

If there is an adequate and available en-route alternate (ERA), the contingency fuel carried may be reduced but there must be unambiguous instructions that a technical stop is made at the ERA unless the fuel remaining at the descent point for the ERA is sufficent to complete the flight safely with all the reserves (1), (2), (3), (4) and (5). In this case, the OM should contain specific instructions on the in-flight fuel checks to be made and the replanning calculations to be made to ensure that the flight can be completed safely. In no case should the reduction of contingency fuel prejudice the basic need to have sufficient fuel to allow arrival at the ERA with all the reserves (1), (2), (3), (4) and (5).

Alternate fuel requirements

These should provide for a diversion from Decision Height (DH) or Minimum Descent Height (MDH) above the intended destination to a suitable alternate using a realistic route and en-route altitude. It is the usual practice to provide a table or graph to assess the alternate fuel requirement. This is done in Data Sheets 33 and 34. The basic entry will usually be total distance and the average wind component and the total fuel, time and the cruising FL will be extracted. The figures will probably allow for an optimum procedure for diversion – a climb to the FL shown, possibly a cruise at this FL and then a descent to the destination. An allowance may also be built into the table for overshoot and holding. It is necessary to check the notes for the particular table. Diversion tables have to make various assumptions concerning temperature, aircraft weight (often maximum authorised ldg wt), altitudes at the beginning and end of diversion (usually sea level) and that the aircraft will operate up to the FL shown in the table. Provision may be made for making corrections if these conditions are varied. For example a percentage correction to the fuel quantity for each 10 t that the aircraft weight is below the one assumed for the table.

Additional fuel reserves
Allowances should also be made for the following:

- taxiing and power checks
- operating de-icing systems, heaters and auxiliary power units (APUs).

Consideration should be given to the effect on fuel requirements in the event of engine or systems failure (e.g. pressurisation) particularly on sectors where there is no suitable ERA.

An extra allowance should be considered when the operation involves a congested air traffic area or when there is a need to climb or descend from the en-route safety altitude whilst in the vicinity of the departure or arrival aerodrome (e.g. Beirut).

Continuing flight without full reserves
The OM may include instructions allowing a flight that is within an hour of a destination and close to a usable ERA, to be continued even if full diversion and holding fuel will not be available. This is only permissible if there is sufficient fuel to reach the destination with contingency fuel and to be able to hold for one hour at a realistic altitude and

- the actual and forecast met conditions permit a visual approach to landing with a visibility over 8 km and no significant cross winds until one hour after ETA
- there are no known or probable ATC delays for the period to one hour after ETA
- there are two independent runways suitable for landing.

Fuel monitoring and balancing
The OM must lay down the rules for fuel monitoring. For a flight of between one and two hours' duration at least one check should be made. On multi-crew aircraft, the instructions for fuel balancing must cover the following points:

- when an abnormal fuel feed procedure is used to balance fuel, the Captain must be informed and at least two crew members must monitor the operation

- with more than two engines, one engine, if practical, should remain on direct feed. Preference should be given to an engine with an operative electrical generator and, where applicable, a hydraulic pump.

Extended range operations (EROPs) twin engine aircraft (ETOPs)

More detailed information on these are contained in *CAP 513 – Extended Range Twin Operations (ETOPS)*. Any expressions that are in **bold** type will be defined in *CAP 513*.

ETOPs flights are taken to be flights that at any time are more than 60 minutes flying time (in still air) at one-engine speed from an adequate airport. Alternatively, the relevant authority may lay down a **threshold distance** and then all flights beyond this will be regarded as being ETOPs flights.

ETOPs flights will be permitted only when certain conditions have been satisfied and then the flights will be subject to further time restrictions. Values of 90, 105, 120, 135 and 180 minutes may be encountered. The factors that the licensing authority will consider before granting an extension of the **threshold** time include:

- propulsion system reliability record
- modification and maintenance programme
- flight dispatch requirements
- training evaluation programme
- operations limitation
- operations specifications
- operational validation flight
- continuing surveillance and engine reliability reporting.

Different authorities will approach the above factors in different ways but in the end they will grant to a particular operator the right to operate a particular aircraft to a given **time threshold**. When the time threshold is known together with the one-engined speed to be used, route planning can be commenced. This is best illustrated by a practical example as in Fig. 14.2.

Obviously the direct flight from A to B is not permissible with a 90 minute threshold. Circles are drawn around all the available bases and a track has to be selected that passes through the areas encompassed by these circles and deviates as little as possible from the direct route. The operator will be hoping that after operating for some time without incident under the 90 minute rule, the authority might be persuaded to extend the threshold to permit a direct flight. Currently the maximum time threshold being granted is 180 minutes but operators usually have to work up to this figure.

ETOPS despatch considerations

The CAP specifically refers to the following conditions to be satisfied before despatch on an ETOPs flight:

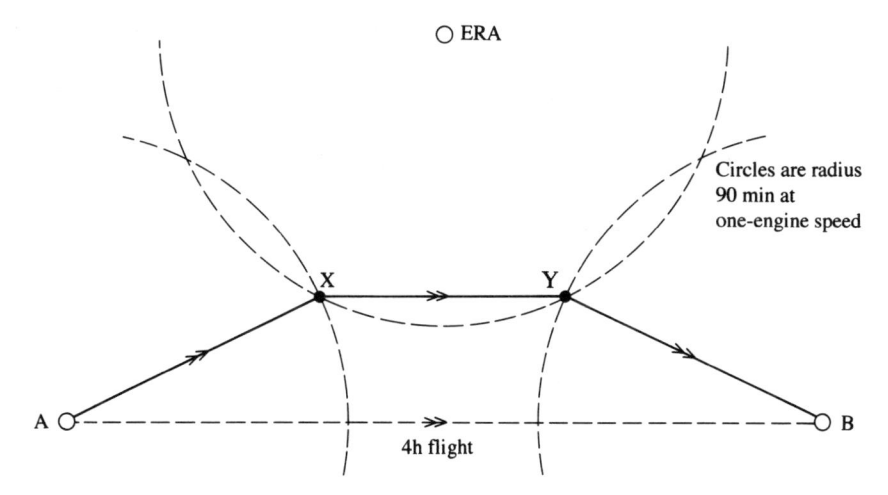

Fig. 14.2 Principle of ETOPs.

(1) **Minimum equipment list (MEL)** will be specially designed for these operations and must be rigorously adhered to.

(2) **Communication and navigation facilities** must be available to give full and adequate coverage for the route and any foreseeable diversion that may be required.

(3) **Fuel and oil supply** must comply with the normal OM requirements and must also be adequate to cover an engine or systems failure at the most critical point on the flight in terms of fuel and oil requirements along the planned route. In this connection the CAP describes a **Critical Fuel Scenario** which requires the operator to consider the implications of a simultaneous failure of an engine and total pressurisation failure at the CP based on time to a **suitable** alternate.

(4) **Alternate Aerodromes** that may be required for any part of the flight that comes within the **Extended Range** part of the operation (often based on a 60 minute Threshold Time) are all **adequate** and available from one hour before to one hour after the likely earliest and latest times they may be required. All essential information about these alternates must be available on the flight deck during flight.

(5) **Aeroplane Performance Data** in the OM must cover all possible requirements for a one-engine diversion including a possible drift-down to 10 000 ft.

Points of equal time (PET)

In Fig. 14.2 Points X and Y will represent the PET between A and the ERA and the ERA and B in still air conditions. A–X–Y–B will represent the best acceptable ETOPs route. If the circles were drawn around the end of a 90

156 *Plotting and Flight Planning*

minute wind vector blowing into the respective bases, the intersections would then represent genuine PETs. Ignoring the wind effect, X and Y will represent the most critical points on the flight in terms of fuel. Between A and X a return to A should be less than 90 minutes at single-engined speed and then between X and Y, ERA would be within 90 minutes.

Fuel planning for EROPs flights

It is interesting to consider the FAA requirements in these cases. The FOB should be adequate to meet the following critical fuel scenario:

(a) fly to the most critical point in terms of fuel required and assume engine and pressurisation fail at this point

(b) cruise at 10 000 ft and descend to 1500 ft at chosen aerodrome

(c) allow 15 min for missed approach, approach and land

(d) allow up to 10% contingency reserve

(e) allow for APU and MEL fuel penalties

(f) allow for possible anti-icing as well as the effect of icing on un-protected surfaces

(g) repeat steps (b) to (f) with no engine failure but cruising at 10 000 ft due to pressurisation failure.

The critical fuel is the greater of (b)–(f) or (g) and it should be checked that the fuel loaded will satisfy this requirement.

Chapter 15
COMPUTER AND ATC FLIGHT PLANS

Introduction

Most modern airlines use computer flight planning. Some have their own system and others will make use of the service offered by several international providers of a planning service. One of the best known of these is Jeppesen Dataplan and it is by their kind permission that the computer flight plan illustrations used in this Chapter are reproduced. Smaller operators may make use of one of the numerous software packages that are available so that an operator can produce his own comparatively simple computer flight planning procedure suitable for running on a typical IBM personal computer.

General principles

All flight planning computers work on the same basic principles. There will be a database which will hold some or all of the following pieces of information:

(1) coordinates and 'idents' of all beacons, waypoints and aerodromes likely to be used

(2) the necessary Met information (winds, temperatures, weather etc. for the areas to be used). In the big mainframe computers this will be automatically fed in from one of the main International Met. Offices (e.g. Bracknell). For simple computers this may have to be fed in manually for each particular flight.

(3) the operator's standard routes (OM)

(4) relevant ATC routeings and altitude/FL allocations – Airways, Advisory Routes, Preferred Routes, SIDs, STARs etc. For areas like the North Atlantic where there is a daily broadcast of the routes to be used, the mainframe computers will have this information fed in automatically.

(5) the operator's fuel reserves policy and when additional fuel will be loaded for economic or other reasons (OM)

(6) details of individual aircraft, weights, fuel capacities, hold and passenger capacities. Individual aircraft performance particularly with regard to speeds, fuel flows and take-off and landing performance (OM)

158   *Plotting and Flight Planning*

(7) aerodrome details probably related to the particular aircraft, the wind, pressure and temperature conditions and the runway expected to be used so that the regulated take-off and landing weights can be extracted (OM)

(8) the operator's preferred alternates, possibly with a priority rating (OM)

(9) the method the operator wishes to use to cost the flight

(10) the operator's preferred method of operating the aircraft – constant speed, constant power, cruise climb etc.

General procedure

There will usually be a standard procedure for feeding in the necessary information that the computer needs when a flight plan is required. Most modern systems are 'user friendly' and the terminal in use will guide the user step by step on a question and answer basis. Fairly obviously the computer will have to know certain basic facts:

- the aircraft to be used
- the proposed time off-blocks
- the departure point and the destination
- special instructions regarding the route, method of cruise control, load required etc.

These would be a bare minimum. It is quite possible for the computer in the big systems to handle everything else BUT it must always be remembered that the computer is an *idiot*. A very sophisticated one, but an idiot all the same. Unless the particular fault that you have committed has been foreseen by the programmer, the computer will endeavour to perform any task given without question. Fairly obviously if you ask the wrong questions you will get right answers to the wrong questions and not the ones that you were expecting. Ask the aircraft to fly from New York to London and it will give a perfect answer even though you really wanted to go from London to New York. Tell the computer that you are flying Concorde when you are operating a Viscount and it will do its best to accommodate you! Remember the computer phrase GIGO: Garbage In–Garbage Out.

General method of solution

When the route to be flown has been decided, either by nominating the company's route identifier or by giving departure and destination aerodromes, the computer will select the route according to any instruction given e.g.:

- best direct track – selected by the computer
- best direct track for navaids – selected by the computer

Computer and ATC Flight Plans

- best direct track on airways – selected by the computer
- least fuel or least time track
- any known constraints of fuel, traffic loads, levels to be flown etc.
- special characteristics of the aircraft if not known to the computer.

The route having been selected, the tracks to be flown and the distances between waypoints are calculated by the computer from the coordinates stored in the database. The calculations are for GC tracks and, in the more sophisticated computers, allowance will also be made for the spheroidal shape of the earth. Using the Met information available either from the direct Met office links or by manual feed-in and the aircraft performance details either from the database or by manual feed-in, the plan is then calculated. All necessary details for the flight are then produced. Figure 15.1 shows a very comprehensive style of presentation and Fig. 15.2 gives a full print-out of a short flight from Gatwick (EGKK) to Frankfurt (EDDF).

Interpreting a computer flight plan

Every computer flight plan program will use its own particular format so it is not possible to give a comprehensive listing of all the abbreviations that will be encountered. However, because the end product in every case must, in general, be giving the same sort of information, familiarity with one style of plan will make it not too difficult to interpret others. Every producer of computer flight plans will provide a glossary of the abbreviations they use and usually an explanation of their standard formats. One company might produce a wide variety of formats to satisfy the particular requirements of their various customers.

Referring to Fig. 15.2, the following notes will help in understanding the presentation.

Line 1   The departure and destination, the aircraft, the cruise control used (Mach 0.8) and the date (American style)
Line 2   The times of computation, ETD and of Met. Prognostic used (0000 UTC on the 30th of the month), weight units used (kg)
Line 3   AV PLD = available payload OPNLWT = operational weight (weight less fuel and payload)
Line 4   POA = point of arrival (EDDF FRANKFURT). Flight time in hours and minutes. Flight distance in nm. Take-off and landing weights in kg. Sometimes hundreds of kg or lb are used
Line 5   ALT = alternate (EDDL DUSSELDORF) COMP = wind component used = minus (M) 15 kt
Line 6   HLD = holding reserve
Line 7   CON = contingency reserve
Line 8   Fuel required (less taxi)
Line 9   XTR = extra fuel being carried (if any)
Line 10 Total FOB at take-off and equivalent time

160 Plotting and Flight Planning

```
                          PLAN  4769  ABC123      EDDF TO KJFK  472C  M85/F  IFR  08/03/00
                          NONSTOP COMPUTED 1102Z FOR ETD 1300Z  PROGS 030000Z  MIT
NAT TRACK
                                                                                             LBS
                          POA     FUEL     TIME    DIST    ARRIVE    TAKEOFF    LAND    AV PLD    OPNLWT
             ALT          KJFK    153994   07/19   3498    2019Z     598204     444210  050000    358408
ALTERNATE    KBWI         014450  00/44    0250    2103Z
             HLD          013652  00/45
HOLD         RES          007700  09/26
             TOT          189796  09/14   NAT J  NA   022

RESERVES     EDDF K1R2F KIR G104 RUWER UR110 MMD UR9 PON UA57 CHW UR11 DIN UR111
             OPR..4808..4815..4820..4830..4740..4650..BANCS NA22 KANNI PLYMM2
             KJFK
ROUTE SUMMARY  WIND M005  MXSH 3/4820
               FL 350/REM 370/CHW...350/4650...390
               LRC FL350 164112 07/05  3498 M005
AVERAGE WIND   ETP EINN/CYQX 03/19  1657NM M007/M019 BURN 0804  N47528W031540
COMPONENT
ALTITUDES INCLUDING   EDDF ELEV  00364FT
STEP CLIMBS           CPT      FLT     WIND    S    TAS    GRS    MCS    DST    DSTR    ETE    ETR    FU    FR    FF/E
                      FREQ
SECONDARY CRUISE   DI8         :       :       :    220.7         :     .015   3483    0/16   ./..   ..   ..   ./..
MODE SUMMARY
                   ECHHO       :       :       :    268.8         :     .014   3469    0/24   ./..   ..   ..   ./..
EQUAL TIME POINT   KIR         :       :       :    274.0         :     .023   3446   ./..    ./..   ..   ..   ./..
                   117.5
WIND SHEAR
                   RUWER       :       :       :    272.2         :     .038   3408   ./..    ./..   ..   ..   ./..
NORTH AMERICAN
PREFERENTIAL ROUTE LUXIE       :       :       :      :           :       :      :     ./..    ./..   ..   ..   ./..

                   KJFK                              255.5                .013   3379    0/16   7/03   140   1758  ./..
                   ELEV   00013FT                    274.6                .048   0000    0/24   0/00   026   0358  ./..

                   EDDF    N50021E008343    DI8      N49503E008191    ECCHO  N49499E007578
                   KIR     N49511E007222    RUWER    N49517E006241    LUXIE  N49373E006122
INS CO-ORDINATES   LONWY   N4933OE005490    MMD      N49235E005075    REM    N49187E004028
                   PLYMM   N42026W070256    PVD      N41435W071258    H70    N40551W072190
                   ERICK   N40470W072445    KJK      N40384W073467
```

Computer and ATC Flight Plans 161

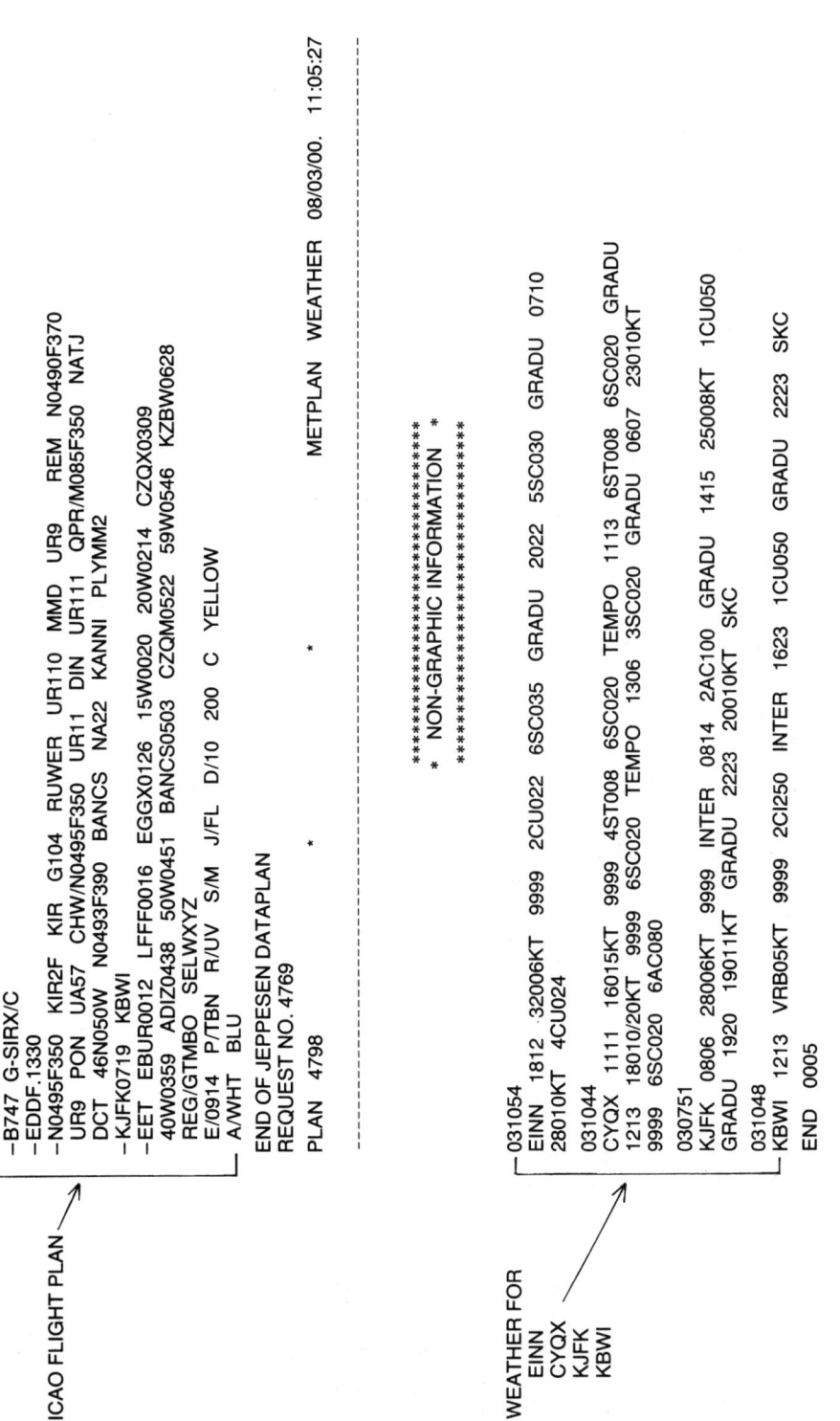

```
FIRS     EBUR/1512    LFFF/1616    LFFF/1420    CZQX    1553    ADIZ/1130
FIRS     CZQM/1823    KZBW/1928

FPL-ABC123-IN
-B747 G-SIRX/C
-EDDF.1330
-N0495F350 KIR2F KIR G104 RUWER UR110 MMD UR9 REM N0490F370
 UR9 PON UA57 CHW/N0495F350 UR11 DIN UR111 QPR/M085F350 NATJ
 DCT 46N050W N0493F390 BANCS NA22 KANNI PLYMM2
-KJFK0719 KBWI
-EET EBUR0012 LFFF0016 EGGX0126 15W0020 20W0214 CZQX0309
 40W0359 ADIZ0438 50W0451 BANCS0503 CZQM0522 59W0546 KZBW0628
 REG/GTMBO SELWXYZ
 E/0914 P/TBN R/UV S/M J/FL D/10 200 C YELLOW
 A/WHT BLU

END OF JEPPESEN DATAPLAN
REQUEST NO. 4769

PLAN 4798            *              *            METPLAN WEATHER 08/03/00. 11:05:27
```

```
                    ************************
                    * NON-GRAPHIC INFORMATION *
                    ************************
```

```
031054
EINN 1812 .32006KT 9999 2CU022 6SC035 GRADU 2022 5SC030 GRADU 0710
28010KT 4CU024
031044
CYQX 1111 16015KT 9999 4ST008 6SC020 TEMPO 1113 6ST008 6SC020 GRADU
1213 18010/20KT 9999 6SC020 TEMPO 1306 3SC020 GRADU 0607 23010KT
9999 6SC020 6AC080
030751
KJFK 0806 28006KT 9999 INTER 0814 2AC100 GRADU 1415 25008KT 1CU050
GRADU 1920 19011KT GRADU 2223 20010KT SKC
031048
KBWI 1213 VRB05KT 9999 2CI250 INTER 1623 1CU050 GRADU 2223 SKC
END 0005
```

Fig. 15.1 Presentation of a computer flight plan.

162 *Plotting and Flight Planning*

line

1	PLAN 6329			EGKK TO EDDF	757B	M80/F	IFR	09/30/92	
2	NONSTOP COMPUTED 1145Z			FOR ETD 1830Z	PROGS 300000Z			KGS	
3		FUEL	TIME	DIST	ARRIVE	TAKEOFF	LAND	AV PLD	OPNLWT
4	POA EDDF	003091	00/55	0362	1925Z	077390	074299	012500	058638
5	ALT EDDL	001485	00/24	0101	1949Z	COMP M015			
6	HLD	001521	00/30						
7	CON	000155	00/03						
8	REQ	006252	01/52						
9	XTR	000000	00/00						
10	TOT	006252	01/52						
11	EGKK DVR6M DVR UG1 NTM NTM1A EDDF								
12	WIND P029 MXSH 5/KOK TEMP P01 NAM 0337								
13	FL 370								
14	LRC FL370	003091	00/56						
15	LRC FL330	003180	00/57						
16	LRC FL410	003111	00/55						
17	EGKK ELEV 00202FT									

18	AWY	WPT	MTR	DFT	ZD	ZT	ETA	ATA	CT	WIND	COMP	GRS	DSTR	REM
19	MSA	FRQ												
20	DVR6M	DVR	092	..	068	0/11	..	..	0/11	...	..	..	0294	...
21	023	114.95												
22	UG1	TOC	097	..	014	0/02	..	..	0/13	...		..	0280	0046
23	023													
24	UG1	KONAN	097	L01	010	0/01	..	..	0/14	27045	P045	502	0270	0045
25	023													
26	UG1	KOK	097	L01	025	0/03	..	..	0/17	26041	P040	497	0245	0043
27	023	114.5												
28	UG1	REMBA	108	L02	090	0/11	..	..	0/28	27030	P028	488	0155	0038
29	026													
30	UG1	NUVIL	109	L01	024	0/03	..	..	0/31	27025	P024	485	0131	0036
31	034													
32	UG1	SPI	110	L01	004	0/01	..	..	0/32	27025	P024	485	0127	0036
33	034	113.1												
34	UG1	LARED	131	L02	009	0/01	..	..	0/33	28025	P020	481	0118	0036
35	034													
36	UG1	TOD	131	L03	007	0/01	..	..	0/34	28025	P021	481	0111	0035
37	043													
38	UG1	NTM	131	..	030	0/06	..	..	0/40	...	..	..	0081	...
39	043	115.3		..										
40	NTM1A	EDDF	089		081	0/16	..	..	0/55	...	..	..	0000	0032
41	043													
42	ELEV	00364FT												

43	EGKK	N51089W000113	DVR	N51097E001217	KONAN	N51078E002000
44	KOK	N51057E002392	REMBA	N50398E004549	NUVIL	N50322E005315
45	SPI	N50309E005375	LARED	N50252E005480	NTM	N50010E006320
46	EDDF	N50021E008343				

47 FIRS EBUR/0014 EDDU/0036
48 (FPL-JD105-IN
49 -B757/M-SXI/C
50 -EGKK1830
51 -N0457F370 DVR6M DVR UG1 NTM NTM1A
52 -EDDF0055 EDDL
53 -EET/EBUR0014 EDDU0036
54 REG/GABCD SEL/WXYZ
55 E/0152 P/121 R/V S/M J/L D/6 150 C YELLOW
56 A/GREY BLUE

Fig. 15.2 Computer flight plan for G-ABCD from Gatwick to Frankfurt.

Line 11 Summary of route being followed including SID and STAR assumed to be used

Line 12 Average wind component plus (P) 29 kt. Maximum vertical windshear expected in kt/1000 ft and its location (KOK). Shears of five or more could indicate moving to another FL might give some advantage in economy. Windshears of these magnitudes also indicate a chance of Clear Air Turbulence (CAT) being encountered. Average temperature deviation is Plus (P) 1. Air miles to be flown 337 nm. Compare with flight distance and flight time to get the the average wind component (+29)

Line 13	The FL or FLs chosen for the flight
Lines 14 to 16	Summary of fuel burn/flight time at long range cruise for the same route at the adjacent available FLs
Line 17	Departure aerodrome EGKK (GATWICK) and its elevation
Line 18	AWY = Airway. WPT = waypoint. MTR = magnetic track. DFT = Drift. ZD = zone (stage) distance. ZT = zone time in hr/min. ETA and ATA are left blank for the pilots' use in flight. WIND will be a five figure group 27045 27 = 270° 045 = 45 kt. COMP = wind component. GRS = ground speed. DSTR = total distance remaining. REM = fuel remaining in 100 kg units.
Line 19	MSA = minimum safe altitude (as shown on Jeppesen) FRQ = frequency of facility at waypoint
Line 22	TOC = top of climb
Line 36	TOD = top of descent
Lines 43 to 46	Precise coordinates of waypoints in the form for entering into on board auto-nav keyboards
Line 47	estimated elapsed times to crossing of FIR boundaries
Lines 48 to 55	entries required for ATC flight plan. Figure 15.3 shows the plan produced from this. ATC may be prepared to accept the plan as printed on this computer flight plan.

Commonsense checking of computer flight plans

Obviously the computer will produce very accurate plans very quickly but, as already mentioned, errors can creep in because the wrong information was asked for. What can the user do to try to pick up these errors? The answer is to use commonsense checking. Do not accept the answers blindly believing that because the computer produced it, it must be right. Consider the information being produced and test it against your own general knowledge of the situation. Here are some suggestions of simple checks that can be made:

- It is quite probable that the flight is one that you have prepared many times before for the same type of aircraft. In this case all the answers must be reasonably familiar. If the fuel amounts are noticeably different from usual, don't be satisfied until you have tracked down the reason.
- Look at the tracks. Are they in the right general direction?
- Does the average wind component fit in with the general Met. situation?
- Is the total distance about right for the flight?

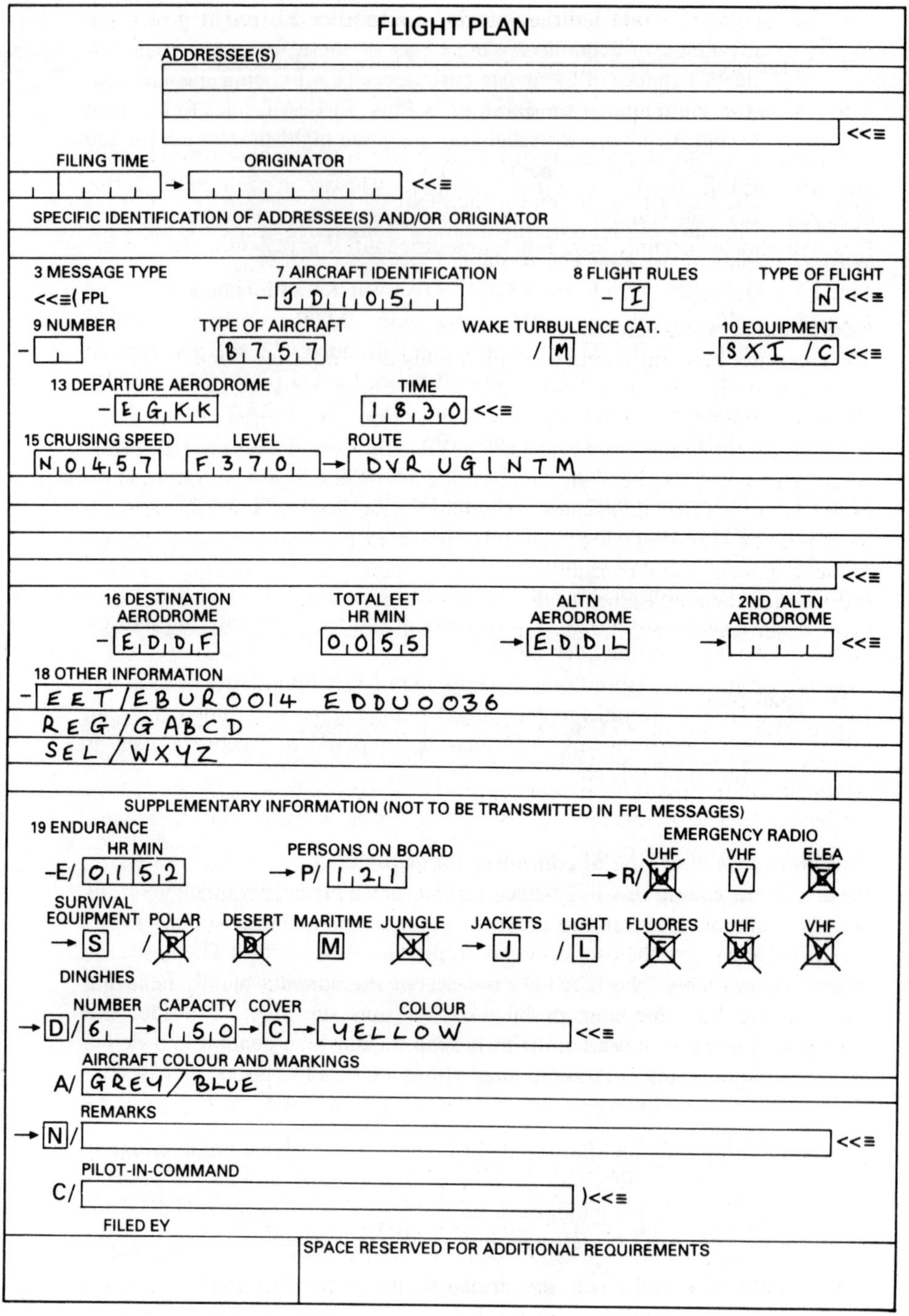

FLIGHT PLAN

ADDRESSEE(S)

FILING TIME → **ORIGINATOR**

SPECIFIC IDENTIFICATION OF ADDRESSEE(S) AND/OR ORIGINATOR

3 MESSAGE TYPE	7 AIRCRAFT IDENTIFICATION	8 FLIGHT RULES	TYPE OF FLIGHT
(FPL	-JD105	-I	N

9 NUMBER	TYPE OF AIRCRAFT	WAKE TURBULENCE CAT.	10 EQUIPMENT
-	B757	/M	-SXI/C

13 DEPARTURE AERODROME -EGKK **TIME** 1830

15 CRUISING SPEED N0457 **LEVEL** F370 **ROUTE** → DVR UG1 NTM

16 DESTINATION AERODROME	TOTAL EET HR MIN	ALTN AERODROME	2ND ALTN AERODROME
-EDDF	0055	→EDDL	→

18 OTHER INFORMATION
- EET/EBUR0014 EDDU0036
- REG/GABCD
- SEL/WXYZ

SUPPLEMENTARY INFORMATION (NOT TO BE TRANSMITTED IN FPL MESSAGES)

19 ENDURANCE HR MIN -E/0152 **PERSONS ON BOARD** →P/121 **EMERGENCY RADIO** UHF[X] VHF[V] ELEA[X]

SURVIVAL EQUIPMENT →[S] **POLAR**[X] **DESERT**[X] **MARITIME**[M] **JUNGLE**[X] **JACKETS** →[J] **LIGHT**/[L] **FLUORES**[X] **UHF**[X] **VHF**[X]

DINGHIES
NUMBER →D/6 **CAPACITY** →150 **COVER** →C **COLOUR** →YELLOW

AIRCRAFT COLOUR AND MARKINGS A/GREY/BLUE

REMARKS →N/

PILOT-IN-COMMAND C/

FILED EY

SPACE RESERVED FOR ADDITIONAL REQUIREMENTS

Fig. 15.3 ATC flight plan.

Computer and ATC Flight Plans 165

- Is the alternate selected the one you would have chosen?
- Is the cruise control the one you would have chosen?
- Does the route appear sensible?

If there seems to be a serious discrepancy which you cannot resolve, your first move will be to ask advice from colleagues who are in the vicinity. If this does not work and you are using one of the computer planning companies, they will almost certainly have a helpline procedure for just such situations.

Additional services offered

The computer planning companies will usually offer many additional services. Referring to Fig. 15.1, it will be seen that weather information in the form of TAFs and METARs can be appended to the plan. In addition provision can be made to supply the latest relevant NOTAMs affecting the proposed flight. Arrangement can also be made for providing more extensive Met. information in the form of full colour charts. Handling arrangements can also be dealt with and the transmission of the ATC plans to the appropriate authority. These companies are constantly reviewing their services so as to provide every conceivable assistance to the airlines of the world, so you may well find many other ways in which they can be of service to you and your company.

ATC flight plan

Figure 15.3 shows an ATC plan derived from the flight shown in Fig. 15.2. Full details of how to complete an ICAO flight plan are in a current yellow Aeronautical Information circular and also in CAA publication *CAP 511* (see Appendix 3). The following notes highlight some particularly important points to watch out for when preparing an ATC flight plan.

Item 7 Frequently this will be the flight number, in this case JD105 – the aircraft registration is then shown under Item 18 (the scratch pad) – REG/GABCD
Item 8 Invariably I for IFR for most public transport flights. Type of flight will be N for non-scheduled or S for scheduled
Item 9 Number – only used for formation flights
Type – only ICAO-approved abbreviation to be used.
Wake Turbulence Cat. – H, M or L – see AIC or CAP for the weight limits
Item 10 S for standard is always used. In the UK this would indicate the full requirements for airways operation and there is no need to elaborate further. This aircraft was also carrying INS and the automatic navigation fit required for flight in MNPS airspace (X). Omission of the X would result in a rejection of the plan if this were a North Atlantic flight. C indicates that the SSR has an altitude transmitting capability.
Item 13 Only use ICAO identifiers for the aerodrome. Provision is made

166 *Plotting and Flight Planning*

for cases where none exists but this is unlikely with public transport operations. The time is the *estimated time off blocks* in UTC (four-figure group)

Item 15 Cruising speed will usually be either N (for knots!) and a four-figure group for the speed – in this case 0457 for 457 kt or M and a three-figure group for the Mach No. i.e. M082 for Mach 0.82.

Level will usually be F (for FL) followed by a three-figure group. In this case the FL is 370. If it had been 90, it would have been shown F090.

The speed and FL group must be regarded as one entity. If there is a FL change or a significant (over 5%) speed change en route, the whole speed/FL group must be shown after the point where it occurred. For example, if it was intended to change the cruising level at SPI to FL 330, the entry would read SPI/N0457F330.

Route – here the minimum necessary detail to describe the route unambiguously. Each waypoint must be shown where the route nomenclature changes. Every section of the route must be given a name. If there is no ATC title DCT is used to indicate a direct track between the two named waypoints. Waypoints are described using beacon callsigns or the published five-letter names for points without beacons. Provision is made for using latitude and longitude or bearings and distances from known positions – see the AIC or CAP for examples.

There is no need to include SIDs or STARs in the route. ATC will decide which of these you are to use at the time. For this reason the route will usually terminate at the holding beacon for the airfield. From here the ATC will direct.

Item 16 Use ICAO code for the destination and show the estimated flight time from airborne to arrival at the final beacon. ATC can then make their own calculations using the notified airborne time and their own estimate of interval from arrival at the beacon to landing at their airfield. Provision is made for showing two alternates. It is not always necessary to nominate two alternates.

Item 18 'The Scratchpad' is used for miscellaneous information. Each piece of information will have to be identified by an abbreviation. Acceptable ones are listed in the AIC and CAP; mostly they are self-evident. In this case EET stands for estimated elapsed time at the international FIR boundaries which are identified by the ICAO codes for the respective ATCCs. The times are four-figure groups giving the hours and minutes from airborne to reaching the boundaries. The aircraft registration has already been mentioned under item 7. The other entry indicates that the SELCAL code for this aircraft is WXYZ.

Item 19 Endurance – the maximum time in hours and minutes (four-figure group) that the aircraft can remain airborne on this particular flight.

Persons on board – frequently TBN (to be notified) is used. The pilot will give the actual number on board over the RTF probably when asking for taxiing clearance. Emergency Radio – just cross out the frequencies not available with the *emergency* radio equipment on board. Survival equipment – just cross out the equipment not available.

Dinghies – the total number of dinghies and their total capacity.

APPENDICES

Appendix 1
GLOSSARY OF ABBREVIATIONS

a/c	aircraft
A/D	aerodrome
ADF	automatic direction finding equipment
ADIZ	air defence identification zone
ADR	advisory route
agl	above ground level
A/H	alter heading
alt or Alt	altitude
amsl	above mean sea level
APS	aircraft prepared for service (weight)
APU	auxiliary power unit
ASI	airspeed indicator
ASR	altimeter setting region
ATA	actual time of arrival
ATCC	air traffic control centre
ATD	actual time of departure
ATZ	air traffic control zone
AUW	all-up weight
Brg	bearing
BS	broadcasting station
°C	degrees Celsius, hitherto called Centigrade
°(C)	degrees Compass
CA	conversion angle
CAA	Civil Aviation Authority

Appendix 1

CAVOK	weather fine and clear
CAS	calibrated airspeed
ch lat	change of latitude
ch long	change of longitude
CL	chart length
cm	centimetre(s)
C of G	centre of gravity
Comp	component
COAT	corrected outside air temperature
CP	critical point
CS or cs	call sign
CTR	control zone
cwc	cross wind component
Dev	deviation
DF	direction finding
DH	decision height
dist or d	distance
DME	distance measuring equipment
DR	dead reckoning
EAT	expected approach time
EET	estimated elapsed time
ERA	en route alternate
EROPS	extended range operations
ETA	estimated time of arrival
ETD	estimated time of departure
ETOPS	extended range twin-engined operations
ETW	empty tank weight
FAA	Federal Aviation Authority
FIR	Flight Information Region
FIS	Flight Information Service
FL	flight level

FOB	fuel on board
ft	feet
ft/min	feet per minute
°(G)	degrees Grid
GC	great circle
GCA	ground controlled approach
GD	Greenwich date
GMT	Greenwich Mean Time (see also UTC)
Griv	grivation
GS	ground speed
H24	operates 24 hours daily
Hdg	heading
HF	high frequency
HJ	daylight hours
h m s	hours minutes seconds
h	hour(s)
ht	height
hwc	head wind component
Hz	Hertz (or) cycles per second
IAS	indicated airspeed
ICAO	International Civil Aviation Organization
IFR	instrument flight rules
ILS	instrument landing system
INS	inertial navigation system
IMC	instrument meteorological conditions
in	inch
ISA	International Standard Atmosphere
kg	kilogram(s)
kg/h	kilograms per hour
kHz	kilohertz, or kilocycles per hour
km/h	kilometres per hour

KT or kt	knot(s)
Lat	latitude
ldg wt	landing weight
LD	local date; also landing distance
LF	low frequency
LMT	local mean time
Long	longitude
LRC	long range cruise
M	Mach
°(M)	degrees Magnetic
Mb or mb	millibar(s)
MDH	minimum descent height
MEL	minimum equipment list
METAR	aerodrome routine weather report
M–F	operates Mon to Fri only
MF	Medium frequency
MHz	megahertz, or megacycles per second
min	minute(s)
M_{ind}	indicated Mach number
mm	millimetre(s)
MN	Mach number, magnetic north
MNPS	minimum navigation performance specifications
mph	statute miles per hour
msl	mean sea level
MZFW	maximum zero fuel weight
NDB	non-directional radio beacon
NM or nm	nautical mile(s)
OM	outer marker/operations manual
P	port
PA, Press Alt	pressure altitude

Glossary of Abbreviations 175

PET	point of equal time
PL	position line
PNA	point of no alternate
PNR	point of no return
posn	position
PPI	plan position indicator
QDM, QDR, QNH, QTE	defined in the text
RAS	rectified airspeed
RBI	relative bearing indicator
Rel	relative
RL	rhumb line
RLW	regulated landing weight
RMI	radio magnetic indicator
RTOW	regulated take-off weight
RW	runway
sg	specific gravity
S/H	set heading
sm	statute mile(s)
SSR	secondary surveillance radar
Stb	Starboard
Stn	station
t	tonne, time
°(T)	degrees True
TAF	aerodrome forecast
TAS	true airspeed
Temp	temperature
TMA	terminal control area
TMG	track made good
TO	take-off
TOC	top of climb
TOD	top of descent, take-off distance

Appendix 1

TOW	take-off weight
Tr	track
TVOR	terminal VHF omni-directional range
twc	tail wind component
Tx	transmitter
UKAIP	United Kingdom Aeronautical Information Publication, known as the UK Air Pilot
UTC	co-ordinated universal time (see also GMT)
UHF	ultra high frequency
u/s	unserviceable
Var	variation
VDF	VHF direction finding
VFR	visual flight rules
VHF	very high frequency
vis	visibility
VMC	visual meteorological conditions
V_{NE}	never exceed speed
V_{NO}	normal speed
VOR	VHF omni-directional range
W/D	wind direction
wind comp	wind component
WE	wind effect
WS	wind speed
wt	weight
WV	wind velocity
ZFW	zero fuel weight

Appendix 2
CONVERSION FACTORS

Imp gal	to	litres	multiply by	4.546
litres		Imp gal		0.220
Imp gal		US gal		1.205
US gal		Imp gal		0.833
gal		cubic ft		0.161
cubic ft		gal		6.250
lb/sq in		kg/cm^2		0.070
lb		kg		0.454
kg		lb		2.205
ft		metres		0.305
metres		ft		3.281
sm		nm		0.868
nm		sm		1.152
sm		km		1.609
km		sm		0.621
nm		km		1.852
km		nm		0.540
in		mb		33.860
mb		in		0.030
°C		°F		use formula (°C × $\frac{9}{5}$) + 32
°F		°C		use formula (°F − 32) × $\frac{5}{9}$

Appendix 3
NAVIGATION EQUIPMENT, CHARTS, ETC.

Plotting gear
Can be bought at a number of shops providing for draughtsmen, but is best obtained from those specialising in pilots' requirements. Airtour International, at Elstree Aerodrome, Herts WD6 3AW has a large stock; they have other branches.

Dividers: buy the compass-divider type (those vast contraptions that look like instruments for getting the tops off bottles of pickles are strictly for the yachties).

Protractor: 5-inch square (e.g. Airtour PP2).

Rule: a 30 cm clear plastic ruler is a good investment, with inches, tenths, and centimetres, millimetres.

Scale ruler: 20″ showing nm for 1:1 000 000 scale (e.g. Airtour NM4).

Computer: there are numerous types, avoid movable wind-arms, make sure it goes up to high speeds and has all the refinements like sg, Mach, etc. on the circular slide rule (e.g. Airtour CRP 5).

Electronic calculators: simple scientific as recommended for GCSE. It is worth considering a model with solar cells so removing the dependence on batteries.

Maps and charts
Obtainable from CAA Chart Room or accredited agents (see green AIC) including Edward Stanford Ltd, 12–14 Long Acre, London, WC2E 9LP; Airtour International, as above.
Instructional Plotting Chart UK (Lambert's) 1:1 000 000 and Instructional Plotting Chart Europe (Lambert's) 1:1 000 000 are also available from CAA Chart Room, CAA House, 45–59 Kingsway, London WC2B 6TE.

Aeronautical Information Circulars
These are obtainable from Civil Aviation Authority Printing and Publication Services, Greville House, 37 Gratton Road, Cheltenham, Glos GL50 2BN on payment of annual postage. The circular on aviation charts is a handy reference, and it has a list of chart symbols.

180   Appendix 3

Data Sheets (currently numbers 33 and 34) for Flight Planning,
CAP 360 Air Operators' Certificates, Part 1,
CAP 505 Objective Testing for Professional Licences,
Specimen Examination Questions and Papers,
CAP 511 Instructions for Completion of the Flight Plan Form;

these are all also available from CAA, Greville House, 37 Gratton Road, Cheltenham, Glos GL50 2BN.

AERAD charts
The useful one for this book is any fairly recent EUR 1/2. Available from British Airways AERAD Customer Services, AERAD House, BLDG 254/490, Heathrow Airport (London), Hounslow, Middlesex TW6 2JA or from Airtour.

Jeppesen enroute charts
The principal symbols which appear on Jeppesen enroute charts which differ from those on AERAD comprise:

(1) *Indication of FLs*   If FLs disagree with the semicircular rules, on Jeppesen the routes are annotated O> or E> depending upon whether ODDs or EVENs are in use respectively.

(2) *Total distances between radio facilities*   In addition to distances between reporting points and/or sector points, Jeppesen include values in hexagons to show the total distance between successive radio facilities.

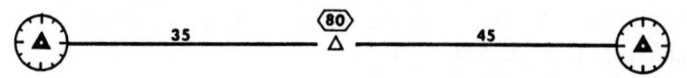

Copyright 1988 Jeppesen & Co.

(3) *DME ranges*   The letter D indicates DME range in nm, either as

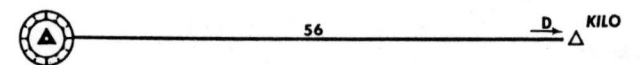

Copyright 1988 Jeppesen & Co.

indicating that KILO would be determined by radial and DME range 56 nm from the station, or as

Copyright 1988 Jeppesen & Co.

where KILO is on radial 274 at a range of 95 nm from XYZ DME/VOR, frequency 114.5.

(4) *Direct tracks*   A capital D in a blue square is used.

(5) *Danger/restricted/prohibited areas*   Identity includes ICAO two-letter locator, and, unless space prohibits, the activity is specified in the area on the chart. SFC means surface. In '● EG(D)136', the '●' indicates always active, as scheduled.

(6) *Minimum off-route altitudes*   (MORA) Although they may be shown as grid values (1° lat/1° long), MORA are given in feet along routes followed by a suffix a. e.g. 3500a. The clearance within 10 nm of the route centreline given by MORA from terrain and known obstacles is

> 1000 ft for MORA up to 7000a and
> 2000 ft for MORA greater than 7000a.

(7) *Radio frequency sector boundary*   Shown on Jeppesen by an outline of 'telephone hand-sets' in green: ∪ ∩ ∪ ∩ . Within the boundary, the common authority callsign and frequency are given, an asterisk (*) indicating not H24 service and (R) indicating Radar.

ANSWERS TO MULTI-CHOICE TEST QUESTIONS

Chapter 3
Q1 (c), Q2 (b), Q3 (b), Q4 (a), Q5 (d), Q6 (c), Q7 (c), Q8 (a), Q9 (d), Q10 (d), Q11 (a), Q12 (d), Q13 (d), Q14 (a), Q15 (d), Q16 (c), Q17 (d), Q18 (c), Q19 (a), Q20 (b).

Chapter 4
Q1 (a), Q2 (b), Q3 (c), Q4 (c), Q5 (b), Q6 (c), Q7 (b), Q8 (c), Q9 (c).

Chapter 11
Q1 (b), Q2 (d), Q3 (c), Q4 (a), Q5 (b), Q6 (d).

Chapter 12
Q1 (a), A2 (d), Q3 (a), Q4 (d), Q5 (b), Q6 (c), Q7 (d), Q8 (b).

INDEX

ABAC scale, 46
ADF, 24, 45
advisory routes, 58
AERAD, 52
Air Pilot, 64, 65
airplot, 37
air position, 37
airspeed, 12
airway, 53, 54, 60, 62
altimeter setting region (ASR), 57
answers, 183
approach chart, 65
APS weight, 108
area navigation (RNAV), 102, 104
ATCC, 57, 60
ATC flight plan, 164, 165

burn-off, 95, 107, 153

change of latitude, 5
change of longitude, 5
chart work, 21, 29
choice of route, 102
circular position line, 23
clearance altitude, safe, 55
climb, navigation on, 31, 93
closing speed, 71
COAT, 13
cocked hat, 34
compression of the earth, 3
computers, 13, 17, 19, 158
computerised flight plan, 157, 159, 163
constant bearing, line of, 77
contingency reserve, 152
controlled airspace, 53
Control Zones, 57
convergence, 27, 47
conversion angle, 46, 47
conversion of units, 7, 8, 177
critical fuel scenario, 155
critical point, 121
    comparison with PNR, 127
    graphical solution, 125
cruise control, 87, 89, 147
    stepped, 85, 88, 147

danger areas, 59, 181

data sheets, 89
dead (deduced) reckoning, 31
decision height (DH), 152
descent, navigation on, 32
deviation, 14
    temperature, 90
distances and units, 7, 22
diversion, 98
divert, latest time to, 80
DME, 23, 56
drift, 16
DR position, 31, 38

economy, cruise control, 148
effective wind component, 19
enroute alternate (ERA), 152
equal time point (PET), 155
equatorial plotting, 44
estimated elapsed time (EET), 29, 166
    flight time, 29
    time of arrival (ETA), 29
extended range operations
    (EROPs/ETOPs), 154

facilities, 52, 56
fan marker, 56
FIR boundaries, 57
fix, 27, 33
flight level (FL), 61, 93
flight plan, 85
    ATC, 164
    computer, 157, 159
fuel on board, 95, 108, 151, 156
fuel, weight calculation, 93, 151, 153, 156

graticule, 4, 44
great circle (GC), 3, 159
    and rhumb line, comparisons, 6
Greenwich meridian, 4
grid navigation, 50
grivation, 50
ground speed, 16, 18

headings, true, magnetic, compass, 14, 18, 29
headwind component, 19
high altitude chart, 65

Index

high speed (HS) cruise, 87
hold, 61, 98, 151
Howgozit charts, 116

indicated airspeed (IAS), 12
interception, 77
island reserve, 151
isogonal, 51, 53, 60

Jeppesen, 52, 157

kilometre, 7
knot, 11

Lambert's conformal, plotting on, 21, 44, 52
latitude, 4
line of constant bearing, 77
local wind, 30
long range cruise, 87
longitude, 4

Mach number, 12, 14
mean wind, 30
Mercator, plotting on, 45
meridian, 3, 4, 44, 50
military ATZ, 57
minimum descent height, 163
   equipment list, 155
   flight level, 54
   navigation performance, 165

nautical mile, 7
navigation computer, 17, 19
navigation on the climb, 31, 93
   on the descent, 32
non-directional beacon (NDB), 24, 55

oblique Mercator, 43
operations manual (OM), 147

parallel of latitude, 4
plotting on Lambert chart, 21, 44
plotting on Mercator chart, 44
point of equal time (PET), 155
point of no alternate (PNA), 79
point of no return (PNR), 112
   comparison with CP, 127
   graphical solution, 115
Polar Stereographic, 43
position lines, 23 *et seq*
   transferring, 33, 35
position report, 55
pressure altitude (PA), 13
prime meridian, 4
progress charts, 116, 126
prohibited area, 59

QDM, QDR, QTE, 23
QNH, 57
questions, 40, 49, 66, 68, 82, 119, 129

radials, 58
radio bearings, plotting, 23, 45
radio navigation charts, 52
range position line, 23
Rectified Airspeed (RAS), 13
regulated landing weight, 108
regulated take-off weight, 108
relative bearing, 75
relative motion, 71, 80
report (airways), 55
reporting points, 55
restricted area, 59, 181
rhumb line, 5
RMI bearing, 25, 45
RNAV, 102, 104
route contingency reserve, 103
running fix, 33

safe clearance altitude, 55, 153
semi-great circle, 3
simultaneous fix, 27, 30
small circle, 4
specific gravity (SG), 106
standard temperature, 90
   deviation, 90
stepped cruise, 85, 88, 147

TACAN, 56
tailwind component, 19
take-off weight, 88, 103
temperature deviation, 90
terrain clearance, 55
time threshold, 155
TMA boundary, 60
track, 16, 54, 59
   measurement, 23, 54
transition altitude, layer, level, 65, 66
transverse Mercator, 43
triangle of velocities, 11, 16
true airspeed (TAS), 12, 14
true wind component, 19, 20

variation, 14
vector scale diagram, 11
VOR, 55

weight calculation, 93, 106
wind components, 19
wind velocity, 12, 30, 150

zero fuel weight (ZFW), 108